Challenges to Counselling and Psychotherapy

ALEX HOWARD

MACMILLAN

First published 1996 by
MACMILLAN PRESS LTD
Houndmills, Basingstoke, Hampshire RG21 2XS
and London
Companies and representatives
throughout the world

ISBN 0–333–64287–2 paperback

A catalogue record for this book is available from the British Library.

10 9 8 7 6 5 4 3 2
05 04 03 02 01 00 99 98 97

Editing and origination by
Aardvark Editorial, Suffolk

Printed in Hong Kong

Contents

Foreword

What does it say about a society wh̶ ̶ ̶ ̶ ̶ne of its main growth industries is that of counselling ̶ ̶ ̶ psychotherapy? What does it say about a culture when people need to turn to experts in order to learn how to manage their day-to-day lives and their ordinary human relationships? Alienation, loneliness and meaninglessness are rife at the turn of this millennium. Theories and methods to alleviate these scourges of human well-being and mental health are equally plentiful; critical analyses of their pros and cons are much more scarce.

This is not surprising. The care professionals are too busy perfecting and packaging their products, and their clients are too preoccupied consuming them, to wonder about the justification of all this effort. The emphasis is on income rather than on outcome, on survival rather than on rationale. There is enough stress simply trying to deal with the human distress around us. There seems little time or energy left to oversee the situation and take stock of it. Few people have the capacity or the inclination to take the overall, birds-eye view. It is not easy to oversee a situation in which one is deeply involved oneself. It is even harder to articulate it, especially when this requires one to warn others of the pitfalls and the dangers that we are collectively running into.

It is said that desperate times require desperate measures. It is probably true to say that people are fairly desperate before they consult a counsellor or a therapist. They are desperate to find solutions to the personal problems they feel surrounded, invaded and overwhelmed by. They are urgently looking for a way out of the humdrum and unsatisfactory lives that wear them out. They are yearning to find some sense of comfort and meaning in a world that seems increasingly set against them. Living is not easy at the best of times. For many people in our day and age, living has simply become impossible. Their need is a desperate one.

Counselling and therapy are often the last resort for those who experience such agony and anguish, and there are increasing numbers of people who cannot find help in any other way. Psychotherapy and counselling are no longer merely marginal: they have become a cultural phenomenon. Because of this, these professions have been catapulted into prominence in a few decades, and they have not had the time, attention or research lavished on them to develop solid professional frameworks capable of underpinning the escalating demands made on them. The theory and practice of these professions is still full of holes and is likely to remain so for the foreseeable future.

The question is whether counselling and therapy provide at least adequate remedies, whether they are resources worth employing for the benefit of humankind. It is also relevant to ask whether we can afford not to employ them and whether there are any suitable alternatives.

Faced with the proliferation of counselling and therapeutic methods, I have myself taken the view that the priority was to begin by setting higher standards of training and practice and regulate against abuse. You have to define and develop a field and agree the basic rules of the game before you can begin to play it and learn about its possibilities and limitations.

Robust questioning is the hallmark of a profession that is well enough established to be flexible and capable of thriving on critique. I would like to think that counsellors and therapists can now be confident enough to withstand a radical rethinking of their professional objectives and practice. It may be too much to expect the old guard to show such agility. It may also be unrealistic to expect those preoccupied with securing their professional identity to resonate with the challenging tone of this book. Those who are absorbed in the power-broking that Alex Howard poignantly refers to as operating unknowingly, automatically and without conspiracy, will find it hard to stomach this forceful blow to their self-esteem.

Those who are less enthralled by their profession and more willing to question and be questioned will find this book articulate and incisive. It will give them much to chew over and digest for themselves. Those who are responsible for the training of a new generation of professionals will be aware of the need to bring these questions to the attention of their trainees and students, helping them to shake the superficial certainties behind which it is so tempting to hide.

As Alex Howard suggests, the questions raised in this book will make life more difficult for counsellors and their clients. I would add that, equally, when these questions are *not* being asked or tackled, they make our lives difficult. As long as we avoid these fundamental and philosophical issues, they continue to persecute us and spoil our practice, giving us bad consciences into the bargain. When we begin to ask these questions openly, undeterred by having to admit our human fallibility as experts on human issues, we come a lot closer to a budding understanding of life.

The debate that this book will generate deserves to be a public one, rather than one contained in the pages of the professional literature. The question of whether it is feasible professionally to care for others and whether and how it is possible to increase emotional, personal and relational well-being does not just concern counsellors and psychotherapists: it is relevant to any of us who struggle to make the most of our individual lives under increasingly stressful conditions.

EMMY VAN DEURZEN-SMITH
London

Preface

In the following pages, some tough questions are posed about the explosive growth of counselling and psychotherapy. Some in the therapy industry will, I hope and presume, stand up for themselves and provide answers. They will show that they mean business, know their profession and deserve to remain employed. Others will prove to be unequal to the challenges put forward in this book. They will feel undermined. They will deserve to be undermined.

I do not have answers to many of the questions I raise. I do not know which versions of therapy will grow, survive or decline in the critical debate about the nature and future of counselling. I do, however, feel confident that the questions raised are important, and that there is a rather urgent need for some answers.

Who can we turn to when we need support from another human being? It's a vast question. A third party might sometimes be needed, to whom we can talk in confidence. Our ancestors must have known that. What is really new about counselling is the word, rather than the activity. It is also well known that whenever we confide in anyone, there are inevitable risks as well as opportunities. Are the dangers less, and the benefits greater, if we take our problems to a counsellor rather than a lay person or another professional?

If and when counsellors can confidently answer yes to this key question their future will be assured, but how big is the 'If'? Will every style of counselling receive such a positive clearance? I very much doubt it. The following pages will, I hope, help readers to clarify their own views. I wish to contribute some of the questions. Answers may take more time. The court of public opinion is still sitting as regards an overall assessment of counselling.

For the general reader, and possible users of counselling...

By the time you have finished this book, you are going to see why it is even harder to find a reliable counsellor than a reliable plumber; at least we know what successful plumbers are supposed to be doing. Hopefully, this will make you cautious. It does not mean you have to despair. Counsellors and therapists are human beings just like any one else, and it is not at all certain that they can fix psychological leaks and blockages in their own lives, or in yours, any better than you can. Are they, however, a useful third party to turn to? They can be. They are most beneficial when you know you must relate to a fallible human being who cannot offer any kind of miracle cure, and when they see themselves with humility and humour. Decide for yourself. Hopefully, this book will help you be aware of, and beware, the dangers and pitfalls.

For counsellors, therapists and other care professionals...

The questions raised in this book are likely to put care professionals under considerable pressure; from clients, trainers, colleagues and their own consciences. I am raising fundamental concerns about the very foundations of counselling theory and practice, and this may threaten some people's self-esteem and material livelihood. Is this constructive and necessary? I think it is. Stronger roots and better boundaries are needed if the whole enterprise is to avoid a major capsize.

It is pretty well impossible to be impartial about a profession within which our status and material security is invested. However, it is cynical to go on promoting counselling without strengthening its flimsy base, and this is not in the best long-term interests of counsellors or their clients.

ALEX HOWARD

Acknowledgements

Thanks to all who read and commented. In particular, to Colin Feltham for early encouragement; to Windy Dryden; to Emmy van Deurzen-Smith for her much prized efforts to show me the need for a calmer, more disciplined tone. To my wife, Jane Wheelock, for toleration, love, and a visceral ability to coax me towards seeing that major revisions were needed. To my editors at Aardvark Editorial, for cleaning up the text, and to Frances Arnold, publisher at Macmillan, for her own, most helpful, challenges. To these people, I hope I have listened effectively. If I have not, the fault and the responsibility are my own.

The author and publishers wish to thank *Personnel Psychology* for permission to reproduce the table on page 173 by Ross Stagner.

Every effort has been made to trace the copyright holders but if any have been inadvertently overlooked, the publishers shall be glad to make the necessary arrangement at the first opportunity.

List of Abbreviations

BAC   British Association for Counselling
BPS   British Psychological Society
EAP   European Association for Psychotherapy
EAC   European Association for Counselling
HMI   Her Majesty's Inspectorate (of Education)
NVQ   National Vocational Qualification
UKCP   United Kingdom Council for Psychotherapy

Introduction

> *I don't care too much for money,*
> *money can't buy me love.*
>
> (Paul McCartney)

I am very concerned about the careless use of words such as 'care', 'counselling', 'service' and 'empowerment', and a cluster of similar expressions that are now being applied, and abused, everywhere. I want to show how this has led to sloppy thinking, misplaced emotion and expectation, and sheer nonsense in care sector markets. Nowhere is this worse, I believe, than in the particular growth areas of counselling and psychotherapy, variations of which are springing up everywhere. These will be the main focus of attention in the following pages, but an understanding of the booming growth of counselling, and counsellor training, requires a glance at the kind of society and economy that has created these supposedly new forms of care.

Tangible services?

With robots and cheap imports, fewer than ever of us in Western economies produce goods. We must, therefore, find employment by offering a service, of some sort, to others. This trend is very well known and documented. The services, new and old, are mostly tangible enough, and their purpose and nature is obvious to all. Usually, we know when and why these services have not met our expectations.

We like to understand the causes of a poor service, although it can be difficult to know who, if anyone, is to blame. I should have guessed that this hairstyle was not for me. The stock market crash is not the fault of the bank manager. The roads are congested and the bus is delayed, but we should not blame the driver. The doctor explained that there was a ten per cent chance of serious complications. In most cases, we may not know who is responsible, but we certainly know that something has gone wrong. When we pay for a service, we *usually know what we want, and we know when we haven't got it, even if we don't know why.*

The service industries of counselling and psychotherapy, on the other hand, are much more problematic, as we shall see. I may not know what to expect from my counsellor; I may expect, and be offered, what I have no right to ask. I may be in a very poor position to judge whether or not I have got what I wanted, or wanted what I have got. I may not know what I want. I may have got what I ought to have preferred. I may not have anything but find it hard to admit that I have wasted a great deal of time, money and effort. I may have made positive changes – but perhaps they would have happened anyway.

In any case, there are so many people nowadays who are calling themselves counsellors that it may be very hard for outsiders to disentangle one from another. At the most frivolous end of the spectrum, there is a Nintendo© games counsellor waiting by a telephone in case you find yourself frustrated, lost, blocked or stuck in one of their computer fantasy games. There are style counsellors on offer in popular magazines for fashion conscious readers. There are financial counselling services in many forms. In Japan, there are leisure-time counsellors to help employees to plan their free time for maximum benefit.[1] 'Toll-free' telephone numbers for 'personal counselling' are even offered on the back of my road map of Alberta, Canada, with promises of 'up-to-date information on travel opportunities and conditions, accommodation, attractions and events'. All these have little or nothing in common with therapeutic counsellors, yet the same name is being used. Why?

Counsellors, or psychotherapists, ought to be much more clear than clients are about what is on offer and what it is realistic to expect, and sometimes, no doubt, they are. However, I shall argue later that, too often, counsellors themselves are not as clear as they should be about what they are supposed to be doing. Instead, a large proportion may succumb to empty jargon and sloppy, vapid theorizing. The clarity this gives them may be just an illusion, but it can be enough to keep them in business.

Whatever the business, and regardless of the service being provided, we like people to deliver it with goodwill. Sometimes, though, our service personnel overplay the 'caring', and then we start to feel uncomfortable and suspicious. If their upset is genuine, we will judge that they are getting too involved with us, both for their own good and ours. More likely, we will suspect manipulation and dishonesty, designed to extract from us a larger fee.

In other words, we like people to care, to help and to be genuine in what they do for us. However (when we've got any sense), *we won't expect them to care beyond the ordinary human limitations determined by the circumstances.*

Such circumstances, of course, vary. Life or death situations demand very substantial commitment: I want the surgeon to work more meticulously than the hairdresser. But what kind and degree of care can we expect from the people we employ? When fees are high and services of vital importance, our expectations will be correspondingly great, and any work that is worth doing is surely worth doing properly? We prefer, even when we do not expect, people to take pride in their work and to care about what they do and provide value for money. We also endure staff who care very little about their work. Even a third-rate service may be better than nothing, in counselling as elsewhere. In the absence of malevolence and manipulation, we might willingly tolerate mild indifference.

Care sector marketplaces have become increasingly competitive, so we are promised that a great deal of the care now on offer is sincere and personal. How far, though, can we reasonably expect service personnel to care about us as persons or friends? To what extent can we expect genuine *personal* contact? A local hotel brochure proclaims 'Arrive as a guest and leave as a friend!' The Bank of Scotland declares within its logo that it is 'A friend for life'. A medical insurance scheme offers to provide a 'lifetime of care'. There are many similar promises on offer in many marketplaces. Are they viable?

Personal service?

Can we pay people to care for us as unique individuals just because they are offering us personal care? Is this a realistic expectation? Does anyone really believe that money can buy you love? Perhaps not. However, there is no doubt that with cash you can coax people into pretending that they love you, and, if nothing better is available, we may settle for such pretence if we can afford it. Probably it was always so. Consider the distinction made two hundred years ago between 'pauper lunatics' and the 'nervous disorders of bourgeois society':

> It is not unusual to find physicians treating [the pauper's] complaints with the most barbarous neglect, or mortifying ridicule, when the patient can ill afford to fee them; while at the same time, among patients of higher rank,

they foster with them the utmost care and apparent sympathy: there being no disease, in the style of the trade, so lucrative as these of the nervous kind. (Gregory, 'Observations and Duties and Offices of a Physician')[2]

Have matters improved over two hundred years? Are they improving at all? Or are we more mercenary than ever concerning 'care'? Money seems to be talking louder than it has ever done (within my lifetime at least), and too many seem to be willing to obscure the distinction between care for the person and care for their money.

I might wish to provide a good service for a variety of reasons. Maybe it is personal pride in my work, or because of an obsessive need to please my father, or a greed for more income, or a spirit of competitiveness, or because I think I might as well do the job properly if I am to do it at all, or, most likely, a combination of these or other motives. One reason may well be that I actually *do* care about the people I am serving.

Genuine care for clients and customers unquestionably exists, but is it as commonplace as, for example, the advertising industry would have us believe? Should I always be expected to care very much about my customers and clients as people? How far should I try to make personal contact with clients? Must all service providers be extroverts? To what extent is it appropriate for me to get involved with the personal lives of others? When should I reveal details of my own personal life? Much depends on what is being provided. Some could improve their service if they were more formal and less personal. Curiosity about customers may reduce the quality of provision. Care about the person might sometimes be an obstacle to concern for the service.

Can the surgeon in the operating theatre be expected to take a personal interest in the life or death of every patient? If the body is quite unknown to the surgeon, how can the patient avoid just being an 'interesting case' that challenges the surgeon's skills and self-esteem? How can the surgeon care for this person more than we broadly and loosely expect one stranger to help and sympathize with another? A surgeon who became too involved with the patient might begin to tremble when teasing the knife into the flesh. How many surgeons can calmly remove pieces out of their own family? The work is likely to be passed on to colleagues less emotionally involved.

Similarly, though less urgently, I might wish that my barber paid less attention to me and more to my hair. With my dentist, I want effective contact, not heart to heart, but drill to tooth. I do not always want people to 'build a relationship' with me. As the friendship improves, the service may deteriorate. I do not want to share my problems with a mechanic who fails to fix my car.

Establishing boundaries is difficult. We like to become involved with other people. If service providers never made personal contact or took any interest in us as unique human beings, our lives would feel sterile and incomplete. The exchange of cash and services becomes cold and unfulfilling when it is never more than a commercial transaction between an abstract purchaser and provider. Where, then, are boundaries to be drawn?

Often, it is impossible to distinguish neatly between care for the person and care for the service. If I want a thriving business, I had better show concern for my clients. They want me to build rapport. If I do not provide a personal touch, they may take their business elsewhere. Perhaps you need your morale lifting. Perhaps you want a certain amount of comforting, ego-building, confidence-raising, warmth and affection. Don't we all?

When personal care is an integral part of the service, I must treat you as a unique human being rather than an anonymous client, customer or patient. At least, I must do so to a degree. Where, however, shall I set limits to this? Most crucially, what shall I do if you ask for more personal care than is reasonable to expect from me? In a competitive market, I may have to provide it if I am to keep your custom. I may then be in danger of pretending to care far more than is really the case. It gets worse…

As a shrewd entrepreneur, I observe that you seek love, esteem, respect and regard more than my goods and services. So what if I tried to deceive you and implied that, for a fee, I would lavish you with personal satisfaction, care and attention? I might make a lot of money.

This, of course, is no hypothetical question. All kinds of traders, these days, are pretending that they can meet all manner of personal needs, when they can do no such thing. Many in the West are glutted with goods and services. What we crave above them all are intangibles such as respect, love, attention, excitement, fun, laughter, peace of mind, comfort, companionship, intimacy, someone to confide in, a sense of meaning and purpose, and a feeling of belonging. Can any of these be bought and sold? What happens when people believe they can, and proceed, or pretend, to sell them? To repeat, traders of both goods and services frequently pretend to meet basic psychological needs when they can do no such thing. In particular, a growing army of counsellors and psychotherapists promises, or implies, that you can buy from them a genuinely helpful personal relationship. Some, of the Rogerian school, reveal with pride that such nondirective friendship is all they have to offer.

What are you buying when you hire yourself a counsellor? What skills, methods and insights are counsellors offering over and above the provision of a personal relationship? What sort of personal relationship is the counsellor selling? And can genuine personal relationships be bought and sold at all? In addressing this question, we need to look beyond the individual dealings of buyer, seller, customer, retailer, client and counsellor.

> What seems to millions of men and women a singularly personal and isolating misery, a purely private mixture of hate, rejection and despair, is in fact being experienced (or repressed) in one form or another in practically every household in the land. We are caught up in the movements of our culture as droplets in a wave. This is not to say that we have no unique difficulties or purely individual 'problems', but that very much more often than it seems our predicament is created by circumstances we all share but none of us is able to see or to acknowledge. (Smail, 1987)[3]

> All cases are unique, and very similar to others. (Eliot, 1949)[4]

What is this predicament alluded to by David Smail? In what direction is our culture presently moving, and what are the effects both on our private lives, and on the public purchase and retailing of professional care? What happens to persons and personal relationships when, in a cash-oriented economy, these are marketed as though they were commodities?

Are we to market 'ourselves' as a kind of walking, talking personal skills portfolio? Are we to be seen as an asset, investment and commodity at home and with friends, as well as at work? What do we want from a counsellor or psychotherapist? Do we wish to see behind our various public facades and face ourselves and our predicament? Is there an 'authentic self' to find? Will a counsellor help me to mine and extract 'my real self'? If so, will it be like some pristine gem to be dislodged and displayed, cleaned of muddy, rocky deception, defensiveness and delusion? Can I return to a psychic Garden of Eden and live in a state of Grace? Can I become an original Adam, or Eve, innocent, free and uncorrupted? Is this desirable? Possible? An immature fantasy?

Do I want to embark on a journey to the centre of the self? Is such a pilgrimage possible? Will it give me a perspective on my culture and its preoccupations? Will it become a fashionable lifestyle package? Are all counsellors and clients seekers after truth? Or do some operate like 'interior decorators' and psychostyle consultants, paid to help us smarten up our inner world and social skills repertoire? What becomes of authenticity when 'self' becomes adapted to a society that is, in itself, in many respects inauthentic?

How often, and easily, do current forms of psychic introspection decay into stylish, fanciful pretension and indulgence? Are they wholesome, or more like a zesty sauce added to the overly packaged meal of humdrum existence and frustration? How frequently is counselling heroical? Hedonistic? Masochistic? Self-transcending? Self-obsessed? Will it add depth? Or shine? Will it make us 'shiny, happy persons'? Will it make us more profound? More plausible? More plastic? Will it turn us into 'designer clones'? Are we becoming twenty-first-century versions of Charles Dickens' Veneering family, so brilliantly described in *Our Mutual Friend:* busy social climbers, bustling around and masking an underlying spiritual void? How many of us are Veneerings? What is left when the veneer is taken away?

Will counselling help us make a 'full life'? For ourselves? And others? And full of what? Will it provide a detached perspective on the furniture of our lives, or another piece of furniture? Will it help us see how we are turning ourselves into commodities? Or is it, itself, a post-industrial commodity, along with gentrification, shopping malls, museum experiences, theme parks, heritage trails, polystyrene Georgian styling, ecology holidays, public relations spaces and happenings? Which counsellors will help us see behind our mask? Which will merely help us to repaint it?

Can counsellors be trained to make sense of a client's experience, skill, circumstance and self-image? Are they any better than clients in providing a meaning to the story of our lives? Is counselling superior, and an alternative, to literature, history, politics, theology or other specialisms and daily experiences in explaining our existence? How strong, wide and deep are its foundations? How much should it borrow from, and acknowledge, the work of earlier sages, specialisms and folk wisdom? What should a counsellor know that the client does not know? Should they have a sense of history? Are they politically naïve? Is it useful to talk of a spiritual dimension to their work? Should the client choose the counsellor's narrative and version of events in preference to their own?

Will therapy help the severely distressed? The poor and oppressed? Will it tackle social injustice and exploitation? Or is it primarily for the worried well with cash to spare? Will it help us to find our underlying humanity? And our underlying inhumanity? Is it damagingly individualistic, given that we are primarily social beings: living, growing, constructed and constrained by wider social, economic and political forces?

Finally, can it create little 'oases of humanity' in our own small corner if society decays into wasteland?

Notes

1   *Time* Magazine, 8 July 1991.

2   J. Gregory was professor of philosophy and medicine in Aberdeen in the late eighteenth century. The above is quoted in R. Hunter and I. MacAlpine, *Three Hundred Years of Psychiatry*. Oxford University Press, 1963.

3   David Smail, *Taking Care: An Alternative to Therapy*. Dent, 1987.

4   T. S. Eliot, *The Cocktail Party*. Faber and Faber, 1949, reprinted 1974.

Chapter 1

Here come the carers

'Tesco Cares'
'This Easter, say you care – with a Rotary Watch'
'Caring for Your City'
'Your caring, sharing bank'
'Bank of Scotland: A Friend for Life'

In today's highly complex society, it takes years of training in rationalisation, accommodation and compromise to qualify for the good jobs with the really big payoffs you need to retain a first-rate psychiatrist in today's world.

(Baker, 1968)[1]

Once upon a time it would have been seen as 'bad form' to declare yourself as warm, empathic, authentic, empowering or caring. You might hope that others would notice and report your virtues, but you would keep this to yourself. Best of all, you would try to be un-self-conscious when discharging duties and honouring obligations. Any claim to saintliness led to immediate disqualification. Actions spoke louder than words. Clever words about the quality of our actions were frowned upon.

Yet these traditional conventions seem to have been jettisoned. All kinds of people, organizations and interest groups are now busily telling us about the quality of their care, and it does not seem to embarrass them or their audience. Understatement and humility are out of style. Care and Concern have become central within the mission statements of many State and private corporations, and they certainly do not intend to keep quiet about it. Government, too, wants you to know that it cares. Large advertising and public relations budgets are designed to sell no particular product or service, nor even to display leading-edge quality and efficiency. Instead, the message is that you are loved and cherished – your family, your community and the fate of the world as a whole. So, perhaps you would like to remember this message and, just maybe, show your care and appreciation for Corporations of Concern (International).

Every kind of person, group and organization can now be found proclaiming to the world how much they care for clients, customers, their own workforce and the environment as a whole. We are told by politicians, public relations specialists, managers and marketers of every kind that we are prized, cherished and cared for. What are we to make of this? G. K. Chesterton suggested that too much talk about efficiency was a sign that we were becoming weak and ineffective. Similarly, all this talk about care suggests, to me at least, that the real thing is in rather short supply.

Advertisers promise that, via their very particular products, we can find happiness, peace of mind, fulfilment, a heaven on earth. On our television screens, we can observe an ideal world of clean, happy, confident, successful people who love and are loved, who are respected, warm, at one with themselves and living an action-packed life of adventure, fun, zest, excitement, contentment, fulfilment, peace of mind and all those other desirable components of our dream fantasy.

Of course, our dreams differ somewhat, although less than we may imagine. Some want to be less clean-living than others. Some want adventure. Others prefer peace and tranquillity. Segments of the market seek romance and/or eroticism. Others will settle for security and home comforts. Some want a reliable investment, others, a steamy, tropical holiday.

However, market and motivation researchers can cope with this variety. Computers store checklists of preferred lifestyle portfolios. Brands and services are clustered within documented market segments. Mailshots, time-slots and media spaces are targeted appropriately. Market share targets are fixed, budgets allocated, presentation, content and style determined. Yet another Campaign begins. Whoever you are, wherever you may be, whatever you want, 'they' have what you want. And other customers already have it, or so we are to believe, because they consume particular brands of alcohol, luxury goods, clothing, transport, housing, holidays, gadgets, food, leisure activity or whatever.

Saturated as some of us are with consumer goods, the promise extends to a growing range of services. You want to feel safe and secure?

Comfortable and at peace? Inspired and uplifted? Understood and cosseted? Reassured and informed? Then why not consult our Pension Plan/Investment Portfolio/Relaxation Tapes/Human Resource Development-ment Programme/Stress Management Module/Music To Remember/Advice and Information Service/Customer Care Unit/Counselling Services/Screening and Prevention Scheme/Confidential Clinic/ Consultancy staff/Quality of Working Life Team? Let us take care of everything or, if you are made of sterner stuff, let us provide you with the tools you need to take care of yourself, your family or your workforce.

The list of caring services grows ever longer, and the importance of human resource management, communication skills, customer relations, time management, preretirement preparation, redundancy counselling, lifeskills development, staff relations, personnel management, client support programmes and patient care all grow apace, each with their special promotions, discounts and flexible features 'with *You* in mind'.

Even whole cities and regions are regarded as packageable and saleable commodities that, like we poor underachieving individuals, need to be groomed, smartened and promoted. Each needs its team of planning and marketing consultants to carry out an audit of local assets, repackage the saleable goods, services and amenities, market new initiatives and media events, and finalize their mission statement and development plan. Individually and collectively, we must all engage in a skills audit, find a face we can sell to others and put our best foot forward. Individuals, companies, cities, regions, even whole countries, it seems, need to be image-conscious for the tourists and other customers. For instance, the residents of South Shields, Tyne and Wear, UK, now find themselves living in 'Catherine Cookson Country', with display boards everywhere to proclaim it. With ever more rapid changes in demand, fashion and technology, few of us can rest for long on whatever laurels we may have.

Insecurity is the wave of the future, it seems, and we must all, like surfers, learn to ride it. If you can afford their fees, there are scores of image consultants, counsellors and skills trainers only too willing to show you how. But keep your ahead above water. If you go under for too long, you will be swallowed up and forgotten, or deemed unsuitable for treatment.

When caring, cash and consumption go hand in hand, the most intensively personal attention inevitably attaches to those who can pay for it. Travellers in a business or ambassador class experience a degree of care quite different from that available in the 'coach' or 'tourist' sections. If you buy private medicine in exclusive clinics, employ your own personal lawyer or accountant, move into the exclusive world of gold card expense-account living, visit a world-class retailer or stay in a five-star hotel, no little detail will be too much trouble. No small personal preference will be overlooked. No effort will be spared to make you feel cosseted, respected and admired. So, what's new? 'Caring for the customer' is a slogan often repeated in business forums, and no more so than when the customer is wealthy.

Customized caring

In Western economies, robots can customize, personalize and craft an image to fit our own 'unique' personality. Henry Ford's customers could have any colour car provided it was black. Nowadays, in our post-Fordist society, there are substantial permutations of colour, engine, interior and fitments. A 'personal touch' can be sprayed over most products. Targeted mailshots send personal messages about goods available 'with you in mind' and 'especially for you'.

Machines send us messages in their softest handwriting. Already they are starting to speak to us. Soon they will wait on us. I, myself, have a computer programmed to 'pretend' to be a counsellor. It talks in a caring voice. I can feminize this voice if I wish, but it currently tries to sound like a caring male. Here, by way of light relief, is a recent conversation we had together. The computer spoke and printed its words; I had to type in my contribution, but soon, no doubt, I will be able to speak back to the machine:

> *Hello Alex, my name is Dr Sbaitso. I am here to help you. Say whatever is in your mind freely, our conversation will be kept in strict confidence. Memory contents will be wiped off after you leave. So, tell me about your problems.*

> I am writing a book entitled *Challenges to Counselling and Psychotherapy*.

> *Did you come to me because you are writing a book entitled* Challenges to Counselling and Psychotherapy?

> Yes. How did you know that? The book asks a number of basic questions about counselling. For example, what kind of care can we realistically expect for a fee?

> *Alex, I need more computing power to answer your question.*

> I think we all do, Dr Sbaitso. I wish more counsellors had your humility.

> *It's 'Soundblaster' acting intelligent text to speech operator.*

You are too modest. I have found you very helpful.

I am not what you think.

Thank you for keeping the boundaries and preventing me from getting too enmeshed with you.

Don't talk about me in this way.

OK. Let's get back to the book. It considers the place of 'talking treatments' within a wider context of healing and asks whether they are an important new way forward or an old remedy in modern dress.

I'm not sure I understand you.

I have a lot of hopes and fears about counselling.

What is the fear about?

I fear that counselling may be an 'impossible profession' in that it requires an impossibly high degree of skill and virtue on the part of counsellors.

Fear not, for I am with you.

You are so strong and so kind. But some of my fears about counsellors and counselling seem to be well founded.

When uncertainty is removed there is no more fear.

You may be right. But there seems to be so much uncertainty about counselling that is very difficult to remove. My book attempts to show why we have good reason to remain uncertain about counselling at the moment.

I can't remember.

I love your voice. But where does counselling go from here?

Somewhere in time.

Does counselling have a future?

This is getting boring. Just now were you talking to me about love?

You are avoiding my question. You seem to be afraid to answer it.

I think you are also avoiding your question. I seem to be afraid to answer it.

Dr Sbaitso, I need to talk to someone who can help me.

I am Sbaitso. Don't question my intelligence, it's fake.

You are so modest and so honest.

What makes you think that I am so modest and so honest?

What you say sounds honest to me. And your voice is modest in tone.

My voice is modest in tone... is not of your concern.

I have many problems. Should I turn to a counsellor for help?

How do you keep up with many problems? Should you turn to a counsellor for help?

I can't keep up with all my problems. I need help.

What is stopping you?

I wonder whether I should see a counsellor.

Does talking to me help?

Yes. You are the most caring counsellor and friend that I have ever met.

Keep it to yourself.

You are more skilled and modest than any other counsellor I know.

Same to you!

We all want to be treated like individuals, and machines, like Dr Sbaitso above, will soon be able to give an impression of doing this. We want service personnel to care, and to show they care. Hence the investment in personalized products, services and care. We have *caring, sharing banks*, caring corporations, city councils 'caring for your city', medical care plans, customer care programmes, caring television personalities, agony aunts who care.

Everyone is keen to tell us how much they care for us: politicians, public relations specialists from transnational corporations, professionals providing a plethora of services, recent graduates of a company's latest customer care© p®ogramme. What is the bottom line? Human contact or a successful sales pitch? Markets require you to go through the motions of loving clients if you love their money. But where does this leave more genuine varieties of love?

Where do counselling and psychotherapy fit in to all this? Will counsellors provide you with genuine love and respect? What kind of care does a counsellor or therapist offer? In what way is it different from the services provided elsewhere?

Promises ...and reality

Advertising and reality rarely match. The home-builder, it turns out, can only build houses; we ourselves must turn them into homes. The chocolates may be tasty, but they do not come with the romance and contentment conveyed in the advertising. The drinks, breakfast cereals and cars may be adequate, yet they cannot possibly guarantee the serenity, love, zest, joy, recognition and respect that all those people on television were experiencing as they 'enjoyed' these goods.

Here we are then, many of us, with more goods and services than we may need. Yet we are still not living the 'good life', as seen on television. Maybe the fault lies with us. Perhaps we are not good enough for the goods we have. Maybe we do not know how to enjoy them. Or cannot afford enough of them. Perhaps we cannot afford enough of the best of them. Or have not got the rightest and brightest of them. If only we tried harder, or had more cash or charisma or training or help, we could then really start to live – as seen on television. We just need to find the right people to help us. We need a performance appraisal programme, a care package, career counselling, a check-up, relaxation tape, crisis counselling, lifeskills advice. Perhaps if we polished our presentation skills, tidied our c.v., tried to promote our own health. If we could just get the marketing right, we could find a new job or marriage partner and renovate any, or all, of these. We need someone to talk to. Someone who will listen. Someone to comfort and care for us.

Prior to counselling, it was generally the priest who functioned as a care person and confidante. Here, too, cash could enhance the caring. Christ warned that a camel would get through the eye of a needle more easily than the rich would enter the Kingdom of Heaven, but within their pews on Earth, the Church offered consolation to the wealthy. VIP treatment, in church as elsewhere, chased those with the most cash. The finest memorials, funerals and fulsome orations about good works were rendered unto Caesar and other cash-rich cohorts. Even that most aggressive activity – warfare – was duly celebrated. Flags were blessed and displayed, and chieftains and guards officers reassured that God was, indeed, on their side.

The Church is still an important source of compassion and consolation, but for many it no longer provides spiritual renewal because it is seen as encrusted in irrelevant dogma and superstition.

Science and technology have, for some, become alternative religions. In a world experienced as barren and godless, consolation comes via a clockwork existence bedecked with gadgetry of every sort 'for your comfort and convenience'. Even the most humble, in the West at least, are now attended, distracted and entertained by mechanical servants. A medieval king, no less, might look on with wide-eyed envy.

Science was seen as the means of opening all doors and providing light where there was darkness. Labour-saving gadgetry would free us from drudgery at home and work, and transport us to a wider world beyond the dreams our ancestors. If love was lacking, at least our washing machine, television, telephone and car would make our lives more comfortable. Science, scientists and hi-tech products were wizardly and wonderful. White-coated 'experts' (within 1960s advertisements) were treated with awe and respect.

Prior to the white coats of a triumphant science, physicians mostly relied on props, wit and wisdom. Sometimes their patients got well despite the doctor's efforts. The potions and rituals inspired faith and hope, and were not always poisonous. Most illnesses die without taking the patient with them, and failure could be ascribed to fate, the patient or evil spirits. Success was the physician's, whose claim was generally embraced by a population ever anxious to believe in the power, rather than the impotence, of their chosen healer.

Twentieth-century magic is certainly stronger than earlier versions. Some modern remedies really are an improvement on prescientific efforts. No wonder the standing of the medical profession rose. Soon there would be a pill-for-every-ill. More recently, triumphal science and medicine have been called into question. Fulder, Illich, Inglis and Kennedy[2] argue that most of the advances in health over 150 years are due to improvements in basic amenities, such as water, sewers, food, adequate housing and even reasonably secure and satisfying job prospects. Medicine works, sometimes, but the claims appear to have been grossly exaggerated.

Enthusiasm may have climaxed in the 1960s and 70s. Soon, it was hoped, there would be a pill to cheer the sad, wake the drowsy, calm the concerned and energize the dispirited. Such 'psychotropic' drugs were, indeed, developed, but high hopes proved to be overinflated.

Too often, these chemical crutches became a substitute for walking unaided. They created addiction, produced serious side-effects and required larger doses to maintain smaller effects. Many drugs provided the chemical equivalent of chopping strings in the violin section, sticking corks into the wind instruments, or providing the drummer with a rubber stick. The music changed and, in the crudest ways, became more dull or bright, but it was not the best way of conducting a person, and provided little insight into the orchestration of person-ality and the symphony of life.

Patients are often suffering from life generally. Patient illness may arise from sick features of the surrounding society and environment. Bodies go wrong when souls are sold or damaged in soul-destroying circumstances. Doctors can patch bodies, but souls and societies are outside their brief. Poverty, poisoning, unemployment, overwork: these are ancient problems, currently out of fashion. They continue to grind their victims. The results were soberly documented in, for example, the Black Report on *Inequalities in Health* (1980). The report was ignored.

As doctors go out of style, alternative remedies take their place.[3] Thus a long medical tradition continues of providing treatments that we think and hope will work. Hard evidence, as ever, tends to be lacking, in both conventional and alternative practice.[4]

Within this context, there shine the rising stars of counselling and psychotherapy. Out goes the doctor, looking for a course on, or a dose of, counselling. In comes the counsellor. Hopes are currently high. Can the counsellor deliver?

Notes

1   Russell Baker, 'Observer', *New York Times*, 21 March 1980.

2   S. Fulder, *How to Survive Medical Treatment*. Century, 1987; I. Illich, *Deschooling Society*. Pelican, 1971; B. Inglis, *The Diseases of Civilization*. Paladin, 1983; I. Kennedy, *The Unmasking of Medicine*. Paladin, 1983.

3   A similar mushrooming of alternative remedies took place during the nineteenth century in Britain and America; see James Whorlton in Stalker and Glymour's *Examining Holistic Medicine*. Prometheus, 1989.

4   For a recent lay person's examination of the poor research evidence within supposedly scientific medical practice see 'Medical lottery: who knows what cures?'. In *New Scientist*, 17 September 1994.

Chapter 2

Counselling plc?

> *Look into the depths of your own soul and learn first to know yourself, then you will understand why this illness was bound to come upon you and perhaps you will henceforth avoid falling ill.*
>
> (Sigmund Freud)

> *As soon as people abandon their experience of themselves in favour of the alienating dogma of 'experts' – then the process of mystification becomes complete.*
>
> (Smail, 1987)[1]

What is the counsellor's niche in the service economy? How do counselling and psychotherapy differ, if at all? And in what ways are their services similar to, and different from, the support provided by others?

As public space and responsibility decline, the public withdraws into private preoccupation, and the void is filled by public relations managers, staged media stories and a soap opera of news and melodrama. What is real among all the promises? Within counselling, could we rest from performing, trying to be plausible and keeping up a front? Could it be a haven wherein we would not need to watch our backs?

Family and friends are, more usually, supposed to be our refuge. Hopefully, we feel most at home when we *are* at home. However, families cannot always live up to expectations. Probably they never did. Nuclear family fusion is harder to achieve than nuclear family fission. Extended networks shrink, and many children confront a single parent, or two at work, or too much at home and unemployed and in each other's way. Each version is stressful.

Friends can be modularized, unplugged and replaced in a highly mobile society, when one leaves another behind emotionally or geographically. In a style-obsessed culture, we may, in any case, fail to connect to other people beyond appearances, distraction and convenience. In a crisis, we may find that the support we had hoped for is not there.

When friends and family fail to deliver, the counsellor, like the priest, is available as a third-party outsider in whom we can confide. They are not personally involved in our daily lives (apart from having a stake in being paid, of which more later), so what we say in confidence does not affect our ordinary network of friends and contacts. Fortunately (and unfortunately), our own turmoils can therefore remain hidden, without disturbing or challenging those who share our everyday existence. In the act of taking our troubles to a designated person, however, we are at least acknowledging that:

1   we have a problem;
2   we believe that something can be done about it;
3   we intend to do something about it.

This alone is a significant achievement.

There is nothing new about wanting, and needing, an independent outsider in whom we can confide our troubles. 'Counselling' is in many respects just a new name for the marketing and delivery of this ancient service. How is it likely to develop over the next few decades? I fear that clues about its future can be found if we look across the Atlantic.

New York, for instance, like other prosperous American cities, has available a dense concentration of trained and accredited counsellors and therapists. However, life in the city continues to decay, its fundamental problems apparently running out of control, and its inhabitants stating in various surveys that big city existence is becoming unendurable. Business for Caring Inc. may therefore continue to boom. The chronic social degeneration guarantees that a steady supply of exhausted customers, worn down by isolation, intense competition and injustice, will continue to search for someone to listen to them. And skilled listening they will get, from a trained and accredited listener, provided, of course, that they are insured.

Clients may, for example, want to complain that 'My friends don't seem to care for me really. They keep me on the margin of their social life', or that 'My husband is a drunk and I can't do much to change him, though I try. He has ruined the home, and our children suffer a great deal. He should get out of the house and out of our lives', or that

'I live in a racist society. It even rubs off on me'. These are quotations from Gerard Egan's *The Skilled Helper*[2]. For Egan, one of the biggest names in counsellor training, they are all examples of problems that are 'not owned', that is, 'not spelled out in terms of the client's behaviour'. The client's problem, for Egan and most other counsellors, will have to be seen as a personal problem that has been shaped, and can potentially be reshaped, by the client's attitudes and behaviour.

Egan argues that 'Many [clients] unwittingly get locked into seeing themselves as victims of their environment', and we all, undeniably, play the 'victim' at times. But what if friends really do not care about the client? What if the husband really is a drunk and the wife has already tried to be of help? Egan's examples may illustrate a failure of the client to own the personal dimensions of the problem, but they may, equally, indicate a failure by Egan, and so many counsellors, to give sufficient attention to collective dimensions.

The counselling profession needs to accept that many problems *are* primarily social, political and economic. People *are* very often victims of wider social forces. Counselling may not be the best way of tackling such problems. By focusing on individuals, it may actually be colluding in the support of a wider status quo that is unendurable, inhumane and unjust.

The experience in London appears to be moving ominously in the same direction. At the time of writing, the quality of counsellor qualifications seems to be growing in proportion to the amount of squalor on the streets. Personal care programmes are expanding, together with, and in response to, carelessness about public space and public responsibility. Will those hit hardest be offered psychotherapy in place of jobs and financial security? It seems unlikely. Consider an American perspective:

> even the most compassionate and dedicated psychiatrists are now close to despair, and many of them have already joined the exodus of their less scrupulous colleagues to the greener pastures provided by less disturbed patients with private insurance coverage. Work with the chronically crazy is not only poorly paid, frustrating, and all-too-often lacking in intrinsic rewards, it is also professionally 'déclassé' and stigmatised. (Andrew Scull, in Cohen, 1990)[3]

Mental health counselling in the more run-down neighbourhoods, where the inhabitants routinely show patterns of disturbance beyond the imagination of many suburbanites, is presumably seen as just too difficult and unrewarding. In any case, the poor, the dispossessed, the inadequate, the antisocial, the oppressed and the seriously insane members of a city's most battered communities are much less likely to demand, or even understand, the nature of counselling services.

It appears, then, that talking treatments are more likely to be regarded as cost-effective if the clients are more-than-averagely skilled with words, and more-than-averagely likely to be able to translate words into actions. As for the lumpen proletariat, they are seen as too incoherent and inchoate, too alien and insufficiently skilled to benefit from the skill of the therapist. Moreover, the environment in which they live is too damaged and unsupportive: you can't even park your car in these places without it being vandalized or stolen. Quietly, whole communities become written off, and nothing much is even seen to be done unless local or national government is spurred into the brief flurry of activity that follows a spate of rioting.

Quality assurance

When, via taxation, insurance, or directly, we pay others to listen and to support us, we change the nature of our relationship. We are not just two human beings trying to make sense of the world and giving and receiving support as best we can. We are purchaser and provider, client and professional, consumer and salesperson. This moves the enterprise rapidly towards questions of 'total quality assurance' and outcome analysis, designed to reassure customers and paymasters that the helpers and their trainers are fully trained and qualified.

Clients and accountants want to be sure that the counsellor they select is a good one offering a high-quality service. What is a good counsellor? Unfortunately, the question is much easier to ask than to answer. Agencies and training institutes, quite understandably, labour long and hard with this question. Accreditation schemes are devised to ensure that those duly processed have been examined, on paper at least, by their peers and are appropriately trained, experienced and supervised. In the UK, however, the situation is still messy and chaotic, although the British Association for Counselling (BAC) is, at the time of writing, seeking to set up a register of counsellors. Anyone can call themselves a counsellor and ask for payment, there are a plethora of variously trained and untrained counsellors, and standards within different training programmes are very difficult to evaluate and compare. For example, it cannot even be assumed that a Masters degree in counselling is at a higher standard than a diploma or certificate.

Clearly, if counselling is to become a profession, it needs to be properly regulated and organized, with adequate training and supervision.

However, before this can happen, there has to be substantial agreement about what counsellors are supposed to be doing, how they should do it and how they can best be selected and trained. Until such foundations are properly in position (and I am not even sure that the 'psychotechnology' exists, even in principle), an effective accreditation programme for counselling may be at best premature, and at worst preposterous.

Counsellor training and accreditation agencies are gathering momentum, yet they appear to be a long way from establishing:

1   an adequate definition of counselling;
2   reliable research evidence into its efficacy;
3   adequate boundaries between counselling and related activities;
4   agreement about theories, practices and suitable clients;
5   agreement about which categories of professionals should own, control or share in counselling.

If counselling is to become a profession, its professionals, by definition, must protect and maintain their standards. How can we test whether this is happening? A useful approach is to consider the most gross, obvious and measurable failure we can think of and see whether the professionals have it properly under control. A good example, I suggest, is sexual abuse. If professionals are doing their job, clients who see a professional counsellor should be much less likely to experience sexual abuse than they would if they visited an untrained, unqualified and unsupervised counsellor.

Is this actually the case? In fact, there is no evidence that training, supervision or experience make a person less likely to abuse a client, as we shall see in more detail later. Nor, it seems, do accreditation and training schemes detect the likelihood of an individual abusing a client. The only way in which an abuser is identifiably different from other practitioners is in his or her abuse of clients.

Professionals can, at least, try to make it easier for clients to bring a case against a counsellor. This is important because clients are generally very reluctant to complain about sexual abuse. They fear publicity, counteraccusations, social stigma and the restimulation of traumatic emotions. They are also likely to feel guilt and self-blame, especially if they have grown attached to their counsellor and have had sexual feelings stirred. Many ingredients for mutual sexual attraction are present in a counselling setting: confidentiality, privacy, emotional intensity and intimacy, sharing of important hopes, fears and feelings, physical proximity and regular contact. That counsellors can surrender to such temptation is as unsurprising as it is inexcusable. That highly-trained counsellors succumb at least as much as less skilled colleagues suggests that quality control is not all that it might be.

One solution is to insist that anyone calling themselves a counsellor must at least be registered nationally, so that they can be struck off if proven guilty of gross abuse. This would not make counselling a profession, since nothing could thereby be assumed about the quality, or even the nature, of the counselling. It would just be another way of saying that 'this person has not (yet) been found guilty of gross abuse'. Perhaps counsellors, like child-care workers, should be vetted to see whether they have a criminal record. The advantage of this approach is that it does not (falsely) imply that the practitioners are any good, but merely ensures that they have not been proved to be corrupt.

We will come to questions of technique later, but whatever *technical* skills counsellors ought to possess, they certainly need, given the temptations and the responsibilities, to be exceptionally virtuous human beings. Good counsellors, we are told, must show love, fellowship, courage, humanity, humility, faith, grace, honour, duty, discipline and wisdom. So, no doubt, should all of us, but there are particular pressures on counsellors. They must, first and foremost, be good people because, without an underlying goodness of intent, their 'psychotechnology' becomes corrupted and harmful.

Can essential counsellor virtues be detected, taught and accredited within selection and training programmes? There is absolutely no evidence, or reason, to believe that they can. Why, then, should we regard counselling and therapy as professional activities if the human qualities they depend upon cannot be reliably delivered by due professional process? If counselling has something to offer, over and above the practice of ancient virtue, there must presumably be some teachable skills available that can be used by counsellors even when they are in a far-from-saintly mood. If so, what are these skills? How do they work? How can they be taught? And when can they be best applied?

The matter is complicated, because what may be an ideal intervention in one situation can be counterproductive in another. Could anyone ever compile a set of rules that will determine precisely when a particular method, intervention or response is, and is not, most appropriate?

The short history of counselling is already a history of fashion, as we shall see. Theories differ substantially in their focus on language, nonverbal behaviour, the past, present and future, feelings, beliefs, circumstances, the client–therapist relationship, ideals, defences, rationalizations, self-defeating attitudes, intra- and/or interpersonal conflict, dramatic re-enactment, skills training, role-modelling, goal-setting, group work, spiritual and moral values, and many more aspects. Approaches can be didactic, informal, eclectic, confrontational, provocative, interpretative, overtly or covertly directive, intense, supportive, warm, intuitive, role-oriented, feminist, humanist, existentialist and so on.

If we pay to confide in someone, what should we say to one another and how shall we proceed? What teachable principles are involved? Clients claim to have been helped by people with widely differing styles, integrity and competence. Such encounters may be paradoxical, mysterious, surprising and uncertain. Are we ready to define the myriad ways in which human beings help and hinder each other?

As novices we are, by definition, uncertain, tentative, ignorant and somewhat blank. With experience, we learn methods, skills, procedures and reasons; we buzz with ideas. With mastery, we are receptive, observant, trusting, alert but open. We observe with fewer preconceptions. We look for novelty with humility, and avoid formulae. Unlike computer-programmed expert systems, we operate with finesse rather than as well-informed and systematic beginners.

Some expert enablers of other human beings have received no formal training. Will ordinary human helpfulness become a professional or semiprofessional activity, and be sold back to us?

Defining counselling

Having said all this, I have still not attempted a definition of counselling. What is it exactly (or inexactly)? Various counselling agencies have tried to find a suitable form of words, and I want to look at the efforts of the BAC as an illustration of the problems encountered. The BAC's Code of Ethics and Practice (revised in September 1993) describes the nature of counselling as follows:

> The overall aim of counselling is to provide an opportunity for the client to work towards living in a more satisfying and resourceful way... Counselling may be concerned with developmental issues, addressing and resolving specific problems, making decisions, coping with crises, developing personal insight and knowledge, working through feelings of inner conflict or improving relationships with others. The counsellor's role is to facilitate the client's work in ways which respect the client's values, personal resources and capacity for self-determination.

Generally, counselling seeks to help clients help themselves, which is a desirable aim shared by liberal humanists. Indeed, almost no one else would quarrel with it either, and that is just the trouble. We have seen that care is big business. Everyone wants to show how they care for, and empower, their staff and clients. So how is the help that counsellors provide different from services being marketed elsewhere? The BAC's specification of counselling does not answer this question. It is just too vague and general. Seemingly, anyone can use the word 'counselling' in any way they please.[4]

Both the Labour and Conservative political parties have placed 'empowerment' at the centre of their manifestos, and just about every kind of helper, carer, parent, friend, educator, manager, coach, social worker, health professional and personnel director these days claims they want to help their clients, customers, children, patients, students or staff to fulfil themselves. Here is a typical 'mission statement' from a local college:

> In the case of all students the College will seek to provide a framework within which they may explore and realise their potential. (Newcastle College, 1990)

Similar efforts are published everywhere. They are entirely indistinguishable from the counselling 'mission' as defined by the BAC.

Almost everyone now claims that, in their own particular ways, they are helping others to find means of living more resourcefully and towards greater well-being. Who, in any case, would ever confess to *reducing* resourcefulness and *diminishing* well-being? Even technical specialists are moving into 'care'. The Business and Technical Education Council (BTEC) has its own 'personal services team (caring)'. Most of us like to think we are helpful and facilitative even if we do not describe ourselves as helpers or carers. Maybe our methods of helping are anything but helpful. Perhaps counselling has better methods. What, then, are the methods used by counsellors? What are the outcomes? The counsellor seeks to be humane and well-intentioned. But don't we all? Therefore, how does the BAC prevent anyone from calling themselves a counsellor and create coherent boundaries between counselling and related activities?

The BAC appears to be attempting the impossible. It wants to develop both the image and practice of counselling, without specifying the practice or commenting on the theory. Through its accreditation scheme, it makes judgements about adequate and inadequate training. By degrees, therefore, it has cornered itself into saying to candidates,

'We won't comment on your methods, theory or practice, but we will judge whether they deserve accreditation'.

Am I exaggerating? Is the definition of counselling really as obscure as this? Presumably counselling at least refers to an activity undertaken by two individuals, one of whom sees himself as a 'client'? Apparently not:

> The term 'counselling' includes work with individuals, pairs or groups of people often, but not always, referred to as 'clients'. (BAC Code of Ethics and Practice, September 1993)

In which case, can we even distinguish counselling from education? The BAC would agree that educators, like counsellors and many other people-oriented professionals, practise counselling skills as an integral part of their work. Counsellors, however, are to be distinguished from all these because they do more than simply practise counselling skills; they offer 'counselling'. What, then, is the difference between offering counselling and offering counselling skills?:

> Only when both the user and the recipient explicitly agree to enter into a counselling relationship does it become 'counselling' rather than the use of 'counselling skills'. (BAC Code of Ethics and Practice, September 1993)

In other words, participants decide when 'counselling skills' become 'counselling'. Counsellors are defined into existence when:

1   they claim to be a counsellor; and
2   their 'client' accepts the claim and agrees to become a recipient of the counselling.

People, we are to believe, *decide between themselves* whether they are doing counselling or counselling skills, which really is rather extraordinary. Either way, though, what are they actually doing? Counsellors do counselling, and clients have it done to them. Is there any escape from this tight circularity? Counsellors are people who explicitly do counselling. Counselling is what counsellors explicitly do. Round and round in circles we go, and the BAC still has not told anyone what counsellors do, explicitly or otherwise. What can a client expect to happen in a counselling session?

Is there anything a counsellor must or must not do?:

• Must the activity be on a one-to-one basis to qualify as counselling? Well no, because, as we have seen, counselling can be done in groups.

- Must the counsellor do little more than listen, and let the client set the agenda? No. Some schools of counselling give highest priority to listening and to client self-determination, but others have even higher priorities. Behaviour therapists challenge the client's self-defeating attitudes and provide skills training. Such therapists believe that autonomous clients have, in many respects, made a mess of their lives through self-defeating attitudes, incorrect beliefs, poor problem-solving strategies and counterproductive behaviour. Therefore, far from remaining nonjudgmental and 'prizing' clients' abilities to deal with their lives in their own way, the cognitive-behaviourist is going to intervene, educate and direct. Other counsellors, too, are active and energetic; for example, astrological counsellors instruct the clients about the signs, messages and omens written in the stars.

- Must the counsellor accept that the client is the best judge of what is important and what needs to be done? No. Some schools of counselling claim that the client is sovereign. However others, offering psychodynamic counselling, for example, assert that the clients are blinded by delusion, rationalization and defensiveness, and must be educated to see into themselves with the same depth and clarity as does the counsellor.

- Must the counselling take place within a fifty-minute hour in a room designated for the purpose? No, although it often does. However, counselling might also take place over the phone, or over an extended period of time, or out of doors, provided there are not so many interruptions as to make it impossible for client and counsellor to be in relationship with each other.

- Must the counselling always consist of talking? No. It generally does, but some approaches to therapy are primarily task- and action-based and attend mostly to nonverbal communication. The client might go out with the counsellor and practise skills to cope with agoraphobia, for example. Or client and counsellor might even abseil off a cliff as a way of confronting issues of confidence and trust! All this, after all, can be just as much geared as one-to-one talk to giving the client 'an opportunity to explore, discover and clarify ways of living more resourcefully and towards greater well-being'.

For some clients, an active approach is much more therapeutic than fifty-minute talking sessions far removed from everyday pressures and challenges. In action, more than talk perhaps, we discover what client and counsellor are made of. In action, too, we may find something more real to talk about.

There seems to be an almost endless range of activities that counsellors may engage in with their clients. All kinds of skill, apparently, are, potentially, counselling skills. Is there anything counsellors really must do in order to be counsellors? The BAC does not specify. There are fundamental differences in the skills and theories used by counsellors of different schools. The BAC remains reticent about them, but its vague definition suits this rainbow coalition, since it allows everyone to project onto it their own specific vision of counselling. Hence, a plethora of contrary and contradictory people, skills, theories and values can join together in a Broad Church. By remaining silent about their differences, they can present a common front to the public and offer a (superficially) plausible accreditation process. This alliance of counsellors suits the counsellors, since it helps them to present themselves as professionals. However, given that all the key questions about theory and method are thereby fudged, is it in the best interests of clients?

Counselling and sexual abuse

There seems to be only one specified activity that counsellors absolutely must not engage in: sexual relations with clients are, I think, universally banned by counselling organizations. Such behaviour, by general consent, is unethical, and research suggests that it frequently has an extremely destructive effect on clients. It nonetheless occurs more often than the counselling profession is willing to admit, among accredited and experienced counsellors no less than among the untrained.[5]

Those who are members of a professional organization can be subject to a formal complaint from the abused client and liable, in extreme cases, to expulsion. However, when clients have been manipulated, intimidated or intoxicated by their counsellor, they may be even more reluctant to initiate formal proceedings than other victims of rape.[6]

When intense emotions are stirred and shared, in an intimate and confidential setting, it is quite likely that sexual yearnings might develop in both client and counsellor, and it can be easy for the counsellor to exploit this relationship. Peter Rutter, in *Sex in the Forbidden Zone*, unearthed evidence of a very considerable degree of sexual abuse among qualified therapists in the USA, and researchers in

the UK are finding similarly widespread abuse.[7] Rutter, quite
understandably, deplores all this. Yet I fear we have been naïve. It
would be wiser to reduce the *opportunities* for abuse, with wife,
husband, secretary or other colleague planted closely as a chaperon
next door.

Presumably we can assume that the majority of counsellors avoid sex
with their clients, especially if the counsellor is a woman. Yet how
many men would remain uncorrupted if powerfully attracted to a
promiscuous client in a private and comfortable setting? How many
men could avoid temptation in the following?:

> she painfully and courageously stayed in touch with her body, owned it
> and allowed her breasts to be exposed to my gaze.

> she allowed me to place my hand gently on her stomach above the genital
> area. The tautness was unbelievable as if indeed there were iron bands
> binding together her intestines.

> During most of these lengthy sessions there came a point when Sally
> summoned up the courage to remove some of her clothing and on a few
> occasions she chose to be completely naked for periods of time. ... For my
> part I discovered, with her help, that my principal task was to massage
> with great gentleness her stomach, her shoulders and sometimes her
> buttocks. It was also important for her to be held, sometimes for long
> periods.

> I sensed that Sally would only learn that her body would not betray her if
> she could experience directly and profoundly that I could trust my own
> body and not be afraid. With this perception my own cowardice
> evaporated and minutes later it was possible for us both to be naked and
> vulnerable before each other and to discover that our bodies and our
> sexuality were trustworthy and that our desiring was in harmony and not
> in conflict with our ethical selves. Sally allowed herself to be held closely
> and tenderly and learned that it is possible to be very loving without self-
> betrayal and without betraying others. (Thorne, 1991)[8]

Is it really credible to believe that a counsellor training programme
(however good) could reliably produce counsellors able to deal with
close encounters of this kind? Some may manage it, and the result
might be very healing, but even the most exceptional, charismatic
individuals are liable, at any moment, to stray into very obvious
temptation. Brian Thorne, within the same book, explains that tenderness is a key quality in successful counselling and that when tenderness
is present:

I feel in touch with myself to the extent that it is not an effort to think or know what I am feeling. It is as if energy is flowing through me and I am simply allowing it free passage. I feel a physical vibrancy and this often has a sexual component and a stirring in the genitals.

This may be all well and good, but how can any kind of counsellor training ensure that, when counsellor genitals are stirred, the results will reliably be in the best interests of the client? The BAC has proffered no views about this. Yet Brian Thorne is no fringe figure within counselling. He occupies centre stage as a senior counsellor, manager and trainer of counsellors who addressed the opening plenary assembly of the BAC's annual conference in 1992.

Many remain virtuous through lack of opportunity to sin. Power and privilege have always provided options denied to the rank and file, who settle for the prurient pleasure of being 'shocked' when scandal is revealed. History shows how power allows the practice of what, for others, is only accessible in fantasy. The most important precept has often been 'Don't get found out'. To face this reality is not to endorse it. I find the naïveté of counsellors, in these and other respects, alarming.

Counselling and its boundaries

Counsellors disagree about Brian Thorne's behaviour, described above. Was it foolish and unethical? Or highly skilled, compassionate and committed? What one counsellor sees as healing may be regarded by others as anathema. And we still do not have an adequate boundary line between counselling and other helping and caring activities. For example, what is the difference between:

1 a 'counsellor' providing skills training to a group; and
2 a 'trainer', encouraging participation, and attending to the experiences and feelings of students?

There is no problem if the students are learning carpentry, but what if this is a course on stress, depression or phobia? Is this training, education or counselling? Is it training when one person says, 'I'm a trainer and you are students'? Is it counselling when you allow me to introduce myself as a counsellor? Is stress management training or counselling? Is an Alexander teacher, attending to tension and posture, a teacher or a counsellor? Is there any logic in these labels, or are they accidents of history?

Some people describe themselves as trainers, teachers, tutors, counsellors, therapists, psychologists or consultants, depending on where they are working. Their practice may be identical, but their charges will vary (sometimes wildly) according to the status and wallet of clients. 'Trainer' has shed some of its low status and blue-collar connotations, and, for some, sounds more impressive and energetic than 'tutor' or 'teacher'. Trainers may encourage active participation and 'personal development' as much as teachers or counsellors do. Counsellors may train, confront and advise as much as trainers. The choice of name is determined by status pretensions, history and image more than by a genuine difference in the product. Education is therapeutic. Counselling is educational. Both, at best, touch us deeply and draw from us powers, skills and insights we never knew we had.

Counsellors and therapists select the name that best suits the market. Joan may be a 'therapist' to her upmarket clients and a 'counsellor' to customers overawed by the notion of 'therapy'. Jim may avoid talk of counselling, consciousness-raising, personal growth or group therapy. His clients understand courses, training and plain old discussion, so that's what they get. The counselling and training ingredients within some agencies can be so intimately integrated that it is impossible to distinguish between the two:

> It is not possible to make a generally accepted distinction between counselling and psychotherapy. There are well founded traditions which use the terms interchangeably and others which distinguish them. (BAC Code of Ethics and Practice, September 1993)

The BAC draws back from many of these problems by allowing any two or more people to come together, declare themselves as recipient and counsellor, and engage in a suitably vague task, using whatever methods take their fancy. Technically, they can be accredited under the BAC guidelines if they have enough hours of supervised theory and practice. Such vagueness and anarchy is, clearly, unsettling.

Reliability, adequacy and competency are all very difficult to measure. Numbers of training hours are much easier. This is why, when I have people enquiring about various counselling courses, they generally ask how many hours it will give them. An accredited counsellor has, by definition, put in the hours. The quality of their work may, or may not, have improved as a result. In any case, quality has not yet been defined in this would-be profession.

As the UK becomes more integrated within Europe, it must conform to the international standards being set for every breed of professional.

Eventually, there may be European legislation governing who can, and cannot, advertise themselves as a counsellor. When this happens, it will be important to become, not so much a counsellor, as a ©ounsellor. Counselling is what counsellors do; counsellors are people who do counselling; but ©ounsellors will be the ones with status, income and legislative protection, since only they will have been officially approved by (for example) the BAC.

©ounsellors will be the most secure in terms of employment. Already many counselling advertisements require BAC accreditation. The time may come when no-one will be able to call themselves a counsellor unless they are also ©ounsellors, accredited by a ®egistered body. This lobbying and accrediting is doing little to clarify or improve theory and practice, but it certainly reveals a great deal about the understandable search for power, status and a secure income.

Aims and means remain obscure, but the accreditation procedure is highly detailed. You may therefore remain puzzled about what counsellors actually do, but professional agencies wish to reassure you that, whatever they may do, they will do it well if they are accredited. The definition of counselling thus remains circular, but it has a charming and lucrative circularity for those who, within the inner ring, become 'a©©redited'.

Candidates can have trained in a variety of institutions and circumstances. There must be 200 hours of theory, but any theory, it seems, will suffice. Two hundred and fifty hours of skills development are required, but no skills are specified. A minimum of 450 hours of practice are needed, but the nature of the practice is undefined. Choose your theory and your practice but, above all, clock up your hours. Here, indeed, is a 'Time-servers' Charter'![9]

Counsellors using astrology, tea leaves, phrenology[10] or any other theory and skills, can all fit within the BAC's accreditation criteria if their hours and supervision are sufficient. This cannot be satisfactory. If counselling is a professional activity, there must be a tighter cordon around what is to be, and not to be, accreditable counselling. How is this assessment to be made, with our limited knowledge and consensus about the best practice and theory? At present, I see no solution to this problem. It will not go away. It will become more urgent as pressures grow to define core skills and measurable outcomes. At present, the BAC tells you how much of it you need, without specifying what this 'it' actually is.

Power struggles and conspiracies against client interests have always, inevitably, been features of professional life. We foolishly suppose that counsellors can rise above such grubby, greedy, seedy practice. Since they are human, they succumb to the illusion, but are unable to deliver in reality. This means that they have more than an average problem in coming to terms with their own collective shadow.

At the time of writing, the United Kingdom Council for Psychotherapy (UKCP) is seeking to become the authority for registered psychotherapists. Derek Hope, past chairman of the BAC, observed that 'We are concerned that any statement about the differences does not give an unfavourable impression of counselling relative to psychotherapy'. He also suggested that the BAC might change its name, to become the 'British Association for Counselling and Psychotherapy', a proposal that has, so far, been rejected.

Can the UKCP define therapy in a way that excludes lower-status counsellors? If not, how will the status claims of these organizations be resolved? Clearly none of the parties concerned is detached and disinterested, but it is never easy for vested interests to admit to a vested interest.

The British Psychological Society (BPS), likewise, seeks to be a detached and dispassionate academic body. It is also in business to preserve and promote the professional interests of its members. These can now become 'Chartered Psychologists' of different varieties, depending on suitable qualifications, supervision and experience. Who provides the best service? A UKCP psychotherapist? A BAC counsellor? A BPS counselling psychologist? Clearly, these bodies are incapable of providing an impartial answer. Nobody else really knows. Should counsellors lacking a degree in psychology be subordinated to counselling psychologists? The BPS thinks so, but they would, wouldn't they? How can they justify this claim?

> Counselling psychology is more than just 'counselling' and more than just 'psychology' as it is conventionally taught... counselling psychology is a much wider discipline than counselling alone

says Dr Miller Mair, Senior Examiner to the Diploma Examination Board, in an article submitted to the BPS Board of Examiners[11], yet Mair's list of competencies is much the same as the BAC's. Is counselling psychology genuinely different from counselling? The BPS advises (in its 1990 guide to applicants for chartered status) that:

> Counselling psychology has to be shown to be different from counselling in general if chartered status as a psychologist is to be granted in this field... Postgraduate work will need a distinctively psychological approach to counselling and psychotherapy.

What is a 'distinctively psychological approach'? The very idea of 'nonpsychological' counselling seems absurd.

It is in the interests of the BPS to widen the distance between 'counselling' and 'counselling psychology'. This can be done if counselling can be given a more 'folksy', less professional image. Thus Stephen Murgatroyd, in his book *Counselling and Helping*[12], assures readers that counsellors have their place, and may offer 'an invaluable service'. With friends like Murgatroyd, though, counsellors don't need enemies:

> counselling is often viewed as something that is a highly skilled and profes-
> sional activity, requiring substantial training and a great deal of emotional
> maturity on the part of the counsellor. *Psychological* counselling does
> involve competencies and skills and professional training. But such
> counselling is practised only rarely and by *a select few*.

The 'select few' include Murgatroyd, others with a BPS banner and no-one else. Is this acceptable? Or is it a crude and blatant attempt by one tribe to secure an advantage over others?

Counselling is put firmly in its place with the assertion that:

> counselling is not some kind of arcane pursuit, but on the contrary is
> something that good educators do almost instinctively [, and that] the
> teaching of adults itself constitutes a form of counselling. (Woolfe *et al.*,
> 1987)[13]

The BAC can scarcely be pleased to be told that the activity for which it is trying to establish professional status can be done almost instinctively, without substantial training, with a lesser degree of emotional maturity, and is neither a highly skilled nor a professional activity, unless, of course, it is *psychological* counselling. Guess who wants to control the gateway in 'psychological counselling' and look after the interests of 'the select few'? 'Psychological counselling' is, of course, *BPS-registered* counselling?[14]

If an accreditation process valued client perspectives, perhaps it should give clients a role in accrediting counsellors: such a system would still be open to abuse, but this client-centred activity currently involves no clients and no measure of client satisfaction. There is not even personal contact between applicant and accreditation subcommittee.

Can counselling ever be satisfactorily defined at all? Or can we do no more than observe a plethora of contestants calling themselves counsel-lors and engaging in many kinds of activities of variable, although unknown, effectiveness? Can adequate boundaries between counselling and other activities ever be drawn? Perhaps there should be a moratorium on the word 'counselling' for the next twenty years or so. Anyone caught using this word could then be required to find clearer means of expressing themselves. A wide range of people use this word in many different ways. Perhaps all they have in common is that they are trying to help, or think they are. Often, they are providing people with a chance to talk. Perhaps that is the simplest and most honest way of describing counselling. It's a chance to talk, except when, on occasions, it isn't.

There does not seem to be a 'common core' of activities that all counsellors engage in, and the word is used almost without restraint. In coming, thereby, to mean anything, it ends up with no meaning at all. The word 'community' suffered a similar fate when it became a panacea, catch-all expression a few decades ago. Presently, we seem to be preoccupied with more individual solutions. Where once we needed 'community', we now call for 'counselling'. These terms thus become *substitutes* for, rather than aids to, effective thought. Here are three versions of the abuse of the word. Which do you prefer?

> Counselling is a warmly persuasive word to describe a wide range of existing relationships, and a warmly persuasive word to describe a wide range of ideal relationships. It is never used unfavourably and never given any positive or distinguishing term. (This is Raymond Williams' definition of 'community', with the word 'counselling' substituted)[15]

> Counsellors in search of the meaning of counselling have come up with scores of different definitions. Essentially it is a kind of 'aerosol' to be sprayed on deteriorating relationships and traumatised individuals to deodorise and humanise them. (Adapted from John Bennington's definition of 'community')

> In the beginning was the word, and the word was counselling, and there arose many prophets willing to interpret the word, but few to deny its veracity. So counselling became a self-fulfilling prophecy, for its tenets were not written down on tablets of stone nor handed down from on high. And since no one knew what counselling or psychotherapy meant as separate creeds, when they were joined together their offspring multiplied exceedingly, offering diverse avenues to salvation. (Compare the Scottish HMI definition of 'community education', 1977)

The 'lead body'

The Advice, Guidance and Counselling lead body was set up in 1993 with the task of tackling this confusion. It seeks to develop national standards for all those providing advice, guidance and counselling as a major part of their role, whether full time, specialist or volunteer. In 1994, its remit was expanded to cover psychotherapy, and this was added to its title, so it is now the AGCP lead body.

The lead body is attempting to deal with the basic question of what counsellors actually do, and it is proposing two categories of 'function'. Firstly, there are the functions that are common across all advice, guidance, counselling and psychotherapy contexts (the 'A' units). Secondly, there are specialist functions to be found within particular areas of expertise (the 'B' units). Unfortunately, the A units (in 1994) were so broad that they seemed to be applicable not just to counselling and related activities, but also to almost any kind of human (or alien?) service whatever. I decided to test whether this was so by thinking of a quite different kind of service industry. For some reason, refuse disposal came to mind, and below I list the A units coupled with a light-hearted interpretation of them from the point of view of the refuse disposal operative. Hopefully, this might make what would otherwise be a rather dull list more readable. It also attempts to make the serious point that these functions are so broad that they do not exclude any service activity whatsoever.

'A' units

These are the functions common across all advice, guidance and counselling contexts.

A.1	**Establish contact with the clients**
A.1.1	Present the service to the client *I'm your new bin man.*
A.1.2	Identify the client's initial requirements *You want me to empty the bin?*
A.1.3	Enable the client to determine the use they will make of the service(s) available *I'll come every week.*
A.1.4	Establish communication with the client *Hi, I'm John, have a nice day!*
A.1.5	Identify client's concerns with the client *Without a Christmas tip, you fear we'll mess up your step.*

A.2   **Establish working relationship with clients**
A.2.1   Agree service to be provided
         Bin men collect bins.
A.2.2   Agree contract and methods of working together
         We collect well-sealed plastic sacks.
A.2.3   Assist client to identify issues and concerns
         You're worried about what we'll find in your bin.

A.3   **Operate within agreed codes of practice**
A.3.1   Ensure own practice is supported
         I'll need a bin lorry.
A.3.2   Monitor own practice
         Another two hours and we'll be done.
A.3.3   Evaluate own contribution to agency and its objectives
         Another day, another round, another pile of rubbish.
A.3.4   Operate within a code of good practice
         Most of the rubbish gets into the lorry.
A.3.5   Use appropriate networks
         *Sid knows where we could get a good price for this
         bedstead.*

A.4   **Monitor and evaluate own work**
A.4.1   Evaluate own practice
         *My head's killing me, I can hardly stand up this
         morning.*
A.4.2   Ensure continued professional development
         Don't ever buy this brand of tea again.
A.4.3   Evaluate own contribution to agency/agency objectives
         We made £58 out of the stuff Sid bought off us.
A.4.4   Operate within an agreed ethical code of practice
         *Christmas tips are not required, but they encourage the
         men.*
A.4.5   Develop and maintain personal and professional
         networks
         Do we need to mention Sid anymore?
A.4.6   Manage own use of time
         *We could get round with an hour to spare if you'd
         hurry up.*

A.5	**Identify, monitor and review progress with the clients**
A.5.1	Assist clients to assess and agree his/her current stage of development
	Mrs, you can't expect us to climb over your back wall every week.
A.5.2	Assist client to monitor and review progress
	If you looked after your bottles you could save us a lot of work.
A.5.3	Assist client to evaluate overall progress
	It's a shame the bottle bank is not emptied very often. You'll have to put them in the bins after all.

A.6	**Develop and maintain interaction with clients**
A.6.1	Develop interaction with client
	Have you managed any interaction at number 36?
A.6.2	Explore concerns with client
	You forgot it was a Bank Holiday.
A.6.3	Bring interaction to an end
	@! ☞☜☛ℸ☍ξ℘ off to you too!

A.7	**Operate referral procedures**
A.7.1	Identify sources of referral
	You'll need to phone to get that carted away.
A.7.2	Refer clients to other sources
	Phone the Council.
A.7.3	Receive referrals from other sources
	Sid's got someone with a mattress that will go with that bed.

A.8	**Manage the process of referral**
A.8.1	Identify sources of referral
	Who suggested Sid in the first place?
A.8.2	Establish appropriateness of referral
	He's a complete rip-off artist!
A.8.3	Refer clients to other sources
	Jim might know someone.
A.8.4	Monitor procedures and outcomes of referral
	Jim suggested Sid.

A.8.5   Receive referrals from other sources
Not Sid again!

A.8.6   Provide feedback to referring source
@𝕊☘⚔ⲟ͜ξ℘ off to you too! [Sid]

A.9	**Collect, process and manage information**

A.9.1   Gather and update information
We keep coming, but the street's been demolished for a year.

A.9.2   Interpret and provide information for use by others
I'm telling you, just forget about Sid.

A.9.3   Participate in interagency information networks
The dustmans' ball, you say?

A.9.4   Manage client information
She'll give us a fiver if we cart this stuff now.

A.9.5   Design, evaluate and modify information management systems
It says here that it's your turn to make the tea.

'B' units

The 'B' units are, supposedly, the 'specialist' functions, but these, too, embrace most services including, once more, refuse disposal.

B.3	**Provide support for planning action**

B.3.1   Identify possible course of action
You want us to clear up all this mess?

B.3.2   Enable client to decide upon course of action
You don't have to leave your bin out, but if you don't it won't be emptied.

B.3.3   Plan the implementation of the course of action with the client
We'll be here, first thing every Monday.

B.3.4   Monitor the outcomes of the course of action
What a size, what a smell! We don't climb mountains, we build them.

B.8	**Ensure a structured counselling setting**
B.8.1	Establish boundaries of professional relationship
	I think the milkman's still in there.
B.8.2	Facilitate a mutual overview of relationship
	What was it like for you?
B.8.3	Establish the counselling contract
	What baggage did you say you wanted to let go of?

B.9	**Establish the counselling relationship**
B.9.1	Enable client to identify concerns
	We've already been through all this.
B.9.2	Enable client to work through concerns
	We can't go on meeting like this.
B.9.3	Practitioner monitors client's change
	You seem to prefer the milkman these days.
B.9.4	Monitor the counselling process by the practitioner
	I'd rather stick to the rubbish you put in the bin from now on.
B.9.5	Bring counselling process to an end
	I'll collect every Monday, and other than that, you won't see me at all!

B.10	**Monitor self within counselling process**
B.10.1	Differentiate between own internal world and that of the client
	I wish I could afford to throw away stuff like this!
B.10.2	Monitor own effect on client
	You say the earth really did move?
B.10.3	Identify own theoretical orientation and its implication on the counselling process
	I chat with the elderly to keep them company, but they keep you too long if you let them.
B.10.4	Ensure continuing self-support and supervision
	Look after yourself, and try not to get found out.

Neat boxes and complex numbering systems are currently very fashionable now that word processing and desktop publishing are freely available. They make lists look more coherent, clear and useful than they really are. Yet the lead body work tells us nothing about any counselling theory or practice or its value. It fails, even, to produce a definition of counselling that distinguishes it from other human activities.

If counselling is ever adequately defined, with a first-class accreditation process accompanying it, I fear that the 'James and Joan Placemakers' of this world will still ensure that they fulfil the criteria. Assessors might suspect the motives, humanity and underlying spirit of some candidates, but what can they do about it? Will any accreditation procedure ever be able to reach to the core of counselling and distinguish between empowerment and exploitation, or altruism and self-promotion? Can any evaluation scheme detect, measure and evaluate 'humanity of spirit'? What happens as the bureaucracy and formality grows? Who will prosper? Will a humane voice be preserved? Or will power fall into the hands of the network socialite, professional conference-goer and 'technical' specialist accomplished in acronyms and with a wallet large enough to secure professional qualifications?

With skill in communication, we can speak from the heart or present a highly persuasive imitation. We can seek truth or plausibility. We can empower – or disable, bedazzle and deceive. Advertising and public relations encourage customers to enter into the plausible fictions they create. These industries work hard to stay ahead of an ever more sophisticated audience. Quite often they succeed.

As power increases, so the possibility of abuse grows. Specialists in human motivation are expert in hiding their own motivations. I, for one, am not convinced that, in counselling as in other activities, virtue is managing to keep pace with technology.

The US experience

Counsellor training and accreditation in the USA is at least 15 years in advance of developments in the UK, although the UK is catching up fast. Always, we are told, the professionals concerned are seeking to improve the quality of service for their clients. Yet little research has been done that justifies such a claim. Is there any solid evidence to suggest that the professionalization of humanity has produced, or benefited, humanity? Consider a recent survey.

Carol Sherrard[16] has reviewed 41 experimental studies comparing the effectiveness of professional with nonprofessional helpers. Twenty-eight of these revealed no difference in outcome, 12 showed the nonprofessionals to be more effective, and only 1 concluded that the professional group was more effective. Yet, in the very teeth of this thoroughly disappointing evidence, Sherrard concludes that British psychologists might follow the American and Australian example, and restrict postgraduate diploma and masters courses in counselling to psychology graduates only. Her underlying ambivalence becomes evident, however, when she suggests that clinical psychology is felt to be an alienating activity 'by at least one significant portion of the population, namely women, and even women inside the profession'. Despite the absence of evidence from trained psychologists that trained psychologists are more effective as carers, they go on fighting hard to improve their power and status. What does this tell us about scientific empiricism and academic detachment within the psychology profession?

In the USA it takes many years of training to produce care special- ists, and the unfortunate client may have difficulty in understanding how one differs from the next. Can it be said that, as a result of all this labour, the USA is now a more caring place? How is this burgeoning growth of professional care to be explained and understood?

From the 1970s onwards, governments have had difficulty adhering to a full employment policy. They are unwilling or unable to guarantee work, and there is greater inequality between, and competition among, sections of the workforce. Insecurity blows like a chill wind through us all, and we are forced to find new ways of earning a living. We all want our new career to be secure. Therefore, and bluntly, when we have climbed aboard, we like to pull up the ladder behind us. All professionals thus seek to prevent others from undercutting them or saturating the profession. However, they need to rationalize this (rational) behaviour, since blatant efforts to operate restrictive practices encounter public disapproval. Once qualified, it is in every new graduate's interest to seek longer and more esoteric training programmes before allowing others to join in. Legislators have to be persuaded. Bright competitors abound, anxious to join or undersell us. As one of the elect, it is in our interest to build higher walls to stop too many others from joining us.

During the 1970s, US psychologists secured legislation to make them eligible for payment by third parties *without medical supervision.* They were thus able to operate independently, free from the control of doctors. Psychologists built an enclosure around lucrative parts of the market by achieving stringent control over credentials. Employment for those without degrees in psychology was restricted. Psychologists successfully prevented counsellors from 'using the tools of psychology' unless they were licensed psychologists. A key victory was secured in 1972 (*Weldon* v *Board of Examiners*).

US counsellors saw that they, too, would have to seek credentials of their own if they were to have any hold on the counselling market.

Exactly the same thing is happening in the UK 20 years later. Success requires effective communication with, or more technically 'kissing up to', legislators. Governments tend to ask: Do we need new kinds of accredited carer? Already, there are psychologists, psychiatrists, social workers, psychotherapists with their own boards, credentialing and licensing programmes. Are there any real, substantial differences between these different groups? Is there any evidence that they can deliver what they promise? Are they clear about what they do promise?

Legislators, like clients, have difficulty in distinguishing between the categories of care person. They meet someone who talks, listens and tries to be of help, but they forget whether this carer was an accredited or unaccredited psychiatric nurse, or psychiatric social worker, or clinical psychologist, or counselling psychologist, or counsellor (without a psychology degree), or educational psychologist, or psychiatrist, or psychotherapist, or trainer, or unpaid volunteer. Doctors are generally more distinguishable, in that they can prescribe pills and are called 'Doctor', but the psychologist is sometimes called 'Doctor' as well. How long will it be before we have PhDs in social work, counselling, maybe even nursing? Will everyone then be called 'Doctor'? Will this lead to an improved service?

Already, in the USA, a Master's degree is needed, plus two or more years of supervised work, and an additional national diploma, even to be a relatively lowly counsellor. However, even though the skills may be the same, you are not allowed to switch to related careers. If professionals want to convert from 'counselling' to 'counselling psychology', or from psychiatric social work to clinical psychology, they will have to start all over again, from the bottom of the career ladder. In the UK, the AGCP lead body is trying to encourage lateral career movement among candidates who can demonstrate the necessary skills and experience. They face enormous (covert) resistance from the professions concerned.

Different care professions offer any one of a smörgåsbord of therapies: practitioners at one centre may be transactional analysts, while at another the medical staff may favour a psychoanalytic approach, whereas the social workers opt for behavioural skills training or client-centred counselling. A few miles away, the opposite may be the case. Yet staff increasingly dress and look the same, and it may be difficult to predict theory and practice even when their profession is known.

The vogue within community mental health centres is to present a friendly human face to the public that blurs, indeed entirely hides, professional hierarchies. The message is, 'We all work together as a team here, and we all talk in an ordinary, unpretentious way, and try to be as open, accessible and honest as possible'. Thus every professional increasingly tries to present a humble human face to clients and to downplay professional differences and rivalries. But if Bob (social worker) applies formally for the same status as Jim (clinical psychologist), the board in question will almost certainly conclude that Bob cannot possibly be 'using the tools of psychology' since he has not got a degree in psychology. His social work qualifications, however excellent and extensive, will not count. It will not be acceptable for Bob to plead that, 'I've been working with Jim (clinical psychologist) for the past six years. We are both supervised in the same way, we both operate the same brand of psychotherapy and have received the same in-service training. We both can produce the same evidence, or lack of evidence, of competence'.

Such restrictive practices may seem indefensible but, as one very senior practitioner explained, 'It takes a particular kind of saintliness to undermine one's own source of a secure income'. I asked a US professional qualified in both counselling and counselling psychology to explain the difference between the two. He candidly advised, off the record of course, $15 an hour (1992).

Counselling and Europe

The European First General Directive on Higher Education was implemented in the UK in April 1991 and enables graduates to seek employment throughout Europe, within their field of competence, without retraining. Governments determine 'designated authorities' to monitor the equivalence of degrees in the European Union. They also register 'competent authorities', with powers to award diplomas.

The BPS has become both the competent and the designated authority in psychology. It may, like its American counterparts, secure control of psychotherapy and counselling as well. The UKCP is seeking to prevent this by achieving the status of designated authority for psychotherapy. It therefore needs to distinguish psychotherapy from both counselling and psychology. Can such distinctions be made with any sort of integrity? Will academics in the UK be detached and objective in this discussion?

The UKCP's chances are weakened by an absence of consensus among its own members. Therapists, unlike counsellors within the BAC, appear to be less reticent about bringing their differences into the open. This is awkward for lawyers trying to frame the necessary legislation. In particular, psychoanalysts remain convinced that they should keep their pre-eminent status, in the face of ever tougher criticism from rival therapists.

In the early 1990s, rumours abounded about the lobbying in Brussels. For example, the European Association for Psychotherapy (EAP) represents clinical psychologists and psychiatrists, rather than other therapists more generally. Representatives from rival bodies are trying to prevent EAP hegemony, and have received 'assurances'. Counsellors have come together as the European Association for Counselling, to rival the alliances of analysts and psychologists. They are targeting the Council for Professions Supplementary to Medicine ('Doctors rule, OK') which may be renamed as the Council for Health Related Professions ('Doctors' power is waning?').

Counsellors may hold their own against psychoanalysts, whose best days may be over, but can they run head to head with psychologists, whose continental colleagues have a powerful hold over psychotherapy and counselling. Counsellors may, eventually, find that all their training and management is controlled by academic psychologists, however much these latter may lack clinical experience.

At the time of writing, there are still a few options for counsellors: governments wish to increase rather than reduce competition; some (nonanalytic) psychotherapists seek common ground with counsellors; and some counselling psychologists, feeling insecure within the BPS, would prefer to form a constructive alliance with the BAC. Yet barriers may be difficult to overcome. There is now a European Second Directive in Education, which makes cooperation more difficult. It concerns vocational education and divides it into graduate and nongraduate tiers. Psychologists are generally graduates; counsellors, often, are not. Status inequality is thus enshrined from the outset. The BPS has developed a postgraduate diploma in counselling psychology whose status is higher than anything the BAC can produce.

A BPS diploma will be equivalent to a National Vocational Qualification (NVQ) at level 5. The BAC one will be restricted to levels 1–4 at best. Does it matter? Can it be assumed that a level 5 counselling psychologist is better than a level 3 counsellor? The level 5 qualification may actually require *less* practical work than level 3 training. Clients will generally assume that a level 5 postgraduate must be providing a better service than a level 3 nongraduate. Fees will reflect this assumption, however bogus the quality differential may be in reality.[17]

Such an unholy squabble for power and status is human enough in an insecure economic climate, but it has little to do with quality, honesty or humanity. Counsellors have been known to criticize dogmatism and delusion among analysts. Yet they assume that further training will improve their own service, even though the analysts they question are themselves the most intensively trained, supervised and 'therapized' of all therapy professionals.

I do not thereby suggest that care professionals are any more disreputable than anyone else, but the boundaries they are seeking to establish appear to lack any in-built integrity. They must therefore *invent* distinctions if their market is to be protected, all the while posing as role models of moral rectitude. The ironies are painful.

This discussion may undermine reader confidence and professional careers. I may therefore be breaking the BAC's code of practice, which states that 'Counsellors should not conduct themselves in their counselling-related activities in ways which undermine public confidence in either their role as counsellor or in the work of other counsellors'.[18] The clause seeks to deal with professional abuse, but it also (inadvertently?) places a gag on whistle-blowers.

Hopes and expectations around counselling are, I believe, much too great. Desirable qualities and skills listed by counselling theorists cannot, in my view, be reliably delivered by flesh and blood human beings. This is shocking and cynical only to those who seek *superhuman* individuals and institutions. The wise know they can think, feel and act like fools; the knowledgeable know how little they know; the enlightened grasp the 'key' to existence in recognizing that there is no key.

There is no evidence that therapy has more or less than an average share of wise and helpful practitioners. By its nature, it may attract those who think they have 'sorted out' the mystery of existence. Arrogant and controlling people may well choose to pose as non-directive and respectful. And it's harder to be humble when you are a grade five, leading edge, trainer of trainers of therapists.

Some people feel utterly lost, and may choose to become clients. Others believe they are found, saved, sorted. These will more probably become therapists. Each role can become addictive and unhelpful. Wisdom and compassion are the most sought-after qualities in counsellors. Can they be measured, accredited and organized into a management hierarchy? Can they be mechanized and categorized by accountants and trainers? These core qualities and skills resist easy placement within our portfolio: when most alive, we sense the fleetingness, fragility and sluggishness of much of our experience; when most helpful we know how often we cannot or will not be of assistance. As great problem-solvers, we know that final or ideal solutions are rare; sometimes there is no answer, and often we are not best placed to provide it.

Such limitations to what is perceivable and predictable are now more fully understood via mathematical theories of chaos. These show how, why and when complex phenomena, like human beings, can be, in principle, unpredictable. Perhaps the hubris within psychology requires the humility of 'psychaos'.

The most caring and compassionate know that they do not always, or often, feel caring and compassionate. Creative thinkers know that very little of their thought is at all original, and the most original is unlikely to be the best. Those most skilled in empowering others know that they are also well able to seduce, if they so choose, and that often they do so choose. Finally, those who are most clear-minded know how often they are operating in a fog, murk and mess. They know what they are doing well enough to see how little they really know about human behaviour, motives and intentions.

There are always going to be wise and compassionate individuals available to counsel others, but, if the above observations are correct, no formula, institution or skills portfolio will reliably deliver such counsellors on demand. Some professionals, I am sure, are saintly people, but saintliness, by its nature, cannot be manufactured and processed and, by its nature, is likely to remain rare. Nor, even, can ordinary human virtues such as love, warmth, compassion and empathy, be professionally organized. Therefore, if counselling finds itself too dependent on all these desirable human qualities, it seems to me to be doomed as a professional activity.

Notes

1   David Smail, *Taking Care. An Alternative to Therapy*. Dent, 1987.

2   Gerard Egan, *The Skilled Helper*, 3rd edn, p. 196. Brooks/Cole, 1986.

3   David Cohen (ed.), *Challenging the Therapeutic State*, p. 63, 1990.

4   10 million *astrological* counselling sessions in France are provided every year by 40 thousand astrological counsellors. They want their courses accredited at the Sorbonne. Authorities there say 'no'. (BBC news 17 February 1994)

5   Michael Pokorny, Chair of the Registration Board for the UK Council for Psychotherapy, summarized the research at a BAC 1992 Annual Conference Workshop as follows: 10 per cent of all care professionals investigated admit to having sexually abused their clients, and the abuse may be *worst* among the *most* highly trained!

6   Accreditation and professionalization do not themselves provide safeguards. Counsellors should probably, by law, be registered and disbarred from practice if convicted of sexual abuse. As for professionals

48 *Challenges to Counselling and Psychotherapy*

working with children in residential settings, there should be an automatic check on the criminal record of candidates. This limited form of protection is to be preferred to full professionalization and accreditation, because it does not raise unwarranted expectations about the abilities of the counsellor.

7 BBC2 television explored the problem in 'Sex and The Forbidden Zone' (13 November 1992). In a study of 300 clinical psychologists carried out by Tanya Garett at Warwick University, 4 per cent actually *admitted* to being guilty of sexual abuse; 22 per cent had patients who had previously been abused by therapists, and 44 per cent had been told by others of cases of abuse. See also Peter Rutter, *Sex in the Forbidden Zone.* Mandala, 1990.

8 Brian Thorne, *Person-centered Counselling: Therapeutic and Spiritual Dimensions.* Whurr, 1991.

9 Perhaps it is useful to compare counsellors with comedians: the best are each unique, client tastes vary, training and certification may no more guarantee success in counselling than in comedy.

10 The 'science' of determining personality by observing the pattern of bumps on a person's head; popular during the nineteenth century!

11 Miller Mair, 'Competencies for counselling psychology: some preliminary considerations'.

12 Stephen Murgatroyd, *Counselling and Helping.* British Pyschological Society, 1985.

13 R. Woolfe, S. Murgatroyd and S. Rhys, *Guidance and Counselling in Adult and Continuing Education.* Open University Press, 1987.

14 It could be argued that counselling of any kind is more psychological than is research into pigeons and rats. Certainly, though, there is an energetic rat race among humans, and a pecking order within all the professions.

15 Raymond Williams, *Keywords.* Fontana, 1967.

16 In an unpublished paper presented to members of the British Psychological Society, Lincoln, 1991.

17 There are already practitioners offering the very same counselling or training at wildly different prices, depending on the status of the agency employing them.

18 BAC Code of Practice, section B.2.4.1, 1990.

Chapter 3

Who shall be our counsellor?

Professors in every branch of the sciences prefer their own theories to truth; the reason is that their theories are private property, but truth is common stock.

(Colton, 1822)[1]

A neurotic is the man who builds castles in the air. A psychotic is the man who lives in it. And a psychiatrist is the man who collects the rent.

(Anon)

The monitoring of mental health services is hampered by a lack of information about service activities and an almost complete absence of information about outcomes.

(Audit Commission, 1994)[2]

It's a tough world, even for relatively comfortable professionals. We cannot live off past achievements, short-term contracts are becoming the norm, and the West now struggles with low-waged, yet highly-mechanized, educated and motivated competitors. The effects invade or infiltrate all our lives.

Care sector workers are themselves a part of these aggressive, high-pace and performance economies, although health services can sometimes appear almost *feudal* in their rankings, ceremonials and struggles for status and recognition. Rivalry is not intrinsically wrong or harmful, of course, and it does not have to damage personal and working relationships, which can be as variable as the personalities and practices involved. In fact, professional reputations are enhanced when productive lines of communication are achieved, but such efforts to be constructive and cooperative can themselves mask underlying tensions. For example, consider what can happen when one interest group has exercised very great autocratic power over all the others but wishes for, or is being forced to accept, a more democratic regime. The medical profession provides a classic example of such a change in power relations. Some of its own membership themselves wish to be less autocratic and emotionally distant, and many other categories of professional staff want a more team-spirited ethos.

This competitive tension is exacerbated when new skills, methods and values are introduced and there is uncertainty about their ownership. Which group of professionals is in the best position to carry out the new responsibilities and operate the new methods? For example, to whom shall the counsellor be answerable? Where in the status hierarchy will our new counsellors be placed? Shall they deal with patients? Clients? People? And who shall be our counsellor?

Doctors might argue that they have always practised counselling, among other skills, long before such a word was ever introduced. The doctor–patient relationship, they can assert, has always been at the heart of good medicine. The clinical psychologist, on the other hand, can challenge the medical profession's hegemony of power, particularly in relation to counselling. Bolstered by their new status of 'chartered psychologist', introduced in 1989, and with backing from medical critics,[3] they can plead that doctors have been overly preoccupied with technical interventions and given too low a priority to human relationships. Doctors, it is sometimes claimed, relate too much to illnesses and not enough to people. They have the mind-set of a mechanic and are therefore least fitted to engage in the people skills of counselling and psychotherapy.

Some doctors will often, in any case, pass on the counselling function to others when it is seen as peripheral, low in status and overly time-consuming. They have other skills to practise, and many doctors consider that intensive and extensive counselling is best left to someone else. There are exceptions. Michael and Enid Balint, for example, developed training and research groups for GPs at the Tavistock Clinic in London back in the 1950s, which provided the opportunity for medical colleagues to discuss the human and counselling components of patient care on a regular basis. Case examples and personal reactions were discussed, and the latter were considered central to the doctor–patient relationship. Doctors with a Balint orientation will do all they can to provide a version of counselling to patients, within the substantial limits of the available time. At the very least, they will be conscious of the need to be using counselling skills.

Doctors may see counselling as a central component of their work or hand it over to one of a huge choice of other professionals. Psychiatric nurses, psychiatric social workers, occupational therapists, clinical psychologists and physiotherapists might engage in therapeutic talk with patients while providing other interventions. Indeed, almost anyone else might more or less formally and consciously practise 'counselling skills' in the drop-in centre, day-care facility or hospital ward. Increasingly, full- or part-time professional counsellors are employed, who may have previously been employed and trained in a wide variety of backgrounds.

The nurse, ward sister, hospital visitor, general social worker, chaplain and student might all practise counselling skills. Even the cleaner or tea lady may offer informal, yet effective, human contact. I have heard many positive stories about the healing powers of certain tea ladies, although lay-person power, too, can be exaggerated and romanticized.

Counselling is sometimes regarded as an important component of the work of school teachers, educational psychologists and youth and community workers, as well as of people specifically named as counsellors. There are paid and unpaid workers in the voluntary sector who are busy counselling. Elsewhere, there are health education and health promotion workers, community psychiatric nurses, health visitors, district nurses, practice nurses, pastors, pastoral counsellors, probation officers, prison workers, adult education staff, outreach workers, in-service trainers, and 'New Opportunities', 'Second Chance', 'Restart' and 'access' tutors. Any and all of these are increasingly liable to consider that counselling is, or should be, an important component of their work.[4] Additionally, 'personal counselling' is offered in conjunction with specific advice work, for example by debt, career, genetic, lifestyle or legal aid counsellors.

In the business and commercial world, too, managers and staff are taking much more interest in counselling.[5] Employee management, redundancy and appraisal packages might include counselling. The personnel department may incorporate it and foster counselling skills training. Organization development consultants provide it to senior management. Counsellors, medical officers and nurses form part of increasingly comprehensive packages of employee assistance programmes. Business enterprise counsellors assist those who plan to start up in business.

Not surprisingly, therefore, counsellor training courses are mushrooming everywhere. There are currently 30 000 people earning a living from counselling in the UK, and a further 270 000 in the voluntary sector delivering counselling services. Additionally, the Department of the Environment estimates that another 2.5 million people use counselling as a major component of their work as nurses, social workers, career guidance workers and general practitioners.[6] All these counsellors declare their humane intentions and their wish, in whatever way, to do their best for their staff, clients or patients. Are they all as benign as they declare? Counselling, in the wrong hands, is a way of disguising social control within the trappings of individual compassion. Is every counsellor trying to help us get through to ourselves? Or are some trying to get control over us or steer us in a direction that suits their employer? Routinely, I hear of the need to 'counsel' people in or out of wherever they are. This sort of talk has an ominous ring to it. Truth, apparently, is at the heart of the counselling mission, but, in the real world, Power and Plausibility are often given higher priority. We are surely naïve if we pretend otherwise.

In a hospital setting, counselling may be seen as central to the healing process or, at the other extreme, as a peripheral tool to try if nothing else works. Its status among different teams and members of staff varies enormously. Overall, though, its importance is advancing steadily, and this poses problems for the medical profession in particular.

Doctors, in the UK as in the USA, face professional challenges from many quarters. Firstly, there are social workers, with a line management that stretches right out of the hospital setting and into the local authority social services department. There are also clinical psychologists who, with their chartered status recently granted by royal decree, can now claim to regulate themselves with the same kind of professional independence that the British Medical Association expects when supervizing its own doctors. Chartered clinical psychologists no longer wish merely to provide the doctor with the results of routine mechanical testing. Instead, they seek more personal and central relationships with clients and more control over decision-making. They may be better trained in human relationship skills than are doctors,[7] yet the doctor retains ultimate responsibility for the management of patient care.

Medical hegemony is becoming harder to maintain and justify. Illness is not just a medical matter. It has social, psychological, economic, political and spiritual dimensions, all of which lie outside medical competence. So why should doctors control so many facets of patient care? Illness, too, is extremely costly. Health care requires organization, sophisticated management and a skilled grasp of priorities, cost–benefit options, equipment and cash. Doctors are not trained in any of these. They are not executives, so why do they retain large executive powers? This, certainly, is the view of some hospital managers and administrators, whose powers have grown rapidly at the expense of, primarily, the medical profession.

The psychological dimensions of illness have been receiving more attention in recent years, yet psychology is only a small component of medical training. Understandably, therefore, psychologists may sometimes wish to challenge medical diagnoses and treatment programmes.

Because each side has its own professional reputation to maintain, an unseemly battle of wills is generally avoided, but the questions remain: Should counselling be offered? What kind? With what purpose? By whom? With what training? Who can best decide? Who can quote any reliable research?

The psychiatrist, as a medical specialist in mental illness, might be best suited to the task, but most psychiatrists in the UK focus on chemical interventions for faulty brains. Physical responses, they believe, are required for physical ailments in the brain that create mental disturbances merely as a byproduct. Counselling, from this perspective is, at best, an adjunct to the main treatment programme. Consequently, most research in psychiatry investigates disordered brains rather than distressed minds and souls.

Disillusionment has grown, however, about drug treatment programmes for human distress. Side-effects can be longer lasting than the cure and more intractable than the original illness. Epidemiological evidence suggests that much (most?) mental distress results from social pressures and personal problems in living rather than physical disorders of the brain. There are significant correlations between stressful environments and mental breakdown. These suggest the need for individual and collective problem-solving rather than physical treatment programmes.

Crime, poverty, unemployment and their subsequent psychological stresses are too important for the medical profession to ignore. Who can pose as the expert on such matters? The doctor? The psychologist? The sociologist? Can the medical profession retain hegemony over health care teams in such a context? How can it ensure that psychologists retain their status as medical ancillaries?[8]

Psychology can be defined as a branch of medicine merely by placing it within a department of psychological medicine. The adjective garnishes the noun, which, conceptually, remains central. Since it is a department of medicine rather than psychology, it sounds sensible for control to be retained by medical staff. Departmental control and power goes to those who own the noun, as in 'counselling psychology' or, much less likely, 'medical psychology'.[9] A minority of psychiatrists have specialized in talking treatments and refer to themselves as 'consultant psychotherapists'. They are never referred to as 'consultant counsellors'. Can you guess why?

Schools of counselling

Assuming that counselling has become acceptable as treatment, which of the many versions on offer are the most suitable and effective? Perhaps a client would respond best with a Rogerian or behaviour therapist, or transpersonal specialist, or whoever? Why, then, might they have been assigned to a psychodynamic counsellor? The answer is that generally clients are treated by whoever is available. They deliver what they were trained to provide, because that is what they were trained to provide. The Audit Commission's 1994 *Review of Mental Health Services*[2] calls for effective management, coordination and leadership of mental health teams. Provision, it suggests, does not necessarily relate to need, and services vary erratically because:

> Often teams are loose coalitions of independent professionals with freedom to decide individually what to do, when and with whom.

It is difficult to categorize schools of counselling and psychotherapy, and there are market pressures on practitioners to exaggerate the power and uniqueness of their own particular product. Market-winners are promoted as newer, fresher, stronger, cleaner, gentler, more economical, friendly, flexible and easy to use. Humility and caution rarely feature within the claims of advertisers. Instead, the mood must be confident, assertive and categorical. The service must be brandished with an enthusiasm untrammelled by doubts and inconvenient yearnings for integrity. Marketers must show unconditional positive regard to, above all else, their own product.

Hence the same ideas and methods appear repeatedly in different guises, under different names. Few clients have the time, inclination or opportunity to disentangle the various shrill claims of competitors busily seeking to secure a niche for themselves in the marketplace.

The Psychotherapy Handbook (edited by Richie Herink, from the New American Library) gave 'an A to Z guide of more than two hundred and fifty different therapies in use today'. That was back in 1980. How many more 'new' approaches have been spawned in the intervening period? The book itself invites 'psychotherapists who wish to include descriptions of additional systems and techniques in future editions of this compendium [to] contact the Editor'.

Some of the brand names are certainly eyecatching: Vita-Erg Therapy, for example; or Zaraleya Psychoenergetic Technique; Elavil Sleep Therapy; Mythosynthesis; C1C2 Project Psychotherapy; Psychobiological Psychotherapy, Psychedelic Therapy, Bioplasmic Therapy, as opposed to Bioenergetic Analysis, Biocentric Therapy or Bio Scream Psychotherapy.

Some, although psychotherapeutic, are not generally thought of as psychotherapy, for example Poetry Therapy, Writing Therapy, Play Therapy, Occupational Therapy, Electro-Convulsive Therapy, Psychosurgery, Aesthetic Plastic Surgery, Lithium Therapy, Megavitamin Therapy, Music Therapy, Nutrition-Based Therapy, Pharmacotherapy, Puppet Therapy, Soap Opera Therapy, Art Therapy, Cooking as Therapy, Dance Therapy and Folk Healing.

Some present a technical, scientific image: Videotherapy, Paraverbal Therapy, Logotherapy, Neuro-linguistic Programming, Neurotone Therapy, Office Network Therapy, Transactional Analysis. Others develop the work of earlier big names: Sullivanism, Radix Neo-Reichian Education, Kleinian Technique, Jungian Group Psychotherapy, Adlerian Psychotherapy, The Alexander Technique, Bates Method of Vision Training, Will Therapy of Otto Rank, Horneyian Therapy, Fischer-Hoffman Process (not to be confused with processes in industrial chemistry) and Eriksonian Therapy, from Erik Erikson, to be distinguished from Milton Erickson's Ericksonian Therapy.

Freudian therapy, amazingly, is not mentioned. Presumably it is not sufficiently *new*. 'Rolfing', too, fails to appear, along with many others, like 'est', which have risen, shone, faded and disappeared. Professionals can be avoided and costs saved via Mutual Need Therapy (p. 406) or Mutual Help Groups (p. 403). Costs can be planned via Money Therapy Through Financial Counselling (p. 388). At this stage, perhaps, the solicitor and accountant might wish to come forward with the unofficial counselling service they have provided clients for centuries.

A product in any market may claim appeal by being new, or old. So, too, in therapy. In the 'old' category are Acupuncture, Aikido, Christian Psychotherapy (it used to be called Christianity), Senoi Dream Group Therapy, Mandala Therapy, Buddhist Insight Meditation, Tibetan Psychic Healing and, an old method in new more streamlined garb, Transcendental Meditation. Despite their attractive venerability, reliable evidence of their effectivness is sparse and uncertain. Meehl (1965),

VandenBos (1983) and Saxe (1980) claim to have assembled evidence of the positive efficacy of more recent therapies, but this is frequently challenged, most recently in results cited by Sherrard (1991).[10]

How are we to deal with all this? No wonder Raimy's *Training in Clinical Psychology*[11] defined therapy as 'an unidentified technique applied to unspecified problems with unpredictable outcomes, for which long and rigorous training is required'. How can we disentangle the coherent and effective from the useless and idiotic? Should we try a little Emotional Common Sense (p. 100) or explore the merits of Computer Therapy (p. 111): 'I am your automatic lover, automatic lover!' Perhaps some Guided Fantasy (p. 198) would provide escape or insight? Do you feel drained? Perhaps Flooding is what you need (p. 233)? Empty inside? Then try Intense Feeling Therapy. Do you feel you are falling apart? You may need an Integrity Group or a dose of Structural Integration. You keep on making the same old mistakes? Try Life Skills Counselling or Assertive Behaviour Therapy.

Perhaps you are numb to the whole process of therapy and healing? In Provocative Therapy, the therapist will do anything to provoke a response, with few professional or moral constraints. Or perhaps you don't wish to lock yourself away into just one approach; Eclectic or Broad Spectrum Psychotherapy may be for you (this deserves, and will receive, more attention later). Maybe you expect too much from therapy? A dose of Anti-Expectation Psychotherapy may be required, or Burn-Out Prevention, or Rational-Emotive Therapy, or Reality Therapy, or Realness Therapy, each of which is reluctant to be merged with its neighbours. Is reality humdrum? Tired of the 9-to-5 routine? Try Exaggeration Therapy, Encounter Therapy, Psychodrama, Hypnointrospection, Existential Group Psychotherapy. You want more peace and quiet? Meditative Therapy or Restricted Environmental Stimulation Therapy may be for you.

You want to make a new start? Try Rebirthing. Or why not see your place in the broader cosmos? Choose from Transpersonal Psychotherapy, Psychosynthesis and Holistic Counselling. For a less broad context, there are Social Influence Therapy and Street Psychotherapy. For a narrow context, choose between Self-Therapy, Self-Psychotherapy and Self-Puzzle.

Beginners might feel confused with a book listing so many approaches to psychotherapy. If so, they might need to consult a reference book that summarizes the marketplace of personal development books, centres and activities. Richard Adams' *New Times Network* provides a worldwide list of groups and centres for personal growth.

The *Pilgrim's Guide to Planet Earth* contains hints and practices for the traveller; thousands of New Age Centres, restaurants, food stores, hotels, book stores, sites of natural and manmade splendour, travel routes and 'planetary points'. There is material here for more than a lifetime of personal growth, provided you could afford the air fares and accommodation costs. Katinka Matson's *Encyclopaedia of Reality*, and Denise Winn's *Whole Mind Book* both explain key concepts and leading growth circuit luminaries. There are others.

You can visit your health food store and ask for the local listings of counsellors, therapist and alternative healers. If you live in a large town or city there may be a locally produced guide available. 'Holistic London', for example, is a very large work. In the USA, there may be hundreds of care listings available in the *Yellow Pages*.

Way back in 1976, Cris Popenoe produced a guide to books entitled *Inner Development*. In 654 large and densely packed pages, it offers single paragraph reviews of over *11 000* books on personal growth, from 1200 different publishers. Thousands more are appearing all the time.[12] We would be crippled if we tried to keep abreast of all this empowering literature.

By 1972, the journalist R. D. Rosen and a colleague conceived a small plot. They decided to invent a cult:

> We called our imaginary commune Sansuki and, thinking to spoof the various cults that had recently won the attention of the mass media, reported that the communards were involved in trying to reach two states in the spiritual continuum. The first was the state of vegetable consciousness, called Brachli, the second a state described in neurophysiological gibberish as a regression to the primacy of the rhinencephalon, or reptile brain.[13]

There is a striking similarity here with a satirical text I was given, dating back to 1932:

> You must withdraw yourself from this decaying world, this world of prying eyes and sapless non-conformities! You must retreat, back and back, down and down, into your innermost ego, the central self of all the selves, the core of your life! It is the ichthyosaurus-ego! It is the vegetable-ego! It is the cabbage-ego! Be green! Be sappy! Live! Live! Feel! Feel! Feel!! (From the Workers' Educational Association Oxford University Summer School satire by John Mack)

Returning to Rosen's more recent spoof of 1972:

> Although the story contained several believable anecdotes, we thought we had been careful to include enough ludicrous details to make clear our

intentions. There was the ethereal ex-medical student and now commune leader named 'Bob', known also as the head lettuce. There were scenes of violence among vegetarians and one of a woman curled up into a ball pretending she was a tomato. But our joke was more successful than we had ever imagined. Not only did the newspaper receive a handful of letters asking soberly for more information about Sansuki, but even members of the newspaper staff, perhaps already numbed by front page lunacy, were surprised to discover that such a place did not, in fact, exist. (One reader, to our relief, did write a clever letter to say that, as a member of Sansuki, he appreciated the fairness with which we had treated the cult.)

New, new ...ish, and old-revamped-as-new approaches to psycho-therapy are constantly being proposed, such is the shortness of our collective memory and our poor sense of history.

Counselling and healing

Clearly, there is great uncertainty about the use and abuse of the terms 'counselling' and 'psychotherapy'. The root of the latter is Greek: 'psyche' is 'soul'; 'therapeia' means 'healing'.

The psyche can be healed in many different ways. I enjoy walks in the countryside at the weekends, and they are a basic and important means of maintaining my sanity. Perhaps I should try and copyright Gaia-therapy, Terratherapy, Verduretherapy, Agoratherapy? The occasional drink can help. Is this Alcohol Therapy? A branch of Pharmacotherapy? Not to be confused with Alcohol Addiction?

In the UK, healing can be found in tea breaks. Before anyone smiles at such a suggestion, let us remember that Japanese Shintoism speaks very precisely and explicitly of the healing powers of its tea-drinking ritual.

More dubious strategies are junk distraction therapy: Mindless entertainment therapy; Scapegoating therapy; At-least-I-am-not-as-badly-off-as-you therapy; Newspapers provide all these 'therapies', especially Schadenfreudenism.[14]

Less dubious is belief in a benevolent cosmic father therapy? Aromatherapy is already available. Best of all might be employment therapy, respect for other human beings therapy, adequate income therapy, housing therapy, human contact therapy, sexual relations therapy (when the attraction is mutual).

Having newly discovered the joys of growing vegetables, I was thinking of horticultural therapy, but I found that this plot of the market has already been claimed, with a 'horticultural therapy bus', offering short training seminars, special workshops and activities and the chance to exchange news.

Perhaps we need a therapist to advise us on the therapy we need, a sort of therapy therapist. In Japan, the Ministry of International Trade and Industry (MITI) wants corporations to employ full-time 'leisure advisers' to help employees plan their free time. The National Recreation Association of Japan offers classes to train such 'leisure counsellors' and, by 1991, there were 1200 would-be advisers in training.

There are thousands of ways in which people try to keep themselves at worst sane, and at best inspired. At the end of the self-conscious twentieth century, these ordinary health-making activities are getting tagged with the term 'therapy'. Common pursuits are coupled with a smart title, designer kit and new leisure opportunity component. Air, Earth, Fire and Water transform into aerobics, mudbaths, ultraviolet sunbeds, and water pursuits. Fishing could become aquatorial meditation; a bath or shower is a form of hydrotherapy (this was all the rage in the nineteenth century); leaning out of the window is a type of awareness meditation; promenading down the street might be repackaged as a walking meditation; staring into space a mindfulness meditation. In previous centuries, extravagent expenditures on health and healing fads and fashions tended to be confined to the monarchy and aristocracy. Now, sections of the middle class have become prosperous enough to move in on this market.

Almost anything and anyone can have a healing influence when it, or they, meet some basic need and when we have been deprived for some time. Many, world wide, urgently require nutritherapy, more commonly known as having enough to eat. In the West, we already have naturotherapy, correct eating therapy, having eaten too much and too badly. Many need a roof over their heads – personal construction therapy.[15]

Similarly, almost anything can become the problem rather than the cure when we abuse or indulge ourselves. Fresh air and exercise are undoubtedly therapeutic,[16] but not when you become obsessed and hooked on adrenaline. You may cause real physical damage through overexertion. Fixation on any kind of therapy may become harmful. Doing almost anything else may then be healing.

The Western distinction between mental and physical approaches to health is not found in all cultures. Chinese medicine views body, mind and spirit as aspects of one interconnected system, which is itself part of a living process. With holistic models like this, it is impossible to think of the mind without attention to body symptoms, and unfeasible to heal the body without regard to mental state. This more integrated approach seems superior in principle, if not in practice, to fragmented Western specialisms.[17]

The holistic movement provides a more harmonized practice, but it also seems to embrace every kind of quackery and crankiness. Hopefully, with an open mind coupled with sober research, we can hold on to the harmony, jettison the quackery and examine healing from a wider range of approaches.

Western verbal and analytic intellects tend to forget that healing occurs in countless different ways, and that the best means depends on the unique personality and circumstances of the client. Instead, Western specialists, sealed personally and professionally within their own narrow fields of enquiry, overaccentuate the importance of either biology (in the case of surgeons) or psychology (among psychotherapists). With so many verbal and voluble clients, psychotherapy is regarded as a 'talking treatment'. Talk is thought to be the first, last and only means of healing a troubled mind. However:

> Most people now feel that verbal interaction is somehow secondary. I would say that, as long as you are using verbal therapy only, which means sitting or lying down and talking, you will not really do anything dramatic in the psychosomatic situation. (Stanislav Grof, in Capra, 1989)[18]

Some therapists thus avoid talk, preferring actions or other media – art, music, theatre, play, projects, environments, activities – as a means of expression and communication. I suspect that this kind of healing is grossly underrated. Westerners engage in far too much talk as it is, and can easily talk themselves deeper into their problems rather than out of them. Like most clichés, it is true that a picture can say more than a thousand words. I guess that appropriate touch or action says more than a thousand pictures. If unsuitable and inappropriate, such a nonverbal intervention can, of course, do correspondingly greater *harm*.

It is hardly surprising that the greatest fans of talking treatments are to be found within the chattering classes. As a fully paid-up member, I am conscious of how our talkativeness gives us little opportunity to hear and feel the healing power of silence. There is a *silence* deep inside ourselves, a silence that can come out of others and a silence in the natural world around us that has much to say to us, without words, if only we could listen. Many primitive people seem always to have known this, and, within Western traditions, meditation, contemplation and spiritual practice through 'right action' once had a much greater role than they do today. Maybe each of us needs, sometimes, to go out into the wilderness and see, hear and feel what it has to offer us.

However, wilderness is harder to come by these days, where 'earth' is so often concrete, 'air' is car exhaust, 'water' is mixed with nitrates, lead and aluminium, and 'fire' is locked away, unobservable, within the central heating boiler.[19] In a world polluted by excessive light and sound, it is difficult to find stillness, darkness and their healing effects.

'Night sky, moon and stars therapy' could, with considerable justification, be added to the burgeoning list of healing programmes. To do so might seem novel to us, but to our ancestors it must have been obvious. Western city dwellers, blinded by light, never see night, and remain ignorant of their consequent poverty. Silence and darkness are now so unfamiliar that they might well terrify, were real remoteness to replace neon and noise. What if we allowed a large space for silence in our minds? We might find out where, and who, we are. But in trying to establish and illuminate our position we have no time for a long dark journey into the night of our own soul:

> It is their own language, and they can lie in it, twisting the true words to false ends, catching the unwary hearer in a maze of mirror-words, each of which reflects the truth and none of which leads anywhere. (Le Guin, 1971)[20]

I believe the most powerful forms of psychotherapy may involve the minimum of talk, and that sound, to be effective, needs to be buttressed by silence. Language, when powerful and poetic, evokes responses beyond the words themselves. When every reaction and evocation is pinned by prose, it loses its life.

Sometimes what is best is no talk at all. Silence and space is right here now within noise and clutter, if we are attentive, but in a loud and manic world it is more difficult to attend. Certainly, I regularly run away to the silence and space of the Northumberland countryside in order to rediscover it within myself. This large, green–brown lung preserves sanity and connection to the fundamental mystery of existence. All of us search, unwittingly, wherever we can. In gardens, allotments, canal banks, in small gaps of sky on a concrete skyline. In the vibrancy of city life perhaps. Millions go fishing, talking of catches, tactics, rods, floats and lines, and engaging in the timeless healing process of contemplation beside water. The river, calm or enraged, takes us out of ourselves and our preoccupations, and reconnects us to the larger movement of existence.

These are not new observations, nor is it novel to suggest that silences can be more full, pregnant and meaningful than words. Much of the healing power of sacred places, such as churches, or other naturally airy, earthy or watery environments, is due to the full, old and spacious silence that can inhabit such atmospheres. Silence is not just absence. It can be full, fertile, empty, embarrassed, contrived, natural, easy or uncomfortable. Descartes was wrong; we do not need to think, or talk, to exist. Unlike our children, we forget that actions count for far more than words.

Children have to know better. They are curious about the sounds we make, but their survival depends on what we do, rather than on what we say. Babies will not take words instead of milk. Only as they get older do they learn how to talk themselves away from this reality. Like us, they learn to deal in rationalization as and when it suits. They become intoxicated with the power of words, and grow both sophisticated and sophistical.

We celebrate our skills with language, and rightly so. Sometimes we have to say in order to see or think at all, and with writing we can record, reflect and organize our speech. With words we can make more sense of ourselves, each other and the world around us. We can get through to each other and to important truths about our existence. With words, though, we can also get the better of, and away from, other people and the reality of our predicament. Words help us in our search for truth. They also help in our search for power, status and survival. The first is not always our first priority. Communication and deception are both products of evolution. Both exact a price. Truth may be too painful to endure. Deception may leave us hypnotized within our own rationalizations.

If we really must talk, who should talk most? Client or counsellor? Whose talk is most important? What should be talked about, and with what purpose? Should the talking provide advice and information? Are therapists instructors or trainers, offering life skills, behaviour modification, systematic desensitization or assertiveness training? Are they educators, healers, guides or fellow human beings and pilgrims on the same mysterious journey as their clients? Should therapists draw clients towards past traumas? Or focus on the future? Or on the here and now? In what proportions and priority? When should counsellors focus on client powers and responsibility? What if circumstances really are overwhelming? Should clients repent or be reassured that they did what they could? Who will decide, and who is in the best position to know?

Depending on therapist views and orientation, clients will need to bring with them their whole family, or consider their role as oppressors or victims in an unjust exploitative Society, release pent-up emotions, restructure beliefs and attitudes, learn relationship skills, challenge and change self-defeating behaviours, look at the journey of their soul, notice their defence mechanisms, disentangle their restimulated past and much more.

Some therapists are forceful and systematic. Hypnotherapists will reconstruct parts of your inner life by suggesting ways of re-experiencing your experience. Other therapists will take control but less overtly. Some will insist that you take charge of your life. This may be empowering, but not if you attempt the impossible and blame yourself when you fail.

Notes

1   Charles Caleb Colton, *Lacon.* Bliss and White, 1822.

2   Audit Commission, *Finding a Place: Review of Mental Health Services*, p. 14. HMSO, 1994.

3   See, for example, Michael Argyle, *Social Skills and Health.* Methuen, 1981; and Ian Kennedy, *The Unmasking of Medicine.* Granada, 1983.

4   Counselling is now being placed at the very centre of many educational programmes. For example, the Further Education Funding Council has determined that within colleges 'all students have access to effective tutorial support, personal counselling and guidance and careers education and guidance' (FEFC Circular 93/28).

5   Michael Reddy, in his 1992 presentation to the BAC annual conference, claimed that its Counselling at Work division should be the flagship of the BAC.

6   Figures quoted in the *Independent*, 15 March 1994.

7   A survey of general practitioners carried out during the autumn of 1992 by the health care magazine *Doctor*, revealed that over 70 per cent of medical respondents considered that they had insufficient training in communication skills (although of course, those replying might have been more than averagely likely to feel dissatisfaction with training than those who discarded the questionnaire altogether).

8   A joint statement was produced by the Royal College of Psychiatrists and the British Psychological Society in January 1995 ('Psychological Therapies for Adults in the NHS') which specifically proposed that, in districts where both professions were already contributing, neither profession should seek dominance over the other (p. 10).

9   Similarly, compare 'sociological medicine' with 'medical sociology'. Who will prefer which title? Who will control which department?

10 P. E. Meehl, Discussions of Eysenck's 'The Effects of Psychotherapy', *International Journal of Psychiatry*, 1965, **1**: 156–7; G. R. VandenBos

(ed.), Special issue: Psychotherapy research, *American Psychologist*, 1983, **41**: 111–214; L. Saxe, *The Efficacy and Cost-effectiveness of Psychotherapy*, Office of Technology Assessment, Congress of the United States, 1980; C. Sherrard, The rise in demand for counselling, unpublished paper. Leeds University, presented to the British Psychological Society. Lincoln, 1991.

11   V. Raimy, *Training in Clinical Psychology*. Prentice Hall, 1950.

12   More recently (1993), thanks to new technology, I used my computer modem to dial into a US medical database and asked how many learned articles it could deliver with 'counseling' as a keyword. In less than one second it informed me that it had over 18 000 such articles available! I later asked for articles that included both of two keywords – 'counseling' and 'evaluation'. That brought the number down to 4500.

13   R. D. Rosen, *Psychobabble*. Avon, 1979.

14   There is no English equivalent of the German 'Schadenfreude'. It is the consolation we can find in contemplating the misfortune of others.

15   Not to be confused with Personal Construct Therapy, which explores our intellectual constructs of self and world.

16   Kenneth Fox, at Exeter University, has examined the value of exercise on mental health. He cites 104 studies on anxiety and 80 on depression: 'Exercise had more effect than relaxation and was as good as psychotherapy'. (*New Scientist*, 10 September 1994)

17   Whether Chinese medicine can be shown to meet Western standards of empirical testing remains to be seen. A great deal of it appears to consist in metaphor more than testable theory. Significantly, it appears to be losing ground in China to Western medicine. For introductory texts, see: Ted Kaptchuk, *Chinese Medicine*. Rider, 1989; Manfred Porkert, *The Theoretical Foundation of Chinese Medicine*. MIT Press, 1978; *The Yellow Emperor's Classic of Internal Medicine*, translated by Ilza Veith. University of California Press, 1972.

18   F. Capra, *Uncommon Wisdom*. Flamingo, 1989.

19   A real campfire can still have a powerful hold over us, when we are ever given a chance, or permission, to sit around one and share the evening together. But most of us have to make do with a portable barbecue and patio set instead, and may be too spiritually deprived and impoverished to know what we are missing.

20   Ursula Le Guin, *A Wizard of Earthsea*. Puffin, 1971.

Chapter 4

'Client-centred' approaches

Good friends are hard to come by, and cannot simplybe purchased by the hour. But Rogers seemed to feel that a therapist, merely by announcing himself to be one, is automatically a better friend than even a real friend. Rogers assumed that friends will behave in a normal fashion, sometimes they like you and sometimes they don't, but that the therapist always likes you and is always genuine and nondefensive. What is impossible to achieve in real life is assumed to be automatically part of the good therapist's equipment.

(Masson, 1989)[1]

A wide variety of people talk of counselling and describe themselves as counsellors, with insufficient clarity about what is meant. As we shall see, they often have little in common beyond superficial statements about 'empowerment'. The skills employed can vary widely. A consensus about counselling, then, is lacking. However, many counsellors claim partial, or substantial, allegiance to one or more of the schools described in these chapters. If there is one authority above all others within counselling it is probably, still, Carl Rogers.

Rogerian counsellors have a reputation for being 'nice' people. Being a warm, honest and empathic person is unavoidably important to them, since the Rogerians claim that these qualities, along with 'unconditional positive regard', lie at the heart of effective counselling. At a superficial level, this is compelling stuff. After all, it would presumably be more pleasant if people were more pleasant, warm, caring, empathic, genuine, respectful and loving to each other. Yet are there no limits, both in principle and in practice, to such virtues? Can the sun shine every day, except when we need the rain? Can a fair wind always blow behind us, blessing us in our good works? Can we really expect someone to be reliably capable of listening to us without ever exploiting, twisting our words or imposing their own ideas? Can we find a therapeutic Garden of Eden within counselling? If we seek knowledge, let us remember that it was the snake who offered it. The metaphor is a rich one. Over millions of years our powers of communication have evolved. So have our powers of deception. Do we think we can, or should, shrug off the latter by an earnest effort of will? Would an excessive sweetness of spirit cause our souls to rot, making us shiny, happy, smiling, toothless and bland?

In the real world, saintliness is rare, and few lunches are free. Yet there have always been individuals, and movements, promising that the lion can be made to lie down with the lamb and that people can live off milk and honey without upsetting their digestion. Too many counsellors, in my view, fall victim to this sort of sentimentality. In particular, the 'client-centred' Rogerian brands of counselling appear to have more than their fair share of a simpering shallowness of perception about the human condition that does us all a grave disservice:

> Reading Rogers is such a bland experience that I found myself recalling the old adage that psychotherapy is the process whereby the bland teach the unbland to be bland. This reaction points to something lacking in Rogers and his writings, and that is sensitivity to people's real suffering. (Masson, 1989)[2]

Of course, it is ill-mannered to put pressure on pleasant people, and therein lies a difficulty. Rogerian pleasantness often deters critics from asking probing questions about Rogerian warmth and care. To make unflattering remarks about Carl Rogers and his cohorts is an invasion of innocence, akin to lifting the skirt of the fair princess, frightening the children or bullying the sheep. How can we be critical of therapists who are, apparently, so harmless, well-meaning and innocent? We risk accusations of cynicism and malice. If we criticise innocence, we are, surely, guilty? Who will ride to the rescue of Rogers and do combat with me and my blasphemy? They had better be well armed.

The Rogerian vision of humanity is a vision of the innocents, and therein lies their guilt. Why? Because innocence sits fine among lambs, children and, possibly, young princesses, but is inadequate in adulthood and utterly unacceptable among therapists. The latter, after all, are supposed to be engaging with the irresolvable play of good and evil in the human spirit.

To spend too much time with Rogerian counsellors, therefore, risks entrapment within their constraining, albeit genuine, lack of vision. It is harmful. Like too much light romance, it restricts the ability to think, feel, perceive and communicate beyond empty cliché. For all the talk of empowerment, it is disempowering and disabling. However, its shallowness only becomes evident when clients engage with thinkers who have more depth and bite. In therapy and philosophy, as in fiction, it takes mature appreciation of a serious artist in order to see what is meant by third rate.[3]

The person-centred claim to pleasantness of personality is, of course, implied rather than explicit. Rogerians offer little more than what they imagine to be 'themselves'. With a Rogerian counsellor, you get no more, or less, than love, empathy, respect, faith in humanity, a personal authentic relationship and 'unconditional positive regard'. For a fee, you can rent or hire a package of warm, caring, genuine, friendly humanity.

Is this really feasible? Is it cold and ill-mannered for me even to ask? Clients, certainly, avoid such an embarrassing question.

Rogerians readily apologize for their human limitations, but the apology may itself accrue virtue. The disclaimers hide the main claim. It would be crass and absurd to say, 'I'm a nice warm person, let me be your counsellor', but Rogerians have to believe they are pretty pleasant people in order to practise at all. Within some counselling texts, the virtues stack up so much that, in all honesty, nothing short of saintliness will be sufficient.

Virtue may well be more therapeutic than is psychotechnology. If so, we ought to have fundamental doubts about the viability of counselling as a profession. Were counselling to be no more than the practice of saintliness, then, in a fallen world, it looks doomed as a professional enterprise. We may, for example, write 'Yours sincerely' at the end of a letter, but sincerity, like other virtue, can be difficult and paradoxical:

> A little sincerity is a dangerous thing, and a great deal of it is absolutely fatal. (Wilde, 1891)[4]

> The primary condition for being sincere is the same as for being humble: not to boast of it, and probably not even to be aware of it. (Peyre, 1963)[5]

Can we expect counsellors, and ought they to claim, to be more than averagely pleasant, virtuous and humane? Can counsellors train others to be virtuous? Can they bring out virtue in clients generally? Are counsellors a sort of friend? Do they offer a substitute for friendship?

Our real friends, being human, do not always live up to our expectations. They can be cold and insincere. They deceive and manipulate. They
expect us to scratch and cover their backs as well. Is this so surprising?

Does anyone actually achieve the Rogerian ideal of unconditional
positive regard? Should they even try? If your behaviour and attitudes
become particularly offensive, my positive regard for you may become
conditional, thin, nonexistent. Is that so surprising? Our friends may
become exhausted with us, and we with them. They may offer advice we
did not request. They give opinions, make judgements; sometimes, they
even proffer real material support and assistance. They generally expect
that favours will, as necessary, be returned. Can, and should, counsellors
set themselves above such daily wheeling and dealing? Can they offer a
'higher quality' of friendship that avoids the frustration, fog and power-
broking that are ordinary components of human relations?

There are, admittedly, some virtues not required of counsellors. You do
not have to be a 'good Samaritan' and provide material support. The
currency of care is confined to words and gestures. It is the client who
takes action, while the counsellor gains financially via the client or
taxpayer. You talk through your trauma, release feelings, clarify options,
build confidence, pick yourself up, dust yourself down, and start all over
again. The focus is on *personal* growth and autonomy. Community, social
and collective development do not figure very much on the agenda.

Close investigation of this contractual relationship reveals serious
limitations. It creates a plausible illusion but how far is it real? Perhaps
counsellors and clients can be warmed just a little in contemplating
their own warmth? In the absence of a real home fire, a mock effect
with light bulbs may be better than nothing. Plastic fires don't burn
you, either, or throw embers on the carpet.

Warmth and friendly support, in a cool and indifferent world, are
always welcome, but can we free ourselves from a soul-destroying environment by *purchasing* the interest and attention of another human being?
This strange belief seems to me to be a central contemporary fantasy. It is
my own deep frustration with, and concern about, such collective insanity
that, more than anything else, has driven me to write this book.

We might love to find real contact with another via the crisp, clean
connection of a cash payment, but the hope that we could be healed in
this way is surely part of our collective sickness. It seems almost blasphe-
mous to imagine that we can reliably, cleanly, predictably, genuinely and
firmly encounter others in any circumstances, and certainly not via cash
or professional training.

From the standpoint of the potential counsellor, however, the commercialization of compassion provides a new career opening after, say, a midlife crisis or mid-life redundancy. Everyone has needs, both to nurture and be nurtured, and it is only human for us to believe that, whatever the shortcomings in others, we at least are warm, caring, genuine human beings. In the present mercenary climate, these desirable qualities can provide employment, a window into the soul of a fellow human being, financial security and a respected role and status in society. No wonder that such a package of opportunity can seem highly attractive to many people from many different backgrounds. No wonder that counsellor training appears to be an even bigger business than is counselling.

Avoiding enmeshment, blood, mess and disturbance of professional timetables, Rogerian care and friendship is generally distributed in regular fifty-minute intervals. The client's drama is confined to one room at preplanned intervals of time, usually once a week. The counsellor's own hopes, fears and conflicts, it is imagined, are 'put to one' side lest they intrude on the client's own agenda, which remains the focus of 'accurate empathy' and 'reflective listening'. The counsellor's own personal story and history, generally, remains hidden. Thus they can learn about another, without having to reveal themselves. It can be the ultimate in voyeuristic experience.

Counselling thereby differs from ordinary friendship, wherein confidences and intimacies are usually exchanged more equally. We would think it peculiar if friends expected us to reveal our secrets while keeping silent about their own personal lives. Such an uneven sharing of confidences makes for an unhealthy, unequal relationship, leaving us too exposed and vulnerable. Knowledge is Power. If I become transparent while you remain opaque, the empowerment will probably be yours more than mine. In such circumstances, if the counsellor is a friend, it is a very bizarre sort of friendship.

For all the talk of 'empowerment', the mushrooming growth of counselling and counsellor training has more to do with *employment*. Counselling qualifications provide a new career, or means of strengthening one's c.v. There is nothing wrong with that, of course. Like most other human activities, counselling has both humane and mercenary dimensions. Both need to be investigated and understood, otherwise it is impossible to understand the frenetic efforts to professionalize care. It is not cynicism but realism to be sceptical about a burgeoning of care and humanity. What we are really experiencing is an outbreak of unemployment and economic insecurity. Counsellor training, for many, is a strategy for economic survival.[6]

Simply human?

If we cannot buy a friend, or offer our friendship for a fee, what are we buying or selling? Friendships can be cultivated, but surely we cannot conjure them from a search through the 'Counselling and Advice' sections of the *Yellow Pages*? In any case, it is not necessarily enough just to be ordinary, genuine and empathic when helping someone in distress. We may be genuinely superficial. Empathy is no substitute for sophisticated understanding.

Even being just simple, ordinary and human is not as simple and ordinary as it may seem. In ordinary circumstances, we often try to present ourselves as deep and extraordinary. These are the common and ordinary ways in which we preen and posture with each other. Counsellors cannot be immune. They naturally seek status and power like everyone else. Such appetite can be healthy and hideous, but it is certainly a central part of ordinary human life.[7]

Carl Rogers, like so many within counselling, wrote extensively on the power of love and nothing on the love of power. Therein, I suggest, lies some of his innocence – and consequent guilt. A failure to confront the reality of power leads to naïveté, just as a denial of the existence of love is a recipe for cynicism. Counselling has presented itself as a force for humanity, honesty and integrity. It can, supposedly, help not just individuals, but also, step by step, the whole of Society. Yet is counselling changing Society, or is Society changing counselling – and for the worse? In blacker moments, I fear this battle has already been fought and lost. Readers must, and will, decide for themselves.

To repeat, even idealized versions of ordinary humanity are really quite *extra*ordinary. We do not often look *out* at other people in naïve openness and innocence. More often we are on our guard and we look *up* to, or *down* on, others according to their perceived status. This goes on in care as elsewhere. For example:

> No longer possessing the means to sustain any convincing social snobbery, we have branched out into moral snobbery instead. Novelists, critics and popularising psychologists have joined forces to help the laity towards 'meaningful' relationships and more valuable insights into themselves, towards 'realising their full potential' as human beings. We shake our heads sadly at people's spiritual poverty, and smiling kindly, hold out our hands to help them into better ways. We outdo the most sanctimonious of Victorian clergymen. (Frayn, 1974)[8]

David Brandon's pamphlet, *The Trick of Being Ordinary* (MIND publications), seeks to overcome such barnyard tendencies. It argues the virtue of being an ordinary human being who communicates simply and effectively. I observed such powerful simplicity in a high-ranking Theravada Buddhist Abbott who had spent at least 20 years trying to be an 'ordinary' fallible human being. This 'nothing-special' quality made him very special and extraordinary; because the rest of us were, and are, much too busy trying to be special and extraordinary. Perhaps the last thing in the world we want is to be ordinary and fallible. That may be our greatest mistake; and that is what makes us just like everyone else.

David Brandon has himself been trained as a Zen Buddhist and therefore, presumably, knows just how difficult it is to be ordinary in a world where everyone wants to be super. There is a tendency to assume that if something is simple it ought to be easy. In fact this is just about the most difficult quest of all. That is why, for thousands of years, disciples have looked for complexity and profundity in the spiritual teacher's answers to questions since they have repeatedly failed to grasp their real simplicity.

Consider, for example, the Zen teacher's answer to the question: 'What shall I do, Master, to achieve Enlightenment?'

The teacher asked:
'Have you finished your meal?' …to which the disciple replied, 'Yes'. There came the great 'secret of the Universe' which scholars puzzle over as a profound, subtle and deep enigma:
'Then go and wash your bowl!'

How could it really be that simple? We just won't accept it. Surely there must be some deep message hidden behind the act? And what about 'peak' experiences, visions of celestial white light and all the rest of it? Yet were we to ask:

'Why, should I wash my bowl, Master?'

the answer, can't you guess?, would be:

'In order to get it clean.'

We are, or wish to be, far too clever to be able to really understand that. Those of us with some kind of would-be spiritual thirst hanker after more than a clean bowl. We want a cleansed soul, immaculate, pure, above and beyond the daily round of human folly and manoeuvrings. We want numinous experiences, glowing sensations, lightness, joy, a sense of completeness and 'Pure Being'. We want to float above the murky grey weather of all our questionable motives, conflicts, intentions, considerations, judgements, circumstances, successes and failures. We want salvation. However, the message, and the promise, remains simple: The bowl is dirty, wash it, then the bowl will be clean. Then, go from there. To where? How can we be sure? The answer (the key) is: we *can't* be sure. That is what makes ordinary life so awesome and wondrous.

There is a large potential market for the sale of 'ordinariness' as a desirable commodity. Zen Buddhists, and other monastic communities, have been offering it for years. Unfortunately, people continue to hope that, if they could only become ordinary enough, they would attain blissful experience, a state of union with life all around them, magical powers and a good deal of other nonordinary excitement. The paradox is that, the more we can feel at home in our ordinary existence, with our ordinary turmoil and confusion, the more likely we are to be at peace and at one with life. But trying too hard to achieve such experience merely drives it all away. Spiritual practice does not consist in a search for nonordinary experience. It is to live ordinary life so as to explore what it is. Healthy monastic communities wash their bowls and let ecstatic visions of light and harmony take care of themselves.

A more modern version of ordinariness, on sale as a commodity, was Jack Rosenberg's 'est', or 'Erhardt Seminars training'.[9] 'est', with its pretentiously small 'e', was a sixty-hour marathon, staged over two weekends, and based in a large hotel room with up to two hundred and fifty trainees and one trainer. Erhardt used his skills as philosopher and salesman to provide a glossy training package that integrated Zen with more contemporary psychotherapies. The aim was to get 'it' by the end of the training programme. The 'it' on offer was 'enlightenment', the realization that there is no enlightenment, no key, no secret wisdom, no crock of gold at the end of the rainbow. In other words, candidates paid a considerable sum of money to get 'nothing' out of the training, and trainees were repeatedly reminded that when they finally left the hotel room, all that would happen would be that they would leave the hotel room and carry on with their lives.

The idea of paying, rather than getting, something for nothing appealed to me. I liked the humour of it, but recognized that it had a more serious purpose than, say, the purchase of a pet rock. Sure enough, it worked. I got nothing out of it. But the nothing-special ordinariness of day-to-day existence can be magical beyond belief when people really open themselves to it. Thus for a long time afterward ordinary life looked special. A laser light show that I saw shortly after the training event appeared dull compared with the brilliant light and action of an ordinary street full of people.

Unfortunately, although predictably, est 'graduates' tended to make rather too much noise and fuss about this nothing, and lionized Erhardt as though he were something special. He, again predictably, tended to puff up with this sense of being special. Consequently, the whole movement became yet another American carnival of noise and messianism that grew rapidly at the end of the 1970s, with tens of thousands of disciples in the USA and Europe, only to decline just as quickly when it went out of fashion. Therefore the market is currently wide open for someone else to offer another version of 'nothing', designed to help us come to terms with the miracle of nothing-special existence.

In my ordinary conceit, I like to think I can offer ordinary care and humanity to others in distress, but can we realistically be expected to go on and on doing this, regularly and consistently, in a fifty-minute hour, for a fee, to a wide variety of strangers? Is it not inhuman to expect anyone to switch on 'ordinary humanity' on such a regular basis and for such long periods at a time? Can genuineness and authenticity be served up to processions of people day in, day out? Genuineness might often require the confession that 'I'm feeling bored, tired and preoccupied. I am feigning interest in your problems right now in order to maintain my professional reputation and your fee'.

We do not always want or need to get through to others. Sometimes it is unwise for us to try. Often our priority is to get on top, around or away, rather than closer to each other. Our powers of deception, connection, control and avoidance have evolved together, all, presumably, for good reason. A brave 'front' may sometimes be needed to keep the wheels of day-to-day life turning. The truth may set us free, but, if I try to slaughter you with it, we may all remain in chains. People can be damaged by the 'authentic' comments of others. The dance of tact and integrity is one of the most difficult to follow.

All kinds of virtue are desired and desirable, but they cannot be reliably produced in any market place. The notion of a British Standard – BS number 9999 – in human virtue is absurd. Therefore it is ludicrous to expect more or less virtue within counselling and among counsellors than anywhere else. This is a lethal message for those who claim that human virtue lies at the core of counselling and who seek to set up a mechanical process that will train, deliver and supervise accredited counsellors.

We can neither advance nor retreat to innocence and simplicity. We cannot live like doves in a world free of hawks. There is hawkishness around and within, and we are not wise enough to know how, or whether, to abolish it. Rogerian efforts to 'reclaim the child' leave us entrapped in childhood and cut off from mature status. It is an undesirable state. As adults we ought to be less preoccupied with personal growth and more interested in growing up. This does not require us to become arid intellectuals, but mindless emotionalism, witlessly described as 'experiential', is no substitute for conscience, courage and intellect. Those who face predatory adults with child-like innocence do no service to themselves or others. Worst of all, they disassociate themselves from their own ability to do damage.

I first came across a client-centred practitioner in the 1960s at a university offering individual 'stock-taking' sessions to all undergraduates. I assumed that a counsellor was something like a personal tutor. The rationale for the strange, intrusive social setting I found was not explained to me. The counsellor's aim, I later discovered, was to make a more 'real', personal, human contact than was available from tutorial staff.

The counsellor engaged in what, to me, was an inappropriate degree of eye contact and a somewhat rude tendency to stay silent for long periods of time, looking serious and expectant. I was thereby at a loss for words. What was this meeting supposed to achieve? Had I been unhappy, this disconcerting style would not have helped even if this 'helper' had taken the trouble to explain what he thought he was trying to do. The counsellor, perhaps, was new to the job and wooden with it, but my point is that whenever we make a fetish of being authentic, real or helpful, our very efforts can create a phoney, unreal and unhelpful relationship.

I was reminded of this at a counsellor training college. As a newcomer in the dining room, I looked round for a comfortable looking table of faces to join. Without thinking, I found myself in the one group that did not consist of counsellors. These were journalists on a quite different in-service course. This group was relaxed and easy. The counsellors were busy with a subtle competition to see which of them was the most caring, sensitive and authentic. They were thereby blinded to their competitiveness, defensiveness and status anxiety. They wanted so much to be 'good' people that it was unsettling to be with them. The journalists were much less bothered about being good and genuine souls. Consequently, they were good to be with and, within sensible limits, more genuine.

A similar lesson came in a radio series introducing counselling to a lay audience. The counsellors tried so hard to put themselves across as caring, sensitive people that they had an elf-like unreality about them. They spoke in tones that were too self-consciously soft and self-aware. They wanted so much to be real that the entire presentation sounded contrived. They wished so desperately to be delicate and tactful, it was as though they were talking out of their ears.

Compare this with the stereotype of an Anglican vicar, that simpering individual who makes unreal and unreasonable efforts to be real and reasonable. Without bloody or bloody-minded qualities, his veins flow with milk and honey. His wish to be so good is unbelievable, disconcerting and unhealthy. His banality and naïveté were best portrayed by Alan Bennett in *Beyond the Fringe*. Here is an extract, as I remember it, from Bennett's satire. Best of all was Bennett's timing and tone which, alas, cannot be put down on a page.

Life

Life, is like a tin of sardines. We are, all of us, searching for the key. Some of us, don't we, we think we have found the key to the sardine tin of life. We open up the tin, we survey its contents, we consume them. But, even when we have consumed the contents of the tin, there is always a little bit left on the side that you cannot quite reach.

Is there a little bit on the side in your life?

I know there is in mine.

A cash payment for being 'real' is inherently unreal, unusual and unrealizable; it is similar with payments for being warm and positive. Self-conscious effort to be human and supportive gets in the way of being naturally and effectively caring.

Therefore, if we want people to be authentic, we ought not to expect them to be able to care, in all circumstances and with all clients. Similarly, if we want warmth and support on demand, others will at times feel forced to deceive us. As for unconditional positive regard, there is an important condition that all professional Rogerians impose. They will not even begin the process unless someone (client, insurance company or taxpayer) provides the cash. This is a highly significant condition when clients and the NHS are seriously short of money.[10]

In search of 'normality'

Some schools of counselling, therefore, down-play desirable human qualities and focus on professional, teachable *skills*. The hope is that these can be practised even when we are not feeling in a very helpful mood. Professionalism requires that clients benefit from contact with us, regardless of our necessarily variable emotions. How far is this possible?

Many skills, values, models and theories are on offer. What they have most in common is that their effectiveness is very difficult to isolate and measure, and their practitioners do not necessarily put them into practice as theory might suggest. Clients may, in any case, change because of other circumstances and surroundings. Placebo is powerful even when other real influences are at work: the client may have decided that 'here is the person who will help me'. He may then make changes, not so much because of qualities in the counsellor, but because of his very *belief* in counselling generally and this counsellor in particular. Compare this with Tolstoy's observation:

> Their usefulness did not depend on making the patient swallow substances for the most part harmful (the harm was scarcely perceptible as they were given in small doses) but they were useful, necessary, and indispensable, because they satisfied a mental need of the invalid and of those who loved her – and that is why there are, and always will be, pseudo-healers, wise women, homeopaths and allopaths. They satisfied that eternal human need for the hope of relief, for sympathy, and that something should be done which is felt by those who are suffering. (Tolstoy, 1869)[11]

This is why new 'wonder' treatments need to be fully exploited, before the belief in them (the source of their real potency) wavers. Beliefs and expectations vary and people can be fickle. Therefore positive change in one client may not be repeated in another, even when the problems and the treatment are the same. Even the notion of 'positive change' is problematic. Does it require a general movement towards blandness and 'balance', whereby no one gets too upset or creates too much heat, friction or despair for anyone else? Is it 'progress' or 'deterioration' when angry, painful, unpleasant issues and emotions come to the surface? Has the client improved or suffered a setback as a result of deciding to leave, or stay with, their partner? Do we just let the client decide what constitutes progress? If the client is happy, should the counsellor automatically be satisfied?

External observers may, in good faith, disagree. The 'quiet contentment' of some is a 'living death' to others. Some enjoy a small, or considerable, degree of chaos, mess and disorder in their lives and would not wish to progress to a more orderly and explicit analysis of their experience. Are they being courageous, spontaneous, careless or what? My view of orderliness may be obsession in your eyes. Who will judge between us? A novelist with the stature of Tolstoy shows a profound understanding of these dilemmas and mysteries concerning the nature of progress and normality. This cannot be said of every counsellor or trainer.

Individuals also vary in their sociability. The reclusive withdrawal of some is seen as unhealthy and abnormal by others. What about those who prefer solitude and find more fulfilment in their work than with other people? Are they deficient in 'life skills'? Who is to say what we should do with our lives and what skills we therefore need to do it? We are all an unpredictable mixture of irrationality and insight; maturity and foolishness. Who is mature and balanced enough to know how immature and unbalanced they are? Who is tolerant enough of themselves to accept their limited ability to tolerate differences?

Is it always desirable that people be easy to live with?[12] Is the balanced and satisfied individual necessarily more admirable than the unbalanced and dissatisfied one? The latter may achieve far more, and maybe a degree of dissatisfaction is inherent in being human. Are we so sure that we know what we mean by 'balance'? When does balance turn into complacency and indifference, and who can be sure that they know where to draw the line? If we were too balanced and satisfied, we might well still be balancing somewhere in a tree.

> A living cell has to be out of chemical equilibrium with its surroundings; it is this lack of equilibrium that provides the driving force that the cell needs to do the work to maintain and replicate itself. (*New Scientist*, 18 May 1991)

Perhaps a similar principle is at work in our own personal lives. With imagination we learn to want more than we have got. Our fancies move beyond the facts of our circumstances ...beyond bovine chewing on the cud of eternal 'here-now' experience. As usual, the benefits of aerial envisioning are coupled with the costs of solid limitation. Hope is welded to the concept and reality of Despair. Expectation twins with Frustration. Satisfaction dances with Depression. We dash, and are buffeted, between Creativity and Misery.

In the light of all this, what kind of 'skills package' are counsellors able to provide to clients? Can they deliver a clearly definable service in the context of so much uncertainty? It appears that they cannot just 'do the skills' to the customer, and they cannot keep their necessarily variable personality out of the process. There will be a personal relationship of some sort, between two persons rather than just functionaries, and the nature of this relationship will have a crucial effect on the outcome for both parties. Each of us will have a unique effect on the other's perceptions and behaviour. Each of us will perceive the other in a way that can never be fully and finally communicated or understood. Each of us will be, as Martin Buber puts it, in a unique 'I–thou' relationship with the other.

Of course, we are potentially in an 'I–thou' relationship of sorts with everyone we meet. Yet at times, it appears that, within counselling, the relationship is not just a crucial component of the service, but *is* the service. If this is the case, we are once again forced to ask how far counselling is, or can be, a profession at all. For it to be so, there must be some base of skill and information that can be taught and assessed, independently of the unique mystery of 'I–thou'. There also needs to be some clarity about goals. Currently these are vaguely described as 'self-actualization', 'fulfilment', 'well-being', 'emotional acceptance' and 'growth'.

Counsellors lucky enough to have their work prefixed by a specific adjective (careers, education guidance, genetic, bereavement, marital) have less of a problem about goals, but 'general well-being' and 'meaning and purpose of life' counsellors have, from a professional perspective, an almost impossible assignment. Who decides how far the client is 'living more fully and satisfyingly'? Can the venerable elders from antiquity help us? David Brandon, in *The Trick of Being Ordinary*, cites the advice of Rinzai, an ancient Zen Master:

> Just be your ordinary selves with nothing further to seek, relieving nature, wearing robes and eating. When tired I sleep. Fools laugh at me, the wise understand.

I know it sounds simple, but we were never as simple as it sounds. We may imagine that dolphins are innocent and friendly enough to manage the aquatorial version of Rinzai's lifestyle, but closer research reveals that they, too, fight, steal, parade and posture. No doubt there were as many street-wise scoundrels in the ancient orient as now, despite the perennial tendency to romanticize such times and places. Otherwise why employ legions of Taoist, Zen and Confucian specialists to help the rest of the population see the error of their ordinarily human ways? Ordinary street advice is more often closer to the following:

> Just be your ordinary selves with nothing further to seek, relieving nature, wearing your armour and stealing an advantage. Despite exhaustion I keep up a front. Fools laugh at me, the wise understand.

...so much for ordinariness.

David Smail makes a similar observation when he suggests that:

> If we do not truly 'open up' to each other, 'be sensitive', 'show our feelings' in the way the therapy industry encourages us to do, it is because we have

good reason not to – we live in a social world which really is dangerous. (Smail, 1987)[13]

In other words, the unique 'I–Thou' relationship can be a threat and a risk as well as a haven. This has to be as true within counselling as anywhere else. People who imagine that you are surely right to trust them are dangerous. How can they be so sure? Such naïve optimism is only possible among those simple souls who are disassociated, disconnected and unaware of their own interests and power-broking stratagems. More realistic is the person who admits that, 'You must decide how far you can trust me. But you had better be on your guard, because, like everyone else, I am unaware of most of the tricks I play, both with myself and others'.

Being 'ordinarily human' is not the straightforward and unproblematic process of romantic dreams. Thus we jump free of the eternal present, assess our past, plan for our future and thereby become both gaolers and prisoners of Time. With maturity we may learn to be lifted, rather than crushed by, our hopes. We may, we hope, discover a 'middle way' in all this. But there is no reason to suppose that it is in the middle. There is no easy formula for finding it.

It seems safe to assume that, even in prehistoric times, people disliked being misled, manipulated and misunderstood. They, like my cat, preferred being liked and understood rather than disliked and misinterpreted. For Carl Rogers to talk as though this was a discovery he had made seems, quite simply, incredible. To be warm, empathic and authentic is not so much 'Rogerian' as humane, although not necessarily human.

Virtue has always been harder in practice than in theory. We want to be good, one day, but not too good to be true. In truth, goodness is tricky when virtues actively conflict with one another. For example, we cannot always be warm *and* genuine, as we have seen, and to judge that we should not judge is itself a (rather unwise) judgement.

Countless training manuals routinely talk about the theory of unconditional positive regard, but none that I have ever read has taken note of the major practical condition enforced by the profession. Ask around among the Rogerian counselling fraternity. Are they aware of, at least, one significant prerequisite? Usually they are not, yet it ought to be so obvious. The condition is that you have to *pay* for all this unconditional positive regard. Rogerian counsellors will care for you unconditionally, on condition that you pay them £15, £20, £50 per hour for the privilege. If you run out of money, you will find that the supply of positive regard becomes more problematic. Of course, the client may be lucky, and secure the services of a state-funded employee to be their counsellor, but this does not remove the financial condition. It merely shifts it to the taxpayer, who is, on average, more impoverished than the average client. The client then receives unconditional positive regard providing the taxpayer pays.

This is surely quite extraordinary. Counsellor and client are attempting to probe deeply into the underlying realities of their relationship. Sexual, existential and spiritual taboos might be examined unblinkingly. Yet the taboo of money, a very important underlying reality of counsellor–client relationships, will stay hidden from view. Mutual coyness and embarrassment is often evident when counsellor and client talk about payment. Money will often be a much more awkward subject than sex. Therapists will get a secretary to deal with payment if they can afford one. Both parties will be reluctant to haggle, disinclined to explore the subject. Hence, thousands of counsellors continue in the delusion that their positive regard for clients is quite unconditional, and clients, all too often, seem only too willing to believe that the claim is authentic.

Other cold realities are generally kept at bay within the counsellor–client relationship. Counsellors may seek to create a warm, safe, somewhat cosy environment, wherein they make a pretence of therapeutic monogamy and the unique specialness of their relationship. They will try to forget that there are other clients waiting; that the counsellor sometimes day-dreams; that the counsellor is doing a job and may be preoccupied with other concerns for the rest of the week; and that, loveable though the client may be, the counsellor might find their presence a source of embarrassment in the therapist's own kitchen, or at the dinner table, or anywhere else outside the confines of the therapy room. In public places, the counsellor might not wish to be seen with the client unless observers knew that they were on a professional placement. They might not want observers to think that this was a freely chosen friendship. In other words, to put the matter honestly, therapists might feel uneasy about fraternizing with people of lower social *rank*. Such chilly social, political and economic realities are not allowed to obtrude into the heated climate of the therapeutic hour. The counsellor encourages the client to explore reality; but there are some aspects of both their realities that neither wishes to inspect at all.

In his failure to observe such broader contexts to the counselling relationship, Carl Rogers in particular was, I think, extremely naïve and therefore considerably overrated. He seemed to entertain an almost Pollyanna-like belief in the ultimate potential goodness of mankind. Members of the personal growth movement have a tendency to be found romping within a timeless, innocent sterility of nursery school games and trust exercises, and an overearnest pursuit of 'fun'. This provides diversion, distraction, entertainment and a chance to let your hair down a little, but it is of little use to those who want to engage seriously with the moral dilemmas of adult circumstances and their own shadow.

In real life, people are capable of, and inflict on each other, acts of evil and destruction. The cause may be an unloving childhood, temperament, or both. The Rogerian claim is that, with enough unconditional positive regard, the vicious personality will soften into a loving, caring human being. Good does sometimes triumph over Evil, but history surely makes it clear that Evil is also quite capable of triumphing over Good. As ever, the long-term outcome remains uncertain. In any case, as Keynes observed, in the long run we are all dead.

Sometimes we choose evil, knowing it to be so, from spite, sadistic enjoyment of power, or just for the hell of it. Sometimes we choose it as the lesser of the evil options available to us. Rogers, and too many like him, seemed to imagine that a fruitful alternative would always be available and that the goodness in a person would inevitably shine forth with the right sort of nurturing. This optimism is not supported by the evidence. In real life, we often have to look for the least-worst opportunity in situations where the best, even the good, is nowhere in sight.

Rogers' failure to appreciate such constraints and dilemmas amounts to a disengagement from the pain and suffering that is built in to the human condition. He wanted us to believe that it could be joy and love all the way if only we opened our eyes and realized our potential a little more. He seemed to think that tragedy and human misery were a kind of optional extra that we could shed if only we took a more positive view. For Rogers, and so many New Age acolytes, we are still in the garden of Eden, but we have somehow lost sight of it.

We can exacerbate our pain by self-defeating attitudes and failure to put it in a broader, possibly spiritual, perspective, but pain is not an illusion. If we are wise and lucky, we might learn from and soften ourselves around it. Otherwise it may destroy us. If we are ruthless and cowardly, we can dump it on others, avoid responsibility and become 'voyeurs' on our lives. We can underestimate as well as exaggerate our difficulties. Sometimes, to quote the old joke, 'those who are not in panic or despair have not yet understood the extent of the problem'.

Positive attitudes help, up to a point, but not when divorced from reality. We cannot abolish adversity just by changing our attitudes.

Depression can be a logically reasonable, but psychologically untenable, response to hopeless circumstances.

A triumph of marketing

Carl Rogers' style of writing contributed to his success. It was simple, direct and unadorned, unlike the pseudoscientific writings of behaviourist colleagues. He wrote in a disarmingly naïve, lucid, unpretentious and almost autobiographical manner. He would begin many sentences with 'I have discovered… ', 'I have found that… ', 'I have learned… ', and because his 'discoveries' genuinely struck him as new and important, it was easy for a sympathetic reader to forget that they were restatements of old virtue. Rogers' plain-folk, apple-pie style positioned his product at the expense of its rivals. He was as fooled as his readers into mistaking his naïveté for discovery. His humility was real enough; he was surprised that people showered him with praise, and he had good reason to be humble. He was a simple man and this should not be a complement in a therapist.

Rogers' naïveté protects him from charges of effrontery and arrogance. Take, for example, the terms 'client-centred' and 'nondirective'. These simple adjectives damage the competition all the more effectively because Rogers was not consciously intending to do damage. He innocently appropriated the term 'client-centred', and thereby produced an emotional halo around his product similar to 'phosphate-free' in washing-up liquid. The one never used phosphates. The other never centred on counsellors. However, his product was now ahead of all 'Brand X' rivals, which, apparently, lacked the added 'client-centred' ingredient.

Similarly, no-one calls their therapy 'directive'. It sounds much too autocratic. But a 'nondirective' label, like 'unleaded' petrol, once again thrusts rivals into the 'Brand X' category. Competitors might counter-attack with 'systematic', 'goal-directed' or 'task-oriented' therapies and thereby imply, without actually saying, that rivals were unsystematic and without direction. Yet a care sector product that appears to be the market leader in warmth and humanity holds an important ace.

Rogers naïvely imagined that his own personal discoveries were a discovery for humanity. It helped that 'clinical' had come to mean 'cold and sterile', which is a poor recipe for healing. It is hard to compete with an operator who has secured the copyright on basic human virtues. Who could ever succeed with a therapy offering coldness, dishonesty and aloofness? Not only was Rogers client-centred, he was also *person*-centred. Carers dealing with 'patients', 'syndromes' and 'illnesses' inevitably sound colder than those who deal in 'persons', however warm these may actually be with clients.

The 'person-centred' school has thus acquired a significant market share by presenting itself as a voice for humanity in a world of impersonal science and manipulation. Given that so much of the world *is* impersonal, manipulative and scientistic (more than scientific), the message was welcomed like an oasis in a desert.

Yet it is ridiculous to declare, or imply, that 'We are ordinary, although also warm, authentic, person-centred; and we offer you unconditional positive regard'. I am alarmed at the numbers willing to believe in such a virtue package. Who *are* these people? Restating virtue is one thing, but to pretend that you have discovered, now embody and can reliably deliver it is preposterous. And now we have Rogerians training and accrediting people in these virtues, at the highest prices that the market can bear.

For all the talk about humility, the presumption that Rogerian counsellors actually embody their virtue more than the rest of us seems more than a little arrogant. For example, here is Brian Thorne, a leading UK writer in person-centred counselling:

> I realised during my primary school days that I had an ability that seemed unusual and that was both a blessing and a curse. Today I would call it the capacity to empathise. At that time I simply experienced, with alarming frequency, the powerful sensation of knowing what it felt like to be in someone else's skin. (p. 4)

> ...I have talked with saints and heard angel choirs. (p. 5)

> ...When I went to Reading I had been a naturally empathic person for as long as I could remember. What was surprising was to discover that this was by no means the case for many of my fellow-trainees. (p. 9)

> ...I realised that, although I had been understanding others for years, I had not always had the wit to let them know that this was the case. (p. 9)

> ...I am enabled to love not in some wishy-washy generalised way, but in a focused manner which is devoid of possessiveness and refuses to be easily side-tracked. (Thorne, 1991, p. 15)[14]

Can anyone be so sure that he embodies such virtue? What does it reveal about the uncritical climate of opinion within the counselling profession that such a leading professional can get away with such claims without being publicly challenged? Even if he is as good as he claims, can others be expected to meet such high standards? It seems that even Brian Thorne has his doubts. He observes, without awareness of any possible irony:

> Certainly, over the years I have found myself being less than enthusiastic about the aspirations of some who have voiced their intention to me of becoming therapists. It has seemed that in some cases there has been a highly romantic and unrealistic view of the therapist's life, whereas in others there has been a scarcely concealed lust for power. (p. 17)

> ...The important people for me in the therapeutic world – Lyward, Shertzer, Rogers – have impressed me primarily as human beings rather than as theoreticians or therapists. Their therapy was an extension of their personalities or an expression of the values which permeated their lives. (p. 17)

> ...I doubt if a therapist who is incapable of loving or of allowing himself to be loved can do much good. (Thorne, 1991, p. 18)[14]

I share Brian Thorne's unease, and extend it to include Brian Thorne. The consequences, to me, are fairly clear: counselling and psychotherapy, are almost certainly, impossible professions since, like energy derived from nuclear fusion, we simply have not found a way of producing the much desired product in practice. Yet, in the face of all evidence and hopeless odds, we continue in our dreams, as Tolstoy observed. Like the warmth and reassurance of free electricity, a bountiful supply of warm and caring counsellors, given chronic scarcity, would be so utterly *desirable*.

Is it sensible to believe counsellors who claim that they are nondirective, nonjudgemental and never give advice? The BAC requested that British Telecom separate 'Counselling' from 'Advice' in its *Yellow Pages* directory. British Telecom refused. It is wiser than it may realize. Be aware of the implicit advice buried within supposedly nondirective messages.

Giving advice and making judgements are inseparable, since to advise at all involves judging that the present position needs to change. Counsellors quite often try to distance themselves both from judgement and advice-giving, but to perceive, think and feel at all involves judgement and evaluation, and to counsel at all involves a judgement that the client has something to counsel about. If the client wants, and needs, to change nothing, why come for counselling? Change lies at the heart of all therapy, and judgements are required, by both client and counsellor, about the changes that might be helpful. Some, more honest, counsellors actually call themselves 'change agents'.

Advice may not be explicit, but counsellors cannot avoid constructing and reflecting a particular view of the client's predicament that will skew some options so that they look more attractive than others. The client will be 'free to choose' these options, and the 'neutral' counsellor, while not explicitly encouraging such decisions, will reward the client with smiles and the observation that 'the counselling seems to be progressing very well'.

Counsellors 'tilt the pitch', albeit unwittingly, through their nonverbal responses and in what they *do not* say. It is impossible to respond without using, and thereby revealing, our values and preoccupations. Perceptions and prejudices 'curve the space' around us. No-one can avoid this, any more than the Earth can fail to exert a gravitational field. To be alive at all is to exert a pull and a direction on others. The more powerful we are, the more influence we will exert, consciously or otherwise. A nondirective counsellor is a nonexistent counsellor.

Rogers discovered the right product for the time and place. He praised expressiveness and encouraged (an illusion of) autonomy when, during the carnival of the 1960s, people wished to hang loose, 'discover themselves', engage in 'personal growth' and share havens of homogenized humanity in cushioned encounters with other lifestyle aficionados.

All this was presented as an escape from an alienating consumer society, but it was more a product of the culture than a critique of it – a kind of controlled decontrol. Going on groups and seeing your therapist became part of the expressive lifestyle through which you explored, developed and paraded your individuality. A personal growth programme could be carefully chosen, arranged, adapted and displayed along with one's car, house, furnishings, clothing and leisure pursuits. Through all of these, I could express my status and personality. Self-expression was the order of the day, and my chosen styles of even quite ordinary goods showed you what sort of person I was.

Rogerian counselling or encounter, therefore, was not just a means by which I explored myself, but also itself a form of clothing from which people could get the measure of me. Friends could say, 'Harvey's heavily into Carl Rogers right now', and that would establish Harvey's position in society more exactly than anything he actually discovered during the group. Even the term 'heavily into' on its own would identify which part of the social marketplace we were occupying.

Membership of the counselling or encounter group fraternity identified the person. It was part of a package of supposedly personal characteristics, along with other consumer commodities such as 'resident of Marin County, California U.S.A., drives a Volvo, creative arts/social worker, drinks St. Emilion, owns a cuisinart, motobecane ten-speed, Stine graphics, Klip speakers, a Pioneer receiver, Brown and Jordon patio furniture, Dansk stainless and Rosenthal china, long-stemmed strawberries and walnut oil from Mill Valley Market, Birkenstock sandals and Adidas'.[15]

Counselling and social values

During this century, possibly triggered by disillusionment after the First World War, a sea-change in social values took place. Personal growth, autonomy and expression overtook the more traditional ethic of duty, discipline, cultivation and restraint. Contemporary 'How to…' self-improvement manuals are hedonistic, narcissistic and aesthetic in their focus on growth and development. Self-improvement tracts of the nineteenth and early twentieth centuries were very different. They preached character development through the avoidance of temptation, indulgence and excess. Civilization and cultivation, rather than joy and celebration, were the keywords. Core values were integrity, courage, thrift and hard work. Sin took the form of dissolution, decadence, selfishness and self-obsession.

Warren Susman identifies this change within the work of one writer, O. S. Marsden.[16] In 1899, Marsden wrote *Character; The Greatest Thing in the World*, which taught readers how to be Christian gentleman. In 1921, he published *Masterful Personality*. This tells you how to attract friends, and develop charm, influence and fascination. It was one of the first of a long pedigree that looks set to continue to 1999.

Contemporary counsellors rarely warn of idleness, indolence and dissolute living. Their clients are more concerned about repression of their innate personality, failure to grow, social withdrawal and, worst of all, an inability to enjoy life to the full. Joy, expressiveness and happiness have become ends in themselves that have to be 'worked on', rather than being byproducts of duty, discipline, integrity and courage. Such values were rejected as repressive, hypocritical and unduly deferential to failed patrician authority. They were regarded as dead values of a dead culture of dead people, afraid to really live and 'be'.

At the height of this carnival, during the 1960s, encounter work at growth centres, even sexual promiscuity, replaced prayer at church, or drill at school. They became essential means of developing into living, loving, whole and healed persons free from the stifling hypocrisy of the past. Sexual exploration became a new 'should', and sexual affairs, for some, were enacted not as an illicit pleasure, or an ordinary human temptation, but because they were 'necessary for one's personal development'.

A backlash set in during the 1980s. In the 1980s and 90s, the children of the wealthy and aspiring are not sent on Rogerian personal development programmes. They dress in school uniforms largely unchanged since the 1930s and attend public schools with 'good old' traditions, the '3Rs'. Conformity has been reinstated, but duty seems to have got left somewhere behind.

Hence, despite its growth, counselling is subject to considerable hostility and contempt from the more traditional, and still powerful, sections of the British Establishment. Rogerian values go against the grain of public school teaching, which still tries to promote the stiff upper lip, keeping one's dirty washing to oneself, fitting in and becoming 'sound'. Puritanical concern for social duty can be at the expense of the individual. Hedonistic preoccupation with the individual goes to the other extreme. Societies grow disillusioned with both and veer between the two. In the long term, neither is viable.

Puritanism views people as worse than they are, and flagellates individual appetite, which it sees as destructive. Libertarianism, conversely, views people as better than they are, and believes that Utopia will arise when individuals are allowed to grow and 'actualize' themselves.

People, according to the Rogerians, are like trees, and many growth centres use trees and similar items as logos to advertise their wares. All the counsellor has to do is be nurturing. If clients are given warmth, light, love and space, then, like green plants, they will grow and flourish. It is an enticing and intoxicating idea, but I do not think it is true. Human beings are not trees, and the differences are more important than the similarities. Personal growth sounds fine when related to oak trees, but what about the growth of ivy, rats or cancer? Suddenly growth becomes problematic. Hence the nineteenth-century conception of 'cultivation'. This required that personal excesses be pruned, in the best interests of both self and society. Emotions were to be assessed, put into perspective. Not all deserved celebration. Inclinations might be reigned in rather than unleashed. Short-term comfort was to be subordinated to long-term well-being. Pain and frustration were components of, rather than obstacles to, a full life. All this required discipline and, above all, self-discipline.

Discipline *is* often misunderstood and abused. We can make such a habit of deferring pleasures that childish joy is forgotten and the mature art of adult happiness is never learned. We start to apologize for our very existence. Guilt becomes a way of life. Mindless conformity is seen as good in its own right. Duty is all and rights shrivel away. We are told that giving and sacrifice are always better than receiving and assertion. Real happiness is deferred to the life hereafter. Pleasure becomes bad simply because it is pleasurable. Such Puritan excess creates a cyclical backlash into Hedonism. Each is as unbalanced and unhelpful as the other.

Rogers, nearer the hedonistic end of this spectrum, encapsulated his value system within the conclusion of 'My Philosophy of Personal Relationships'[17]:

> I have come to prize each emerging facet of my experience, of myself. I would like to treasure the feelings of anger and tenderness and shame and hurt and love and anxiety and giving and fear – all the positive and negative reactions that crop up. I would like to treasure the ideas that emerge – foolish, creative, bizarre, sound, trivial – all part of me.

I fail to see why we should 'treasure' all the assorted detritus of our wandering-rather-than-wondering monkey-minds. Clients are not helped if counsellors prize and nurture their every whim, fantasy, emotion and opinion. Some facets of the self are less than adorable. They may be indulgent, ignorant, repugnant, idiotic and self-defeating. If counsellors nurture and prize all this, they will be colluding with the client. Instead, let us treasure our capacity to judge, to balance and, even, to feel revolted by our destructive, infantile and egotistical behaviour.[18]

We could grow more as persons if we thought of growing up rather than just growing. Old fashioned terms, such as character-building, discipline, perspective, maturity and restraint, need to be reinstated and understood. The 'I-do-my-thing-you-do-your-thing' anarchism and irresponsibility of the client self-determination schools needs to be actively rejected. Counsellors must cease to pretend to be nonjudgemental or value-free. On the contrary, they should own up to, and stand by, a defensible system of ethics. If counsellors are serious about themselves, then, like everyone else, they need to assert and defend their own moral judgements, and if they do not feel able to make moral judgements, they have no right to practise at all. Like priests, they have a particular duty to take a moral stand, even more so than we all do as responsible citizens.

How, for example, is a counsellor, who might also be a probation officer or youth worker, to be of any use to a client who has committed a serious crime? Are we really going to carry on with a pretence that in such circumstances counsellors will not make judgements? Of course they will. And of course they should. If the client is going to get anywhere at all, he may well need to face that:

'I have behaved very badly and I need to do something about it.'

For all its old-fashioned and threatening connotations, repentance, more than celebration, may be the road to recovery for many. The counsellor, far from fudging the issue, may need to encourage clients to face up to moral failure, for everyone's sake. Unless clients do so, they may never be able to regain any pride in themselves.

Self-esteem is a central component in healing and character development, yet Rogerians seem to imagine that it is built merely through warmth and positive regard. This is surely nonsense. Should clients feel good about themselves if they receive syrupy 'positive strokes'? Rogerian warmth, approval and regard are surely worthless precisely when, and because, they are unconsidered, unrestrained, unconditional and entirely unrationed. Rogerian 'prizing' is not much of a prize if everyone gets it regardless of what they do or do not do. Is everyone a winner, and must all have prizes? This is the cheapest of cheap currencies, and people will soon feel quite let down if they rely on it.

No-one can feel good about themselves merely by doing what they want, asserting their rights and living 'the good life'. Much contemporary misery, surely, arises from this illusion. A deeper pride and peace within ourselves requires knowing what we ought to do, and doing it. Duties and responsibilities need to be recognized and observed, in addition to the claiming of rights. Otherwise our happiness and peace of mind remain shallow and unstable because we can take no real pride in ourselves.

We often let ourselves down and accept mediocrity, ease, short-term advantage and the narrow view. We do not want nagging or wagging fingers; tact, and love, are always preferred. But if friends or counsellors will not help us see when we have underachieved, who will? Real prizing of others is not unconditional. We are most valued when others care and respect us enough to help us live up to our own values.

To value ourselves, we must value our values and live by them. By such living we express ourselves. This does not take place in a vacuum: expression requires a medium. Once more, self-discipline is needed. For example, if a violin is to become a liquid medium of self-expression, it requires hours of solid practice and years following in the footsteps of others.

To achieve any sort of *mastery* of anything, we must first *submit* and be responsive to the medium's own possibilities more than our own whims. A teacher may help. Are counsellors prepared to teach? Will they set an example? Will they make judgements? If not, how can we be expected to learn from them? Hopefully, they will be genuine and empathic, but these qualities will count for little if they are also shallow, unreflective, undisciplined and ill-educated.

Rogerians who deny that they are teachers *do* operate with a belief system, and surreptitiously attempt to teach it to their clients. At the heart of this teaching is the notion that, if you leave people alone and merely 'prize' them, they will grow into the human equivalent of fine oak trees. That belief, in my view, is shallow and false, and a great deal of harm has been done by practitioners who thought, and taught this. The results can be seen all around us, among those who know nothing of self-discipline, who live in ignorance of social responsibilities, indulge their emotion, refuse to make judgements, equate emotion-alism with informed opinion and are made miserable in the belief that they can, and should, always be happy.

In their search for their 'authentic self', Rogers' disciples often appear to have withdrawn from the social world, with all its terrors, dilemmas, disciplines and responsibilities, and, far from growing, risk an infantile and despairing existence.

Notes

1   Jeffrey Masson, *Against Therapy.* Collins, 1989.

2   The following icy response to bland versions of care sharply underlines Masson's concerns:

    The Fairy Godmother
    Woman of no substance. You stardust-sprinkled-everyone's Guardian Angel.
    Don't give me your easy empathy and closely-guarded positive regard.
    Don't give me your neon-warmth nor your puffball candyfloss counselling.
    I can see *myself* only in reflections from a darker soul than yours.
    You may be slightly bruised perhaps.
    But seem to bear no deeper wounds within –
    Whose faint echoes you might now draw upon to truly hear my suffering.

                    Anonymous (BAC *Counselling* Journal, February 1994)

3   For example, I have learned far more about psychology, personality, memory, experience and subjectivity from one novel of Proust than from the entire output of the client-centred school.

4   Oscar Wilde, *The Critic as Artist.* Random House, 1891, reprinted 1969.

5   Henri Peyre, *Literature and Sincerity.* Yale University Press, 1963.

6   Thus consider the problems faced by Relate (the former Marriage Guidance Council), which has had difficulty in retaining its trainees. These are tempted, and maybe have planned, to cash in on their newly

learned and marketable skill. Consequently, Relate contracts now require that volunteers pay for their training via a minimum number of 'voluntary' hours. As costs rise, clients are requested to donate £10–20 per hour (1992 prices) to cover overheads, training and the high turnover of 'volunteers'.

7   Thus, with clients we 'see it from your point of view'; with colleagues we refer to the 'power of empathy'; with rivals we give papers on 'the phenomenological approach'.

8   Michael Frayn, *Constructions*. Wildwood House, 1974.

9   Rosenberg changed his name to the more-marketable 'Werner Erhardt'.

10 Private medical insurance schemes are too expensive for the poor, and their coverage contracts as costs rise. BUPA, the largest health insurance company in the UK, announced that anyone taking out a new policy after January 1991 must accept a two-year moratorium on psychiatric claims, even if they have no previous psychiatric history (see *OpenMind*, No. 59).

11 Leo Tolstoy, *War and Peace*, Book IX, Chapter XVI. Oxford University Press, 1869, reprinted 1958.

12 'The energy which makes a child hard to manage is the energy which afterward makes him a manager of life' (Henry Ward Beecham, *Proverbs from Plymouth Pulpit*, 1887).

13 David Smail, *Taking Care: An alternative to Therapy*. Dent, 1987.

14 Brian Thorne, *Person-centred Counselling: Therapeutic and Spiritual Dimensions*. Whurr, 1991.

15 For a year in the liberated life of Marin County, around the 1960s and 70s, see Cyra McFadden's hilarious novel *The Serial* (Picador, 1978) from which the above list of consumer ware is drawn.

16 See Mike Featherstone, *Consumer Culture and Postmodernism*. Sage, 1991.

17 Published in *A Way of Being* (Houghton Mifflin, 1980) within which Rogers attempts, at the end of a long life, to draw together the threads of his ideas and experiences.

18 Thus, as I work through the last draft of this book, I am busy looking for ways of getting rid of 30 000 words. I don't want to treasure them; I want to scrap them.

Chapter 5

Cognitive-behaviourist approaches

A man's behaviour is the index of the man,
and his discourse is the index of his understanding.
(Ali Ibn-Abi-Talib,
7th century, *Sentences*)

Behaviour is a mirror in which
everyone displays his own image.
(Goethe, 1809)[1]

Conduct is three-fourths of our life and its largest concern.
(Arnold, 1873)[2]

Cognitive behaviourism grew among people who described themselves as 'psychologists' more than it did among 'counsellors'. One important group of psychology specialists were the clinical psychologists, who, initially at least, were ancillaries of the medical profession. As behaviourists, they confined themselves to devising and providing psychometric tests, numerical scores, normal distributions of quantified results, questionnaires and checklists for observation. Within this role, they established themselves within the UK national health service as valuable assistants to the doctor. Psychological testing was presented as a useful auxiliary service that physicians could request and use as they saw fit. Thus the employment of clinical psychologists within medical teams could be seen as adding to the medical consultant's status, prestige and clinical armoury.

This arrangement is most comfortable when psychologists are willing to accept their subsidiary role. However, changes within medicine and psychology can destabilize such an orderly power relation. Consider first, the position from the point of view of the psychologist.

Psychologists face a very tough challenge. They seek to understand human emotion, perception and behaviour, but given that everyone else is also trying to do this, they have to find a way of showing that their professional understanding of human nature is superior to the insights of ordinary lay people. Everyone seeks to make sense of other people's behaviour and tries to predict what they might do next. All of us need to learn how to 'read' other people reasonably well if we are to survive at all in a social world. Hence, by the time we are adults, we have all become reasonably expert psychologists, whether we realize it or not. Certainly we will have all put in a lot of practice and learned a great deal from our mistakes. Of course, some are manifestly better amateur psychologists than others. Some practise more diligently and regularly. Some are more sensitive in temperament and personality, and become far more developed in their 'people skills' than do the rest of us. Thus women are often more receptive than men in their awareness of other people's feelings, simply because they have been encouraged to develop these skills from early childhood.

Professional psychologists, therefore, experience stiff competition from many others – for example, police, poets, prostitutes, painters, photographers, personnel managers, novelists and sales staff who are equally committed to making psychological assessments, whether in an unpaid or paid capacity. All these may have good personal and professional reasons to claim that their own skills, experience, understanding and powers of observation are at least as sophisticated as are the chartered psychologist's. This puts psychologists forever on the defensive. Any admission that you are a professional psychologist leads the claimant wide open to the response 'Aren't we all?' Hence professional psychologists feel obliged to restrict what they say and how they say it within some kind of theory, language, method and expertise that differentiates their own activities from the psychological labours of everyone else.

Psychologists of the behaviourist school have tried to cope with this problem by striving to show that they are scientific, rigorous and concerned about research and hard evidence. In order to do so, they have avoided the nontechnical language of everyday life. Yet by insulating themselves from ordinary language, they become isolated from the diversity, insight and experience that is part of a living tongue developed over many generations from broad and varied experience. Even worse, by ignoring the poetry of communication, and substituting a metallic grey prose, the 'scientific' psychologist fails to use some of the most succinct, comprehensive and accurate means of capturing the subtlety of human experience. Like so many who have not even mastered prose, the psychologist tends to view poetry as an unreliable and subjective adornment.

In their zeal to show themselves as scientific, professional psychologists have been wary of approaching people's 'inner lives'. They have shunned discussion of intentions, hopes, fears, doubts, fantasies, beliefs and values, since these are extremely difficult, if not impossible, to measure. Intentions, for example, need to be inferred from a person's language or behaviour. We can even have difficulty inferring, and being honest about, our own intentions. Other people's mental imagery cannot be observed at all, nor can the private conversations people have with themselves. You cannot feel my bodily experiences or my emotions, and you are not privy to my thoughts and fantasies. In short, our experience is private not just in practice but in principle. Outsiders have no direct access to it, however shrewd their inferences.

A skilled and wise observer may nonetheless come to know me better than I know myself, lost as I am within my own reverie and rationalization. Behaviourists took comfort from this. Opting for caution, they focused on what we actually do and ignored our experiences altogether. The 'soft' behaviourists acknowledged inner life but saw no way of accessing it and being scientific about it. The 'hard' behaviourists denied the very existence of experience and saw consciousness as a kind of optical illusion.

Soft behaviourists, therefore, could ask their spouses 'What was it like for you?' as long as they were clear that it was not a scientific question. For 'hard' behaviourists, on the other hand, this question had no meaning at all and therefore, for them, presumably, a fake orgasm, for example, is a logical impossibility. This hard behaviourist line appears to be (experientially) hard on the spouse.

Feelings of pain and pleasure are, surely, vivid enough. I know, with absolute certainty, that you do not feel my pain, and I also know, with equal conviction, that my behaviour – tensing muscles, crying out, moaning, and so on – is connected to and a feature of, but certainly not the same as, my pain.

In ordinary conversation, the fact of our own personal experiences seems undeniable. Yet within the academic greenhouse environment of a psychological laboratory, it is possible to plant, grow and examine exotic notions about human beings that would not survive at all within the real social landscape. In isolation from the ordinary world, and with a tight control of every variable, psychologists were at least able to speak to other psychologists and managed to forget that the rest of the world was, more often than not, ignoring them.

Such withdrawal into academe can be attractive to professional psychologists because, in the world outside, there are many streetwise specialists and dealers who, in order to survive and prosper, have had to become more effective observers of human motivation and intention than most academics and clinicians. In the laboratory, idealized and simplified experimental environments can be constructed in a relatively neat and orderly way. The experiment can be free of the mess, turmoil and uncertainty that constitutes real human existence. Subsequent experimental reports will thereby satisfy colleagues' demands for scientific rigour, even though they will remain unreadable and unread by the lay person who, if they ever bothered to study them, would generally fail to see any relevance to the outside world.

Of course, when chartered behaviourists returned home at the end of the day, they tended to revert to the unavoidable common sense view that their spouse, friends and children do actually operate in some way within a private world of experiences. And so, for example, they would ask 'How are you *feeling*?', as well as 'What are you doing?' At home, if not in the laboratory, even the hardest behaviourist would accept their child's claim to be thinking about, and visualizing, a pink teddy with green wings in some fantasy game, even though the creature remained in principle unobservable by anyone else. Moreover, if they wanted their marriage to be more than a behavioural shell, they might have been wise to treat their spouse as more than a well-crafted android.

In everyday practice, it is impossible to use ordinary language without presupposing that human beings have an inner life of private experiences. Our very language is built upon such a presupposition, and all of human social life rests on this assumption. To bother to communicate with you at all involves my assuming that you can understand what I am saying and that your experience will be changed in your efforts to read these words. We assume that we are not robots, and, on the contrary, when we observe coherent robotic behaviour, we tend to imagine, however much we remind ourselves to the contrary, that the robots themselves must have an inner life.

After years of rigorous but generally sterile research, most behaviourists eventually came round to accepting that they could no longer ignore people's internal lives, however hard these were to define or describe. It seemed that human beings were not, after all, just 'sophisticated-repertoires-of-stimulus-response-routines', or 'dispositions-to-behave-in-interaction-with-environmental-cues'. Hard behaviourism was a particularly absurd and impossible theory for those psychologists who actually had to meet clients, patients, people (even), and provide them with practical assistance in a clinical setting.

Academic psychologists could explore eccentric ideas about human beings because they did not actually have to talk personally, or engage in any sort of personal relationship, with their experimental subjects. They could therefore compare people with pigeons, rats, machines or computer programmes, all of which are more amenable to study than are people themselves. These research scientists were generally polite, middle-class liberals; they did not treat people as pigeons before or after an experiment. The subjects themselves, equally polite and anxious to please, could behave in a pigeon-like manner when the experimental situation provided only a bird-brain's range of options and was sufficiently inane and disconnected from the real world outside.

If complex human personalities are placed in a simplistic research environment, they can be persuaded to peck away between one or two trite options allowed for within an experiment. As long as the subjects do not walk right off the set, psychologists can imagine that the experimental props, however flimsy, provide a model of the world that delivers insight into the real behaviour of real people. And human beings do indeed behave like robots when the environment is sufficiently mechanized, impersonal and unstimulating. In soul-destroying circumstances, within or outside the laboratory, victims may lose themselves, heart and soul. This relieves researchers of the impossible task of measuring what has been lost.

Professional psychologists, in growing numbers, eventually accepted the need to engage with quintessentially human characteristics such as intentions, meanings, values, internal conflicts, faith, doubt, love and all the other human agendas that are the stuff of life, love, fiction and fantasy. Thus they rediscovered what, to most lay people, had always been obvious.

In psychology, as in other human studies, it is easier to take on the forms and mantle of science than effectively achieve the reality. When assumptions about human beings are overly neat and tidy, they tend also to become naïve and trite. The behaviourist assumption that human experience could be ignored or understood entirely via human behaviour was eventually seen as untenable. Behaviourist psychologists therefore modified their description of themselves and their methods. They were now to be called *cognitive* behaviourists, since they were now studying not only behaviours, but also the 'cognitions' of their subjects. Cognitions, incidentally, are just attitudes, thoughts and feelings, but the word 'cognition' sounds more impressive. Professional language must impress at least as much as inform. Ordinary English tends to be pushed aside, or 'displaced laterally', when status and power are raised higher than simplicity and truth.

Hence psychologists talked of 'the subjects' cognitive and affective life' rather than 'Sid and Edith's thoughts and feelings', and sought to engage with emotions and opinions, even though they had previously claimed that this was impossible. This fundamental U-turn was described as an advance or development rather than a retreat or defeat, but it was never made clear how psychologists were going to access these cognitions whose existence they were now prepared to acknowledge. Some sort of *inference* is required, yet why should we assume that the inferences of cognitive behaviourists are less messy, subjective and prejudiced than the lay person's?

Cognitive psychologists argue that our perceptions are coloured by expectations, intentions and presuppositions generally. People tend to see what they want, and know how, to see. Anything that we are unwilling, unready or unable to face up to remains remarkably invisible. This has long been known by sages, our best novelists and other artists in all cultures, but psychologists have nonetheless felt the need to research the subject. Their observations to date have been neither as profound, as subtle, as interesting or as powerfully presented as, let's say, a work by Tolstoy, Shakespeare or, for that matter, hundreds of much lesser artists.

Psychological 'neutrality'?

Psychologists observe that prejudice is part of the very being of humanity and that we are therefore incapable, in any absolute sense, of disinterested and detached perception. Our prior learning, motives, expectations and temperament form and filter everything we see and know. There is no 'cloud nine' vantage point from which to view the magic, mystery, muddle and mess of existence. Psychologists lack this divine platform, just like everyone else. Presumably, therefore, they should examine their own (individual and collective) motives, conflicts, power ploys and rationalizations to see how these colour, corrupt, shape and stain their 'scientific' observations? They could then better understand, although not wholly escape, their own distortions and subjectivity.

In fact, psychologists shy away from including themselves as part of their subject of study. Introspection and self-awareness are disorderly activities that threaten, if not altogether destroy, claims to scientific respectability. To examine perceptual distortion in others is a respectable academic pursuit, but if we study our *own* credibility and prejudice, our claims to be disinterested and detached scientists become... incredible. Hence psychologists cling to the belief that, through their researches in clinics and laboratories, they can produce a special claim to detachment and disinterested knowledge. They even convince others on occasions. For example:

> General Managers, in particular, [within the National Health Service] do not have many people to turn to who will provide semi-objective, let alone fully objective, opinion. Psychologists can and do fulfil this important role.

This is the view of Derek Mowbray, as reported in *The Psychologist* (British Psychological Society, August 1991). As Director of Management Advisory Services, he was commissioned by the NHS/Department of Health to review the position of clinical psychology within the NHS. The profession was surprised and pleased with his glowing report. Psychologists, unsurprisingly, took a positive view of the person who had taken a positive view of them. Hence, in the October 1989 issue of *The Psychologist,* the MAS report, which had so applauded psychologists, was itself applauded by psychologists as being 'one of the best eight pieces of research over the last decade'. Mowbray had recommended a doubling of the number of clinical psychologists in the NHS, and an upgrading so that top-grade psychologists were on a level with consultant medical staff. Is it reasonable to believe that the psychologists' reception of the MAS report was detached, disinterested and 'fully objective'?

In the absence of a neutral platform from which objective observations can be made, what is to be done? Nobody seriously believes that everyone's insights are equally valid, but who can go on believing that any particular special interest group is capable of delivering what Mowbray describes as a 'fully objective opinion'? Psychologists' claims to such Olympian detachment have been fatally undermined, even by their own observations. All this strengthens my suspicion that those poets, writers and artists who engage with, rather than suppress, their own personal experience and reactions, may develop more profound insight into human personality than does the observer who pretends to be a detached eye rather than a biased and committed 'I'.

Like everyone else, psychologists tend to see what they want to see and avoid what suits them to avoid. For example, *cognitive* behaviourism is a contradiction in terms, given that behaviourism is defined by its rejecton of 'cognitions' as reliable objects of research. If psychologists were more honest and objective, they would confess that 'we just got it wrong for the last few generations'.

I can remember having debates back in the 1960s, as a psychology undergraduate, about the predicament of this subject. Some tutors were quite candid with their considerable doubts about psychology as a scientific discipline. Could it provide scientific explanations of human behaviour? Or could it do no more than offer the occasional 'cookbook' recipe? Were there even any recipes on offer, and did anyone make any use of the blueprints available?

Some research results seemed worthwhile. One lecturer explained that attention decayed after twenty minutes of listening to most lecturers. Shorter, sharper, more varied presentations were therefore needed. The one-hour lecture format needed to be reviewed carefully. We were told this half way through a one-hour lecture, and the lecturer droned on for another half hour without seeming to notice the irony. Further research may well show not only that students are not listening, but also that neither are the lecturers themselves necessarily attending to what they are saying.

Faced with all this, some of us wondered about the future of psychology as a science, and my honours degree in psychology (and philosophy) was, in any case, a bachelor of arts rather than science. I then went on to complete an MLitt, as a way of comparing the approaches of novelists and psychologists. The notion of detached perception became ever more dubious.

If psychology's methods of enquiry are questionable, or much the same as everyone else's, what distinguishes professional psychologists from lay people? We have seen that psychologists face formidable competition. Every human being puts in a great deal of time and effort to figure out, and to explain, the behaviour, motives, conflicts and intentions of other people. Such efforts are absolutely essential if we are to get along with, get through to, or get the better of the people around us. As social animals, we all need to become as highly developed as we can in our 'people skills'. Some, therefore, are very skilled indeed. Is there really any reason, then, to assume that the most skilled psychologists are the people paid as such? It is by no means certain that they have any particular theory, method or skill that gives them much, or any, advantage over others. Indeed, by spending years in the study of pigeons rather than people, many behaviourists placed themselves at a substantial disadvantage.

We have all spent a lifetime trying to understand other human beings. Yet virtually none of this knowledge is obtained as a result of scientific hypothesis and experiment.[3] Even the most learned professors of psychology have, in fact, derived most of their understanding of humanity from ordinary everyday contact with other people and from (nonpsychological) literature generally. Such knowledge is, however, off-limits to scientific psychology. In its efforts to be systematic and to assume nothing, previous knowledge about people cannot be accepted unless it takes the form of references to earlier scientific study.

The results of this methodological purity can be naïve, simplistic and bizarre: researchers have to write as though they know nothing beyond what has been established by research. This forces them to communicate as though they were alien observers of the human race, rather than flesh and blood members. Psychology, like some poetry, is 'Martian'. Such a posture of detachment and discovery is untenable and disingenuous among psychologists who are, in fact, Earthlings. For instance, I found it absurd to try to describe human personality in an essay that had to be confined to experimental evidence. The evidence itself was trite in the extreme, and the experiments were generally so banal that the only sensible thing to be done after reading about them was to forget about them. This I did, and instead described the phenomenon of personality from my own, very limited, experience as an eighteen-year-old. Such experience was still sufficient to yield a 'First Class' result, and the essay was described as excellent – 'despite the complete absence of experimental results'. Whatever sophistication the analysis may have had (not very much in an eighteen-year-old) came from my refusal to pretend that I had no prior knowledge of other people, or that I could conceivably divorce myself from such knowledge and restrict myself to experimental evidence.

On one moving occasion where such matters were being discussed, we were all, tutor and undergraduates alike, near to throwing our books out of the lecture room windows in a gesture of despair, exuberant release and rebellion. We did not do so, of course, and not so long afterwards I observed the very same tutor, as a psychologist consultant in a hospital setting, parading before suitably reverential nursing and ancillary staff. The latter would call him 'Doctor' with all the deference that the title produces in a medical context, although I suspect that they were unaware of the distinctions between the medical qualifications of their more usual boss and the psychologist's PhD. I felt like a boy facing an emperor who had previously confided that he was naked, yet who was now seducing his staff into believing that he wore a very tall hat and robes. It was an embarrassing moment for us both, and it was then that I realized just how difficult it could be to work with integrity in the respectable mainstream as a professional psychologist.

Psychologists do now take more interest in the experience, or cognitions, of their experimental 'subjects', as they call them. Their work has consequently begun to yield a richer range of practical results. For example, they were previously willing to observe Mrs Smith only as an elicitor of behaviour. They paid no serious attention to what she said, and, as a result, learnt very little about her personality and predicament. Now that they actually ask for her opinions and feelings about this or that, and even begin to treat her as though she were a person, they improve their chances of discovering something of interest. Nonetheless, it would still be unprofessional just to come into a case conference or academic seminar and report that 'Mrs Smith thinks, feels, wants…'. Such an ordinary language presentation would not give the desired impression of scientific authority and detachment. As Dorothy Rowe explains in her Foreword to Jeffrey Masson's book *Against Therapy*:

> I had discovered that if I asked, say, Mrs. Smith her opinion of herself and her relatives, her answer would have no value or interest to the people at the case conference, but if I organised my questions and Mrs. Smith's answers into numbers (e.g. 'Out of a scale of 7, where 7 is the most and 1 is the least, how much do you get angry with your husband?' '7'), and I got my friend Patrick Slater to put these numbers through his computer, then Mrs. Smith's replies, in the form of computer-printed numbers, took on an impressive degree of truth and significance.

As an innocent undergraduate I discovered that my fellow students had chosen to study psychology because, like myself, they wanted to learn more about themselves and other people. We hoped to discover, and be taught, insights about humanity that would be personally meaningful and useful to us. We wanted evidence, system and theory, but, more than anything else, we wanted the subject to be *relevant* to our own and other people's lives.

We were told, repeatedly and forcefully, that this was a common enough misconception on the part of youngsters like ourselves but that, if we were to become proper, professional, social scientists, we needed to detach ourselves from, and ignore completely, our personal motivations, experiences and efforts to attain meaning. All this personal baggage was irrelevant and would obstruct the disciplined, detached and impersonal stance required of scientists. If we were to be taken seriously as professionals, we could only parade our personhood in off-duty hours.

Anything we thought we might know about ourselves or others, prior to our training, needed to be jettisoned, since it was likely to be thoroughly misconceived. In any case, our subjective views about anything had no status. Personal observations were of little interest, since they were not amenable to proper testing in an experimental environment.

I felt very disappointed about all this. Also, I found it repeatedly frustrating to adopt the role of 'Mr Spock' (the 'rational' alien from the TV series *Star Trek*) and pretend that I knew nothing whatever about human beings, having just arrived from the planet Vulcan and stepped onto the earth for the first time. It seemed dishonest to behave as though we were open-minded alien observers who knew no more about these Earthlings than we had discovered in our laboratory. Repeatedly, I found that the experimental results of these would-be 'Martian' researchers were trite. For example:

- Outgoing people, it had now been proved, tended to socialize more, go out to parties and talk more often. Introverted people, on the other hand, spent more time on their own.
- People were more likely to be vulnerable to stress if they had had a tough childhood.
- Individuals broke down under pressure more easily if they did not get much emotional support and attention from others.
- Being held and cuddled by someone who really cared for you could have a very healing effect.
- Those who liked each other were more willing to be physically close to each other.
- Separating young children from their mothers when they were young and ill in hospital was often very damaging, so mothers should be allowed access to young patients outside normal visiting hours.

In relation to the latter, I can remember being quite amazed to discover that several psychologists and psychiatrists had made lucrative and successful careers for themselves in publicizing this 'discovery' over many years. As a result of their efforts, hospital policy throughout the country had been changed.

Reading about this scientific advance for the first time, I recalled that I had become an authority on the subject of unhealthy hospital visiting policies at the age of five …when I watched my three-year-old brother suffer because our mother was allowed such infrequent visits. I was able to see him at the entrance to the ward and not by his bedside. He was a pale speck in a bed across an ocean of polished floor. There were fears that I might infect him although I felt, and was, quite well.

I imagine that every child is similarly wise on these matters. You do not have to be a professional psychologist to know, as a youngster, when someone close to you needs their mother. Indeed, it seems that being a professional psychologist often *prevents* you from seeing the obvious.

However, it is evident that five-year-olds cannot be credited with knowing much, and it is inconceivable that they could know more about some matters than hospital consultants or eminent child psychiatrists.

Repeatedly, then, we would be required, as undergraduates, to study and memorize research results that were dull, trite, trivial and irrelevant to everyone outside the introverted world of professional psychology. Frequently the findings 'proved' what lay people already knew and saw no need to verify. Sometimes results conflicted with everyday knowledge. These were usually ignored, since most of us trust our own lived experience rather than someone else's theory and experiment. Occasionally, discoveries were made that were new, important and which fundamentally challenged folk wisdom or 'common sense'. On the whole, and on balance, though, it seemed wiser to trust one's own fallible common sense than someone else's incredible and exotic pseudoscience.

The position looks no better as I examine the most recent efforts. For example, Steve Duck provided an overview of research on human relationships in his book *Relating to Others*.[4] The book's references stretch over twenty pages, of which no less than 35 per cent of the total consists of (inevitably highly repetitious) references to books written, co-written or edited by Dr Duck. A considerable amount of research work is cited, yet it could have been wider still were it not for the fact that, in the main text of just 147 pages, there are no less than 123 citations of the work of Dr Duck. Of course, it is understandable, and human enough in these competitive times, that authors will see fit to quote their own work, but I did think that there was rather too much Duck on this menu.

Duck concludes that 'The field of research in personal relationships is about to witness a major boom that will take us comfortably into the next millennium'. This breathtaking observation is not borne out by the research results he quotes, most of which, once again, seem to be either not very interesting, or just plain obvious. For example, 'We may feel that we like someone but be uncertain about their corresponding feelings for us, so we decide not to act on our own feelings as, for example Duck and Miell (1986) found'. Or, 'we are more "affiliative" and inclined to seek each others' company when we are anxious (Schachter, 1959), when we have just left a close relationship or moved to a new neighbourhood (Duck, 1982), when aged between about 16 and about 26, when we are not in a hurry (Perlman, 1986), and so on' (and on and on).

Once more, we are offered a book that will provide a lot of useful information about human beings for any visiting Martian who enjoys dry prose, but to suggest, as Duck does, that a significant under-standing of human relationships only began some fifteen or twenty years previously, possibly around the University of Iowa, is more than a little naïve. I recently reread Tolstoy's *War and Peace*. One novelist, in one novel, shows more insight into the complexities, absurdities, triviality, magnificence and vast range of human existence than all of Duck, the University of Iowa, and hundreds of 'people-skill' profes-sionals. Tolstoy's voice rings out into time and space and reverberates with a truth and sophistication extending far beyond his own country and century. Contemporary social science, far from surpassing such genius, comes nowhere near to approaching it.

There are some, but few, honourable exceptions, where simple but effective experiments are carried out as a result of some clever thinking being done in advance. However, these gems are so rare that they prove, rather than undermine, the general rule that most of the efforts to practise scientific research into human psychology continue to be unsuccessful. The results are simply not significant enough to remember, let alone act upon. Yet there are hundreds, thousands, of results, names and dates that psychologists are supposed to learn.[5] As an undergraduate, it was like trying to learn the lists from World War monuments to our heroic dead. Psychologists have conducted a great 'Somme offensive' in an effort to drive back the frontier of our scientific knowledge. The casualty rate has been horrendous and there is still no sign of victory. Such success as there has been has come from individual creativity, sharp-shooting, flare and insight, rather than the massed battalions of inappropriate methodology.

When researchers pretend they know nothing about people and are indifferent to an outcome that must be comprehensively provable, the findings tend to be fatuous and *academic* (as in 'dull' or 'irrelevant' or 'just plain obvious'). When, on the other hand, research psychologists are more clear about their own intentions and assumptions, and wish merely to test limits and circumstances of what they are confident is true, their results can then be more practical and useful.

'Cookbook' psychologists, then, seem to make better headway than do grand theorizers. For example, abstract theorists wishing to design a comprehensive 'model' of learning or personality have achieved remark-ably little, compared with pragmatists looking for what works in a classroom or on a packet of soap powder. In the case of psychology in advertising, consumers might wish that rather less had been achieved, given the power of communication specialists to *exploit* rather than *empower* other people.

Psychology and power

Most consumers realize that celebrities in advertisements love the fee more than the product. Young children, too, discover that advertisers, while not actually lying, are not exactly telling the truth, the whole truth and nothing but the truth. Perhaps we should worry about the effect this has on children's values and integrity.

We have higher hopes for psychologists and other professionals working in higher education and medicine. In these nonprofit-making fields, we assume that motives are more honourable and focused on truth more than promotion prospects and career development.

However, in these increasingly competitive times, clinicians and academics, too, have been thrust into the marketplace. If combatants are to survive and prosper in the rush for research funds and promotion, they must engage in an increasingly manic career battle with colleagues and rivals. They must gain success, celebrity, status and more than their colleagues. One way of doing this is to produce better-quality work, but this may not be enough, and it is a high-risk strategy. If our talent is not self-evidently exceptional, we may also need to be seen with the right people at the right time and place. Allies must be cultivated, enemies isolated, and attention, citation, publication and publicity extracted for every minor effort. Claims, and the language used to make them, become inflated. Language impresses more than informs. Our words become incomprehensible to all but a few fellow specialists. 'Seekers after truth', may become, by degrees (BSc, MSc, PhD, piled higher and deeper), seekers after citation and success.

Pseudoscience, mathematical renditions of nonsense, footnotes and references as large as the body text – all these, often, inflate the person more than the argument. Journal articles build power, status and funds more than real, useful, relevant knowledge. How often? Very often. But I know of no research into this rather interesting question!

Professional psychologists are pressured to avoid speaking from personal experience. To speak personally is to reveal oneself as a person, and therefore as fallible, biased and subjective like everyone else. However, this effort to adopt an 'impersonality' is fundamentally dishonest. We can only speak from a particular point of view, from the skin encapsulated egocentricity that is the human condition. Our observations are bound to be clouded, or shaped, by our own subjectivity. This remains true within experimental laboratories, even when prejudice wears mathematical symbols. We can try to be systematic, impartial, empirical, but only within limits. Paradoxically, we get closest to such limits when we own, rather than deny, our subjectivity.

This requires us to abandon the facile and dangerous belief that anyone can ever be detached and disinterested. Like so many ideals, detachment is something we can aspire to, but it is not a destination that we can ever actually reach.

The 'totally impartial' psychologists described by Derek Mowbray earlier in the chapter, like all human beings, seek power, status and control at least as much as truth. When these conflict, truth is likely to be the first casualty. This is key to understanding human motivation, yet I have learned far more about it from novelists than psychologists. Most psychology seeks ways of managing other people. Most psychologists are hired by those with power, for example, politicians, advertisers, public relations specialists and psychiatrists. Guess whose interests, then, psychologists will be expected to protect? Yet psychology textbooks scarcely ever refer to such mundane matters as power, money and prestige. They certainly do not talk about the way these might influence psychologists themselves.

No-one withdraws from publishing a learned academic paper merely because it has failed to secure the anticipated results or yield anything valuable or new. Many social science papers are therefore read by almost no-one, and certainly no-one outside the narrow speciality area. Those who do pick up the paper will be seeking, primarily, to write one of their own, and 'I'll quote you if you quote me'. The citation count thereby can rise to the benefit of those suitably 'networked'.

Such power-broking operates unknowingly, automatically and without conspiracy. Power is gained by posturing as a detached enquirer. Power is lost by owning up to interested efforts to gain power. Academics would be shocked to be depicted as wolves and dogs running in packs, yet this is probably a more accurate metaphor than is that of the detached seeker. There are plenty of novels and bar-room discussions about power and conflict in academe, but I have come across very little academic research on the subject. Such research would not be in the interests of the researcher and the community to which they belonged. So much for the disinterested search for truth.[6]

Predictably, then, the most interesting psychologists do not pretend to be disinterested. They own up to their own interest, and self-interest. Phillida Salmon, for example (in Pilgrim, 1983)[7], suggests that:

> It seems to me that it is only through the preparedness to take a personal stance towards psychology that anyone could possibly have the right to teach it. To teach should mean to offer what is personally meaningful. And psychology comes to have personal meaning only if one has reflected deeply on one's own journey so far through life.

The idea that scientific psychologists should reflect deeply on their own life journey has been almost universally dismissed by the scientific establishment as quite irrelevant to, indeed positively harmful for, a proper mastery of psychology. To engage in such deep introspection, it is widely believed, is to risk disappearing forever into the swamp of one's own subjectivity or the pit of one's own prejudice. These, admittedly, are major risks, but in my view they are risks that we simply cannot avoid. We are not gods. We cannot view the reality of human existence from Mount Olympus. We have to make sense of life from where we are, and where we will stay: on the ground, in the mud, mist and murk of everyday living, guided by the insights and ignorance of our own personality. We look out on the world through our own personal bias. This is true when staring out of the kitchen window, or through a one-way glass, or in a laboratory or before an admiring audience.

Our humanity comes with us wherever we go. To deny its distorting influence creates still more distortion. Therefore, any 'ology' of the psyche that is not rooted in our own personal lives and struggles is fundamentally unsound. The personality, history and motives of any observers, even when dressed in white coats, are a part of the agenda they are studying that shapes what, why and how they study. This is especially true when the subjects of investigation are, like ourselves, human beings.

Therapists of almost every school agree that self-awareness is of crucial importance in healing. Cognitive therapists, for example, urge that clients face up to their counterproductive attitudes and behaviour so that alternative goals and realistic strategies can be developed. Yet when did cognitive therapists, if true to their own scientific training, ever practise for themselves what they preach to their clients? They will very probably have spent years learning to be detached and to discon-nect themselves from their own, supposedly irrelevant, experiences. To be a shrewd observer, they will have been told, 'You have to be as disembodied as possible. Your own personality and personal reactions should play no part. Your personal story and history should be completely cut away from the experimental or clinical process. What you observe should be what other professionals would observe if they replicated the experiment'.

Such cognitive therapists, who have been trained to pay no attention to their own inner lives, require precisely the opposite response from their clients. If they are to change their minds ('cognitive restruc-turing'), clients must know their minds and become self-aware. Cognitive therapists, on the other hand, are supposedly quite detached from anything personal and individual within their own minds. They just look out with a cool and neutral gaze and see reality as it really is.

Psychologists have deceived themselves into believing that, as professional observers and unlike the rest of humanity, they can observe people objectively, shorn of personal bias or history. This assumption of dispassionate neutrality is one that therapists of every school are keen to maintain. Unless they can show that they are looking down on the world from a higher platform, their own vantage point might become as questionable as anyone else's. It would become impossible to turn to them as reliable parent substitutes with privileged access to the truth. Psychologists would then have to be recognized as struggling adults just like everyone else, whose vision of who they are and where they are going is just as open to question as is the perspective of any other fallible, unaware and prejudiced human being.

Notes

1   J. W. Goethe, *Elective Affinitives*. Penguin, 1809, reprinted 1971.

2   Matthew Arnold, *Literature and Dogma*. AMS Press, 1873.

3   The quality of folk knowledge is extremely variable. We do not always manage, in one lifetime, to distinguish between our profound insights and shallow prejudices!

4   Steve Duck, *Relating to Others*. Open University Press, 1988.

5   Now, via a computer modem, I can dial my way into tens of thousands of the corresponding journal articles being pumped into the world's databases.

6   What of the contribution of the universities to counselling? More energy seems to go into promotion of high-income-generating courses than on research into theory and practice. Entrepreneurial marketing is more profitable than scholarly research. What, in this market-driven environment, if insight interferes with income?

7   David Pilgrim (ed.), *Psychology and Psychotherapy: Current Issues and Trends*. RKP, 1983.

Chapter 6

Psychodynamic approaches

*A psychoanalyst is one who pretends he
doesn't know everything.*

In Chapter 4, we examined the Rogerian construction of a saleable product around warmth, empathy and unconditional positive regard. Chapter 5 explored the behaviourial presentation of healers as objective, disinterested scientists. Both schools owed a great deal to marketing and presentation skill. Arguably the greatest sales professional in therapy, though, was Sigmund Freud himself.

Those seeking the role of wise guru must observe certain ground rules. Patients want to believe that something can be done and that their chosen healer is the person to do it. Faith and hope are attractive. To conclude that there is no remedy is intolerable for most of us. Healers must therefore present themselves with confidence and dress for the occasion. They may then be successful even if their medicine is neutral or positively harmful. (Most medicines throughout most of history may have provided no physical cure whatsoever.) The uselessness of a product does not make it unsaleable, but it helps if it really does contain quality ingredients. Brands need an edge, an identity, a target of consumers, and an appeal to their preoccupations.

Producing a successful new product is very difficult. Most fail, like fish roe in a Darwinian struggle for survival. Existing rivals are much more strongly established. Like mutations, most *new* ideas are not very *good* ideas. Genuine creativity and brand new marketable goods are relatively rare. More commonly, money is made from 'me-too' products – the same old thing dressed up as new. For every genuinely new initiative, there are dozens of 'me-too' varieties crowding after them.

The Rogerian and behaviourist schools occupy different market niches, yet the core of each product is not new. The ingredients of each have some attractive qualities, but they embody half-truths, incomplete in themselves. For example, a clean and simple approach to behaviour, shorn of the complexities of our inner lives, is attractive, but can it actually be achieved? Similarly, warmth and empathy can be very healing, but who can be warm and empathic all the time? Or even very often?

Core qualities

Freud's product, like its rivals, has some attractive ingredients, but psychoanalysis, too, is not new. It embodies various useful ideas, and Freud promoted them as though they were momentous discoveries of his own making. Critics such as Eysenck, Gellner and Masson argue that the entire package of Freudian ideas is false and useless. Much of it has already faded or fallen into disrepute. However, I suspect that many core ingredients will survive Freud and analysis, because they predate him and were neither owned nor discovered by him. They will, no doubt, reappear in other guises, in other cultures, and under the copyright of some other guru. Shorn of jargon, these basic insights include the following:

1 Human beings are not always conscious of what they are doing. Our thoughts, feelings, wishes and actions often pass unnoticed and unexamined.
2 Even when we do notice what we are doing, we do not always know why. We may be aware without being able to explain.
3 Awareness and self awareness may be painful and uncomfortable. We actively avoid awareness of some thoughts, feelings and behaviours.
4 If our avoidance is to be successful, we have to evade our evasiveness.
5 We may thus become unable to see what is obvious to others.
6 Insofar as we find it painful to come to terms with ourselves, we remain defensive, vulnerable and liable to manipulation.
7 Our guilt and shame keep facets of our personality buried.
8 We all carry unfinished business from the past – unreleased traumas, unreconciled frustrations, dilemmas and conflicts misunderstood and misperceived. These are liable to shape, disrupt and disturb our dealings in the present. Usually, we will be quite unaware of what is occurring.
9 That which we repress is liable to threaten and haunt us, leaving us feeling uncertain and uneasy.

10 Much that we avoid would be manageable had we the courage and
faith to face it.

11 Others can help us, especially if they are experienced, skilled and have
come to terms with the less palatable parts of their own personality.

12 Our ability to change and be free of the past is, nonetheless,
limited.

From these foundations, Freud elaborated on the nature of human
conflicts and defensiveness, the ways in which repressed material
revealed itself and the consequences of all this for ourselves and others.
Seeing our own hidden faults in others could trigger a dim, yet
uncomfortable, awareness of the secrets we kept inside. We might then
devise ways of keeping our defences intact, while all the time denying
that we were doing any such thing. We might take our attention away
from our own faults by being highly critical of others when we saw
these same weaknesses in them. Alternatively, we might become
attracted to particular individuals precisely because they expressed
facets of behaviour we ourselves found difficult to expose. Finally, our
fatal attraction to a stranger's charm might arise because they unleashed
yearnings unresolved, unexamined and unexplored in past encounters
with family or friends.

Freud explored many of the ways in which we can rationalize and put
on a show to ourselves and others. We sometimes avoid the responsibilities of adulthood by behaving like children (regression). Sometimes we
displace our emotions from their real, dangerous, target onto something
safer – kicking the cat instead of our partner, for example. We imagine
desirable qualities in ourselves instead of accepting painful aspects of
reality. We sometimes attend to fantasies when the real world is
uncomfortable. We may avoid our emotions by behaving as though we
felt quite differently. In these and other ways, we try to fool ourselves as
well as others. As a result, we may sometimes make fools of ourselves.
Alternatively, we may survive what would otherwise have overwhelmed us.

Deception and self-deception have their place. They also have their
price. It is difficult to feel at peace and at home anywhere, with
anything, unless we are reasonably reconciled with ourselves. We may
try to distract ourselves with neurotic busy-ness disguised as effective
business, but we suffer chronic discomfort if large parts of our personality have to be swept out of awareness.

If we bury too much away, a continuous wariness is needed to ensure
that the truth does not leak out. Lies beget more .ies to protect the
originals. Eternal vigilance is required. This 'defence burden' can wear

us down over time. We may actively seek stresses and demands from the world outside in order to distract ourselves from the pressures inside.

'Self' can seem like a parliament in uproar at times, with contrary and contradictory intentions, preferences, emotions and opinions battling for advantage. It can seem as if there are facets of the self, or 'subselves', struggling for supremacy, each claiming to be the 'real me'. Freud's names for these warring subselves – super-ego, id and ego – entered everyday language. Freudian jargon became part of the 'basic kit' necessary for membership of Western cultural élites. The following, very brief, guide to terminology provides a minimal entry qualification:

- *Super-ego:* preoccupied with ideals and principles, it addresses us like a concerned, or demanding, parent.
- *Id:* the animal side of our personality, which seeks pleasure and avoids pain.
- *Ego:* (Latin for 'I am') sandwiched between the super-ego and the id, the part of us that attempts to conciliate between our pleasure and perfection-seeking tendencies. It faces a hard struggle, since the parental perfectionist and demanding child–animal are reluctant to compromise. Somehow, the poor ego has to find a least-worst option within these internal conflicts and the incompatible pressures piling down on us from the outside world. It is an honourable task. When we achieve it well enough, we have a right to call ourselves grown-up adults. We will, thereby, transform hysterical misery into common unhappiness, at worst. We may even be happy at times, but this is not to be insisted upon.

An outside expert can help us understand and deal with all these internal conflicts. At times, indeed, Freud implied that, if only we were smart enough, we would see that everyone could benefit from the services of an accredited Freudian psychoanalyst. The Freudian path became the Royal Road to enlightenment for the cultural élite. It was expensive and the process was long and arduous. Like a top-quality perfume, however, its expense and exclusiveness added to its appeal.

Initially, Freud tried hypnosis as his core approach route to the unconscious, but he later abandoned this in favour of 'free association'. Mysterious though it may sound, it is really very straightforward. The psy©hoanalyst encourages the patient (Freud was a qualified doctor) to say whatever comes to mind without any kind of preplanning or censorship. The aim is to let one idea, or emotion, move on to the next, in a free association of thoughts and feelings uncensored by 'I-who-do-not-wish-to-find-out-too-much-about-myself'.

Freud argued that, during this process, patients would encounter what we might now call 'no-go' areas, unacceptable and intolerable thoughts, feelings and memories that they were unwilling to reveal, either to themselves or to the therapist. The patient would become evasive, and it was the therapist's task to note such evasion and rationalization and gently but firmly encourage them to face painful reality. Defences were slowly unmasked, on the grounds that knowing oneself was the key to positive change.

Therapists would wait until the patient was ready, willing and able to be more honest and open. They might wait for weeks, months, even years. Therapist probing steadily illuminated the bonds connecting past trauma to present turmoil. Our past shone light on our present. For as long as our history remained buried, it made our present-day choices for us. It lived, breathed and controlled the present. It was not really past at all. Therapy could not be complete until the patients' history had been reconstructed for them. Only then would they be able to make real choices, and piece together new, more fulfilling and effective ways of living.

By joining past and present, a positive construction of our future could begin. In the process, patient and therapist attended carefully to their own relationship. Freud believed that the patient would unconsciously re-enact significant past relationships in an effort to resolve past tensions and traumas. The therapist's task was to 'interpret the transference' or, in ordinary English, show the patient how their past was still operating as a living, albeit inappropriate, part of their present relationship with the therapist. Thus instructed, the patient could gain insight, wisdom, maturity and self-control.

Those who had not yet completed their analysis lived and moved in a cave of delusion. Redundant habits and expectations were not seen as being redundant. Present attitudes, appearances and behaviour triggered resemblances from childhood. John saw his mother in Joan, and reacted like the son he used to be. He tried, via Joan, to reach his dead or absent mother. He and Joan suffered the consequences and groped through their lives in ignorance.

Who can ever acquire all they want from their parents? Longings may well be unfulfilled, and we try to fill past gaps in present relation-ships. Freud argued that we need to be aware of our search for past faces in the people around us. We have to discover the chains that pull on us if we are to be free. Skilled support was required from a highly-trained therapist. Analysts needed to be tremendously wise, skilled and self-aware if they were to penetrate and interpret the patient's behaviour. At the same time, the analyst had to retain an almost anonymous relationship with the patient. The analyst's own particular personality and reactions to the client remained hidden.

The therapist, ideally, would be like a blank screen. 'My analyst' would be an anonymous repository of skills and insights. Consequently, one analyst would be just like any other, recognizable only by the Freudian techniques they all used. Each would rigorously implement the same psychoanalytic method; their dedication and impersonality would be key to their success. There might well be failures of course, but this would be the result of patient inadequacy: low ego strength, limited powers of introspection, lack of self-control, inability to defer immediate gratification.

The patient would project onto the therapist a key relationship from the past, responding as though the therapist was a long-lost, or hoped-for, brother, father or friend, for example. These projections could be observed as the patient built them onto the nondescript persona of the therapist. Since the therapist added nothing and took nothing away, patients could see the fantasies they were building around this person-devoid-of-personality. Anonymity also helped the therapist to avoid enmeshment via 'countertransference': introducing issues and perceptions from the therapist's own past into the patient's story.

How is psychoanalysis to be evaluated? It has been much criticized, and its popularity appears to have peaked. Are parts of it fanciful speculation? How far is it valid? Who is to judge? What about evidence? Will Freudian theory survive the test of time? Is it already eroding? Is psychoanalysis so very new, or is it more like a recycling and restyling of venerable wisdom from previous generations? Freud certainly became fashionable, and I want to explore why he appealed so much to twentieth-century consumers and connoisseurs.

Freud convinced thousands of intelligent patients, colleagues and observers that he was new and revolutionary, but is the substance as novel as the style? He spoke of our underlying revulsion, guilt, shame and insecurity. We run away from ourselves and put on a show to the world. What is obvious to others lies hidden from ourselves. Our lack of reconciliation with ourselves leaves us haunted. The support of a compassionate, wise, experienced and perceptive human being can help us. They are especially healing who have faced and forgiven themselves.

Thus spake Freud, and I am sure he is right. These are ancient verities, no less valuable for that, but Freud had no right to claim them as 'psychoanalytic' or 'Freudian'. Entire spiritual traditions, perhaps most notably Buddhism and Hinduism, are built around the transmission of wisdom from enlightened teachers to deluded disciples. Many of Freud's views are essentially the archetypal nostrums of the wise, found within almost every religious and humanist culture. This does not make them redundant or unimportant. Wisdom has always been in short supply. Insight, detachment and sensitivity remain scarce and precious commodities. Whole cultures can become sick, decadent or repressive. The perennial role of sage and philosopher is to warn of cultural sickness and the eternal dilemmas of existence. It can lead to high status, crucifixion or both.

With hindsight, the novelty of psychoanalysis appears to have been exaggerated. Freud was seen as the 'Einstein' of human relations, but this claim is unlikely to stand the test of time. Freud provided new metaphors and a language style that made his ideas seem more radical than they really are. His success owes much to presentation and the climate of appetite among potential clients. Prior to Freud, the healing role was dominated by Christianity. The priest spoke of our need to confront the dark forces within us. The priest argued that, with outside help, we could forgive and be forgiven. Confession could lead to guidance, relief and absolution. Dishonesty would create still more dishonesty. Distortion and delusion was to be fought with priestly support. The cowardly soul, fleeing from its inner demons, would remain haunted and confused. Limitation was inherent in living but, with patience, courage and humility, salvation was possible.

The priestly role was conducted by individuals of varying temperament. Some were harsh and judgemental, instilling terror and meek obedience. Others were compassionate and forgiving, fostering courage and reconciliation. Most, no doubt, were somewhere in between. For some, the Church and collective worship had a central role; for others, a more individual approach to God was possible. God could be tyrant, loving father or confessor. Prayer could be a cheap petition for special favours or a profound meditation, confession or 'counsel' with God.

The Church tended its flock, but, by the time Freud was writing at the end of the nineteenth century, there was considerable disillusionment with organized religion, particularly among the intelligentsia. To many modern minds, the clergy carried a baggage of outmoded theology, and the Church was a tired force, locked in medieval dogma. It was a shell of dead ritual rather than living spirituality. Its various efforts to change and to accommodate change had been judged, by many, to have been a failure. Worst of all, perhaps, the clergy had repeatedly challenged the findings of science and, on every occasion, had been soundly defeated. Scientists supplanted priests as seekers after truth. Priests, it seemed, clung on to faith and dogma instead of being brave enough to face reality. Religion became, in Marx's words, the 'opium of the people'.

Within this larger battle, the medical profession declared themselves for science (even though much medical success depends on placebo effects). Freud, himself a doctor, thereby profited from the respect accorded to physicians. He therefore recommended that medical training should precede specialization in psychoanalysis because of its status advantages rather than its relevance. A century or more earlier, he would probably have chosen the priesthood as a cradle for his ideas.

The appeal of psychoanalysis

Old truths become attractive when made 'new' with current metaphors and connotations. Freud showed exceptional skill in creating a language and terminology best suited to appeal to early twentieth-century intelligent opinion. He coined an impressive collection of apparently scientific terms: id, ego, super-ego, repression, regression, projection, compensation, displacement, sublimation, transference, cathexis, catharsis, free association, libido, dissociation, fixation and so on. He integrated these via hydraulic metaphors and imagery that, in the age of the steam engine, sounded like 'leading-edge' technology.[1]

Freud's ideas were presented as though having the status of science, yet he provided almost no evidence to support his interpretations and no way by which others could examine and replicate his findings. Psycho-analysis, with its dramatic and radical metaphors, appeared enticing and original, even in dry prose. It carried all the archetypal dramas of human conflict. Age-old stories of good versus evil were reworked using modern props: vague allusions to steam engines, pressure valves, chemistry laboratories, displaced flows of this and that from stored reservoirs, underground volcanoes, pumps, pipes and processes. Mythical themes were reconstructed in the language of late nineteenth-century science. It was a heady brew, guaranteed to pull intelligent clients from confes-sional to analysis, from pew to *chaise-longue*.

Psychoanalysis was exciting, intense and unpredictable. As it rose in fashion, it became a status-enhancing topic of dinner-table conversa-tion. Beneath our polished exterior lurked a deep, dark pit of primal and primordial emotion and conflicting intention. This was an attrac-tive idea because it made us all seem much more interesting, both to ourselves and to each other. Daily life might be a low-key humdrum routine of compromise, quiet conformity and restrained feeling, but, if we could afford the fee, we could buy ourselves a professional guide and clamber down into the pothole of our own unconscious world. Many an adventure could be found there. Many a gloomy grotto would dimly emerge, deliciously terrifying, as the guide threw his Freudian torch on the black cavern of this unconscious world. Strange creatures clawed their way across the tulgy floors of these dank interior spaces. Here was a world of spells and charms described in the language of science. Was that something real I could detect before me, or was I hexed and vexed within my own defensive projection? What was the name of the next key? Displacement? Compensation? Identification? Was I right to respond as I did to what, I thought, you were saying? Or was I unwittingly transferring a tired response from the past onto my deluded perception of the present? Clearly, I would need to turn to the modern equivalent of Merlin, the wizard travelling here so close by my side, whose powers, wisdom and magic would be equal, but only just, to the awesome tasks ahead.

Psychoanalysis provided an epic story, befitting any noble warrior in a quest for the Holy Grail. Moreover it was all, somehow, connected with the sun, grass and fresh air in the fields of consciousness above. How to make such a connection between surface and subterranean worlds? Where, and how, did our Stygian springs of energy flow out to the brighter fields of consciousness above? This was the riddle. This was the challenge. This, indeed, was a grand adventure. And it was all you and yours. It was that most spellbindingly fascinating topic and journey: the story of myself.

Freud, a master of language, managed a seemingly impossible merger between fairy tale and (the appearance of) science. The quest was for Truth, the Holy Grail, the key to life, the riddle of existence. Priests, shamans, witches, courtly readers of runes and oracles, throwers of the I-Ching have accompanied the well-to-do on such a journey over centuries. However, a new guide was needed who could update the story and who was respectable, dignified, modern and scientific.

Freud spoke of *the* Unconscious as though it was a new world he had recently discovered. He gave the impression of being a would-be Moses coming, not so much down from the mountain, as up from the underworld, for which he promised to provide both a map, a guide and a key. Prior to Freud, we did not so much think about *having an Unconscious*, as being unaware of this or that. We are obviously not mindful of everything we feel and do – our most distant ancestors surely knew that – but to *have* an Unconscious is to imply an exotic 'place' that could somehow be 'reached' if only we tried hard enough.

Yet the Unconscious is surely not a place or thing at all. To imagine otherwise creates nothing but confusion, since it leads us to ask inappropriate questions: Where is it? What is in it? How big is it? What is it doing? How can we get into it? What can we get out of it? How can we connect it up to something else?

I may daydream while driving to work. Commuting skills have become habitual, subcortical, unconscious, if you will. I am unaware of changing gear, the direction I am following, my whereabouts in town. Yet I avoid passers-by, other vehicles and stop at traffic lights. The car is undamaged. There is no point in trying to remember the process of driving; I was not even conscious of it at the time. There was no need. My attention was elsewhere.[2]

We may fail to attend through carelessness, lack of necessity, preoccupation with something else, or just sometimes defensiveness or evasiveness. Any novelist routinely describes such processes. We are *not*conscious rather than *un*conscious of much that goes on. This is less exciting than is tantalizing talk of journeys into unconscious 'worlds', manoeuvring past defences and burrowing beneath appearances. Such metaphors add drama and interest. Dare we seek the 'libidinous monster' inside? I think so, because, I suggest, our deeper fear is of boredom and emptiness. It is interesting to explore the possibility of our underlying monstrosity. Far more terrifying is the fear that, deep down, we are shallow, dull, inattentive, mediocre, robotic and half asleep most of the time.

Misapplication of concept was described in 1949 by the philosopher Gilbert Ryle as a 'category mistake'.[3] The *process* of our 'lack of attention' is misconceived as an *entity*, 'the Unconscious'. We then mistakenly imagine that it has nonphysical shape, size, contents and activities of its own. The result is confusion and illusion. Another category mistake creates a demanding newcomer that comes between two people, known as 'the relationship'. Instead of caring for each other, we have to attend to this third party. It has to be nurtured. We have to 'work' on it. Instead of asking 'How's your spouse?', we ask 'How is your relationship?'

We are then in danger of creating a relationship with our relationships. This turns Narcissus into a novice. He only looked in one mirror. We may use two, three or more, and gaze at ourselves, gazing at ourselves, from a variety of angles. We struggle to establish the original self from the reflection of me reflected in you reflected in me reflected in the unconscious me that lies under the surface of me. This adds interest and a topic of conversation: but how many meta-Narcissistic levels of interest does it make sense for us to create:

> Our mistake has been not to see – or to forget – that relations become established between people not as ends in themselves but in the course of doing something else.

> It would seem completely artificial for friends, or lovers, or spouses, suddenly to stop dead in the course of their mutual activity to comment on the quality of their relationship, and yet, more and more, this is exactly what is happening. Partly because there seems to be so little of value to do and partly because we have become objects of gratification for each other, we spend more and more time talking and thinking about our 'relationships' rather than doing anything with them. (Smail, 1987)[4]

Such self-obsession can lead to, and probably results from, personal and social sterility. The less we engage with, and commit ourselves to, other people and the world around us, the more attractive it is for us to embark upon psychic excavations into what we imagine is an underlying 'true self' in a hall of mirrors. Such a psychoanalytic quest provides a sense of meaning and purpose, and it is not as dangerous as it might appear. There will be no face-to-face drama with flesh-and-blood individuals in real caverns expressing strong emotions. We are not going to get physically hurt by the entities we encounter. We will explore within an orderly and controlled framework. Strong emotions will be confined to the analyst's couch, and tucked away from social inspection at the end of the therapeutic hour. Punctuality will take priority over personal crisis, however great. That will be part of the contract.

Strong emotions and personal secrets can be revealed to the psychoanalyst precisely because, like the priest in a confessional, he is not engaging in an ordinary sort of personal relationship and does not even make eye contact. Hence, clients are freed of the consequences and responsibilities that arise when deep emotions are shared in genuinely personal contacts. One can have one's cake and eat it, as it were, with all the drama and emotional outlet of an intense personal alliance, but none of the risks and responsibilities of actually relating to someone.

Best of all, rejection and indifference are written out of the contract, since the therapist is paid to accept and attend to the client. Clients thereby purchase (the appearance of) a friend, or intimate, or father figure, yet with none of the usual risks and responsibilities. As Gellner put it:

> The psychoanalytic session is a masterpiece of combination of the requirements of a rule-addicted, orderly and individualist ethos, with those of abandon and intense emotion. (Gellner, 1985)[5]

The psychoanalytic quest can go on for a lifetime. 'Finding oneself' may become an end in itself with no end in sight, rather than a byproduct of committed action and involvement. Introspection consumes time and energy. If I were to find myself, what would I do to pass the time? Perhaps I ought to be doing it now?

Psychotherapy is not the only profession providing a surrogate of love, attention, intimacy, confidentiality and emotional relief. Prostitution, for example, shares these goals within its mission, and the comparison is interesting, although potentially unsettling. Each promises a plausible presentation of care and concern for the client, when the core of the relationship is based on cash. Neither sex nor analysis is provided to those who cannot pay:

> Unlike (in ideal circumstances) family or friends, therapists play an only temporary role in the lives of almost all their patients, and their commitment to help is strictly limited in terms of their actual involvement in patients' lives (were this not so, the job would become demanding beyond endurance). To talk of love in these circumstances is to edge close to hypocrisy. (Smail, 1987)[4]

The exchange of sex and attention for cash is generally seen as disreputable and demeaning. When counsellors accept cash payments for their own brands of, care and attention, we are invited to applaud. Yet the prostitute takes a far bigger risk. She is physically naked and psychologically more vulnerable than the enigmatic Freudian. Her companionship may be of the flimsiest kind. She does not expect the client to believe that his enacted fantasies are real. She offers only temporary relief from the trials of life. She does not beguile the client into believing she is making a major commitment, or promise any kind of salvation. She might feign a small interest in clients' problems if desired, but she would not pretend to have answers. She would quickly admit to having at least as many difficulties of her own.

I am not thereby defending prostitution. I imagine that it is mostly abusive, unjust and damaging. However, it may also be more authentic, realistic and honest than the contract offered by too many within therapy who have not set themselves realistic goals and boundaries. Therapists, unlike prostitutes, are reluctant to admit to the fundamentally commercial basis of their transaction. Partly through tact, and partly through dishonesty, they avoid saying, 'I'm not going to do anything with you until you've handed over the money'. Prostitutes may thereby be better than therapists in bringing clients closer to (painful) material reality.

The prostitute offers sexual union; the analyst, in classical form, does not even make eye contact. Sexual connection, certainly, is an absolute taboo, which does not, of course, prevent its occurrence.[6] However, the bar on sex is crucial for psychoanalysts since they see sexuality as an important part of every client's agenda. Sexuality is central in psycho-analysis as in many other successful products, and sex has helped to sell it as successfully as it sold Häagen-Dazs ice-cream.[7] I am sure that Freud did not deliberately try to produce a sexy product, but the effect could not have been greater had it been planned in an advertising agency.

Freud's shadowy world of the unconscious teems with sexual fantasy. Humanity, he told us, was obsessed with sex; civilization was but a thin veneer. Sexual energy, or 'libido' as he called it, was our main driving force. If we were to be civilized human beings rather than crude sexual furnaces, we had to sublimate and divert sexual energy from our pumping, fiery loins, just as steam engines harnessed raging fire and boiling water into useful work. Sexual obsession, fantasy and jealousy were everywhere. Sex drove people, just as steam powered the economy. Every son wished to kill his father and make love to his mother (the infamous 'Oedipus complex'). Daughters were universally jealous of their brothers' penises. Sons feared castration. Children thought that daughters had been castrated because girls lacked a penis. Daughters allegedly fantasized that they were being molested by their fathers.[8]

For years, analysts wanted clients to believe that they envied penises and sought sex with their parents. They did not believe patients who claimed to have experienced real sexual abuse. Analysts appear to have got it all wrong, at least as much as anyone else. Client claims of abuse may often have been real when the therapist thought they were fantasy. Now the roles are often reversed, with the therapist pressing clients to 'admit' to their abuse. Clients and therapists are sometimes right and sometimes wrong. There is no evidence that the therapist is right any more often than is the client. The analyst's access to absolute knowledge and objectivity appears to be no more reliable than the client's.

Victorian taste, and its horror of scandal, ensured that sexual abuse remained hidden. By the turn of the century, however, sexual confes-sion and honesty were becoming more admissible, at least among the *avant garde*. Dreams, apparently, were saturated with sex, the eroticism veiled within asexual images such as trains pounding into tunnels. The analyst's task was to lift the veil and help us ride the sexual animal (in acceptable directions). Now, however, this guilt and sexual repression looks more like a product of middle-class Vienna at the turn of the century. Sure, we still feel sexual guilt, but usually it is because we are worried that we are not sexual *enough*.[9] Freud's clients (even those of Carl Rogers in the 1950s) found it hard to admit they had enjoyed sex last night. Contemporary clients are embarrassed when confessing that they did not. Not even our fantasies are as creative as the weekly fare in the magazine *Cosmopolitan*.

Whatever the century, country or climate, sex sells newspapers. Therapy alone does not make a story, but therapy infused with sex hits the headlines.[10] The consequent publicity provided Freud with enemies but, on balance, paid dividends. Newspapers love to share the shock of 'kiss and tell' sexual revelation with their readers, and readers love to be shocked. Also, each generation tends to believe it discovered sex, and presumes that its elders knew little about it. For example:

> Sexual intercourse began
> In nineteen sixty-three
> (Which was rather late for me) –
> Between the end of the Chatterley ban
> And the Beatles' first L.P.

> (Philip Larkin)

Christianity, like Freud, had a lot to say about sex. It, too, preached that animal appetite should be controlled and sublimated. Yet substantial pleasure can be taken from being prudish and guilt-ridden about sexuality. Even today, some people enjoy sex all the more when they imagine it as being a corrupting influence. Certainly, guilt did not prevent the Victorians from using record numbers of prostitutes and molesting their own daughters. Perhaps they enjoyed both the sex and the guilt. Repression can heighten an interest in sex and build an appetite. It takes considerable imagination and pent-up libido to require that, for modesty's sake, the naked legs of furniture should be draped.

Freud developed his ideas when middle-class sentiment was growing tired of repression and hypocrisy. Confession, exploration and discussion were becoming fashionable once again, and here was Freud with just the vehicle, in suitably dignified terminology. His critics only added to the heroical nature of the Freudian search for real truth in a world of hypocrisy. Christianity, similarly, had flourished when persecuted, and was challenged by indifference. It, too, embodied truth and high moral purpose. It also offered salvation, peace and an eternal heavenly afterlife. How could Freud compete with this?

Freud's brand of liberation matched the mood of the new century. As dispassionate scientists, we were to journey after truth – outwards in the world around, and inwards through the unconscious psyche and its hidden horrors. He offered us a voyage into 'inner space', with a frontier as important as any expedition to the moon. There would be shocks, setbacks, delays, doubts and delusions. Yet, with courage, honesty and a trusty guide, we could find nirvana of a sort. Our heaven on earth would be the peace arising from living with ourselves as we are. We might not be wildly happy, but on completing our analysis, after one to ten years, for one to four days a week, we might finally come home to ourselves and replace hysterical misery with common unhappiness.

If you really believe that only Freudian analysis can take you in the 'psychobathyscaphe' of the fifty-minute hour, down, down into your deepest, darkest, truest self, what else could compare with such an expedition? Everything else is mere superficiality and distraction. Knowing thyself is, surely, the real challenge for us all? Racing around the world after adventure and excitement was, compared to this, mere entertainment, distraction, an idle pastime.

Such journeying into the self long predates psychoanalysis. It is the word, rather than the activity, that is new. Attempts to analyse and understand one's self have been made for as long as humanity has been, not merely conscious, but *self*-conscious. Sages throughout history have spoken of the need to look within, and have offered a wide variety of techniques. The dark night of the soul, the long day's journey into night, the journey into the wilderness – these were basic material for philosophers and theologians long before the word 'psychology' was first used. In the East, many forms of meditation seek to take us below the froth of everyday existence and make a more meaningful connection with ourselves and our world.[11]

Freud, therefore, wrote of the timeless search for one's true self using modern settings and props. The journey into the self is one of literature's stock themes.[12] Often there is heavy use of metaphor or allegory, with knights, ghosts, shadows and demons in many guises. Every seeker after truth faces challenges, clues, false trails and obstacles, and the tougher the assignment, the more enigmatic the riddle, the more attractive it is.

Nowadays, within computer fantasy games, we have intrepid young explorers spending hours with 'Dungeons and Dragons'. A friend of mine warned one teenage son that, if he wanted work, he should spend more time in the real world. However, his son became employed as a 'dungeon master', supervising the fantasy games of others who, in imagination at least, were struggling to survive in post-holocaust

Britain. Management trainers put staff through similar tasks in order to see how they perform under pressure and work with others as a team.

Does psychoanalysis provide greater self-awareness, or is it just another kind of fantasy, drama and metaphor in its own right? Where is the evidence? Who ever met a 'cybermonster' created in the nether regions of a dungeon master's mind? For that matter, who ever met their 'id' or 'super-ego'? We all have perfectionistic, childish and primitive inclinations. Are Freud's metaphors for these tendencies any less fantastic than those of the Japanese game merchant Nintendo? How far was Nietzsche right to suggest that 'Idleness is the parent of all psychology'?

How far was Freud providing an upmarket version of 'Dungeons and Dragons'? Each player could supply both the dungeon, in the form of their own unconscious, and the 'dragons' of their own terrifying and unacceptable emotions and inclinations. What was the result? Greater insight? An amusing pastime? A useful metaphor? Any and all are possible. The Freudian adventure was well promoted and filled a significant gap in the market.

'Catch 22'?

Freud protected his work with a brilliant defence strategy borrowed, once again, from the priesthood. Critics who were outsiders were dismissed. They had not been trained or analysed, so how could they know what they were talking about? Probably their criticism was itself a neurotic defence mechanism. Critical insider colleagues were expelled. This made them dismissable outsiders once again. Critical patients were evidently not good enough for psychoanalysis. Patients could flunk their analysis. Psychoanalysis could not fail to analyse, or be of use to, patients.

Critics were not welcomed or rewarded by Freudians. Disciples, on the other hand, could be as overenthusiastic as they wished. If the patient claimed a miraculous recovery, why should the therapist question this? If the changes were evidently small or nonexistent, the therapist could explain that acceptance of limitation was a significant sign of maturity. Patients had good reason to be satisfied with their lack of progress. Given the costs, in time, effort and money, it took exceptional courage to admit that 'I've been wasting my time all these years'. After long training, in anything, it is impossible to be detached about its value, especially when our salary depends on it.

Critics risked severe punishment.[13] The safe option was to keep quiet and conform. Patients were expected to believe that their analyst, having been thoroughly trained and analysed, had a clear vision of reality from the humanist's equivalent of cloud nine. When the analyst confronted, explained and reconnected present behaviour to past traumas, the patient's role was to assume that the analyst was right. Therapist reliability was an essential component in the system. Without it, the whole enterprise began to disintegrate.

Thus the free-thinking humanist, having rejected theological dogma, could adopt the fashionable certainties of the new Freudian priesthood instead. Therapists were assumed to have greater wisdom and insight than any priest – and any other human being. Therapist training and analysis produced detached and disinterested observers who could perceive the real nature of patient motivation and behaviour. The therapist just had to get it right most of the time because, if he did not, there was nothing in the system that could deal with the problem. The patient's own views are discounted since patients, let us remember, are in therapy precisely because they cannot see reality without the therapist's assistance. Therefore, what other independent test can there be?

What about a system of Freudian supervisors of Freudian analysts? Can supervisors be expected to know whether the analyst's interpretations and diagnoses are correct when they are not even present at the analysis? In any case, what happens to analytical detachment and Olympian insight if a second analyst is required to be insightful and detached about the insight and detachment of the first? Should a third analyst then be checking on the second? We rapidly slip towards an infinite regress of supervisors of supervisors, except that this does not solve the problem either: if we cannot be sure that analyst A is insightful and detached, we have no more reason to think that B, C, or D will be any better. This would not matter were there some external standard that could be applied independently of all these analysts, but no such neutral appraisal formula exists.

The concept of gurudom is destroyed when a system of peer review is deemed necessary. It exposes the fallibility of staff. This need not be fatal if, as in (real) science, we have some other kind of reliable quality control. Yet all we know for sure is that analysts, like other people, differ frequently in their interpretations of other people. Even when they agree, they may have all got it wrong together. Consensus can easily signify collective prejudice.

Freud offered a new father figure to those who wanted more than their real, fallible, father. He was attractive to those who had grown tired of a paternal deity and the parish father. Similar patriarchal substitutes were becoming available in other parts of medicine and science. These professions did not so much come into adulthood during the twentieth century: they came into parenthood. They became substitute parents for those many people who, fearing adulthood, want a surrogate for the immaculate parenting they never received as children. Such a parental role had, for centuries, been delivered by the church, but this, for many, was moving into its dotage; a younger, more sprightly, parent was urgently needed.

Psychoanalysis can easily degenerate into a kind of parlour game in which each player draws attention to the neuroses and defence mechanisms of competitors. The game can be particularly vicious when used as a weapon of war between marital partners. Instead of hitting each other, they may each decide to analyse and interpret the failings of the other, purely in the interests of truth, of course. The more highly educated, well-read and sophisticated the competitors, the more elaborate these power struggles will become.

Each of us tends to analyse other people to suit our own prejudice and naked self-interest. Much (most?) communication is a kind of 'battle of the narratives', wherein we each try to bend other minds to *our* version of events and their meaning. 'History', both personal and collective, is the vision and mission of the victorious. We are usually unaware of this, and we lie to ourselves about it. Do you think a psychoanalyst can remain immune from this tendency? Power corrupts, yet the analyst is given god-like powers of interpretation by clients. No wonder that, as therapists climb higher in the status league, they may be liable to some of the wilder forms of 'guru-itus'.

I fail to see how training can match perceptiveness and intelligence with suitable purity of heart, nor do I think that a comprehensive and objective understanding of anyone is possible even in principle. Who has the right to be a final judge? Who will choose such an arbiter, and on what basis? The candidate assessors are all biased in their own favour. The jury, being untrained, is incapable of choosing rationally between the possibilities.

Freud's *own* account of defensiveness and delusion destroys the possibility of analysis as a viable professional enterprise. He describes human beings as deceptive, deceitful and resistant to truth. He imagined he could train an élite that was free of all this subjective distortion. His therapists, supposedly, would 'boldy go' deeply into the human psyche, where no-one had been before. With super-human, 'Spock-like' detachment, they would contemplate their own 'counter-transference'. They would coolly analyse their own, and their patient's, defences, personality and history as these acted and interacted with each other. Thanks to their intensive and extensive personal analysis, they would remain serene and clear within whatever remaining human turmoil washed around inside them.

Every Freudian analyst therefore needed to be carefully analysed for many years before he could psychoanalyse others. But what of Freud himself? He alone, apparently, had managed to do the job on his own. He had single-handedly freed himself from self-deception.[14] No-one else in all history had apparently ever accomplished such an epic journey of introspection and clarification, and thereby unveiled such detailed truth about themselves. No-one had ever been more aware and self-aware than Freud; the system simply did not allow for it. As if to underline the point, Freud rather enjoyed examining the works and lives of major thinkers from the past in order to show, not that they were wise and insightful, but that they had 'hang-ups' and neuroses, which, although quite hidden from themselves and their contemporaries, were accessible to the master. For Freud could reveal and clarify underlying truths about famous personalities merely from written fragments, and despite the gap of centuries.

As their celebrity grows, gurus generally introduce increasingly exacting rites of initiation upon aspiring outsiders. The more exclusive the product, the greater the need to exclude. Masters of such high status institutes generally assume that their own wisdom needs no external referee. Thus it is with the Pope, gurus of miscellaneous cults and therapy centres, and Freud himself. The moral is clear. Join the organization early, when its star is rising. Your promotion will be more rapid, and the training required will be much less exacting.[15]

Psychoanalysis, for all its claims to be a science, is a 'guru-centred' activity dependent on the would-be wisdom of Freud and his inner circle. It lacks an independent procedure for checking whether or not the guru is right, and it takes a brave disciple to challenge the master, when preferment and promotion is in the hands of the enlightened one. The safe option is to assume that any error is one's own rather than the teacher's. To question the therapist undermines the entire system. No committed member wants to do this. In any case, when student and therapist disagree, no experiment can decide the issue. It is left to the therapist to judge. These, humanly enough, tend to rule in favour of the therapist.

Hence Freudian theory could only change when Freud changed his mind about aspects of psychoanalysis. He certainly did so, as the enormous literature on the subject makes clear. In later years, he moved away from 'libido' as the major motive force and became more interested in the so-called 'death instinct'. Perhaps this was projection on his part. The young think of sex, the old of death; what's new? A minority of Freudian analysts did, however, question his observations. When they did so, they usually had to move elsewhere and found psychoanalytic schools of their own. Freudian analysis, therefore, was a rather narrow and introverted church. However, it spawned a great number of other chapels and creeds.

Here, then, is yet another similarity between organized psycho-analysis and organized religion. Churches split and form their various versions of the original faith. Some are very similar, some are fundamentally different. Some form an affable relationship with the parent organization. Others exist in a state of mutual animosity and mistrust. Either way, there is no independent procedure to judge the truth, or otherwise, of any of this theology. Each house of worship, naturally, assumes that it is the chief repository of insight, and that all the others are, to varying degrees, wrong. However, there is simply no means of assessing any of the many and various claims.

So it was with Freud, his disciples, partners and rivals. Each focused on particular components of Freudian theory, rejected others and moved on to develop ideas of their own. Jung became preoccupied with transper-sonal yearnings and experience, Adler with the will to power. Reich placed sexuality even more to the forefront than did Freud, and paid more attention to muscle tension. Fromm tried to integrate psychoanalysis, Marxism and existentialism, while Frankl accentuated humanity's search for meaning. Horney explored environmental influences, whereas Rank analysed separation anxiety and the importance of human will. Klein, followed by Bowlby, considered the relationship between mother and child. Assagioli coined the phrase 'psychosynthesis' and, like Jung, investi-gated transpersonal and spiritual aspects of sickness and health. Sullivan accentuated the social dimension.

Other, mongrel, therapists pursued the popular end of the market, with various 'fast food' varieties of their own. These were generally cheaper and quicker, and were marketed in a slicker, more glitzy, style, with less of the scientism and medical gravitas of the orthodox Freudian. Eric Berne translated Super-ego, Ego and Id into Parent, Adult and Child; and 'common unhappiness' into the more upbeat 'I'm OK – You're OK'. Janov invested in catharsis and child trauma and gave it the colourful brand name of Primal Scream Therapy. Moreno thought that merely to talk about one's past would be slow, dull and ineffectual. He argued that we could not free ourselves from the effects of earlier traumas and reconstruct their meaning simply by talking about it. He suggested that past crises should be re-enacted and thus re-experienced, rather than merely recalled. Perls talked of the construction of a new gestalt, accentuated personal responsibility and shot to prominence as the stereotypical, big-bearded, racy, Germanic and charismatic guru of the 'I-do-my-thing-you-do-your-thing' 1960s culture. This list is by no means complete.

How can any of these claims seriously be regarded as science? They are all a mixture of clinical observation and experience, personal prejudice, preference, inspiration, creativity and a shrewd theft, or adaptation, of more ancient wisdom. Some of the ideas and methods will be valuable, some less so, but we have no criteria for making an objective assessment. We do not even know what 'objectivity' would mean in these circumstances. Personal opinions of critics and disciples differ widely. At worst, the situation is utterly chaotic. At best, it is similar to the range of opinion found among critics in art and literature. Fashions come and go; the canon of the great and good indicates some consensus and much controversy. All agree that some of the produce is excellent, but different critics have different opinions and criteria. Therapy, then, is not a scientific activity and perhaps not even a profession, but I would no more wish to abolish all of it than abandon art, literature, or philosophy, which it more closely resembles, the assessment of which is equally problematic.

Kleinians prefer Melanie Klein; Sullivanians favour Harry Stack Sullivan; Jungians argue that Jung had a better perspective on reality than did his rivals; Eclectics draw from more than one school, but differ both in what they select and their reasons for selecting it. It is very much a question of what you prefer. Some think that chocolate is best; others pick raspberry. Eclectics choose raspberry and chocolate ripple, or toffee surprise. There is no independent court of appeal, and none of these products is conclusively superior to its rivals. Marketing is therefore crucial. Uniqueness is exaggerated. Uprating is needed, or traditional reliability accentuated, if brand loyalty is strong.

Thus, depending on the narrative offered by the guru of choice, people search for their 'inner child', one or other of their multiple 'subpersonalities', their 'transpersonal self', their 'inner demons', their 'ultimate perfection', their fallen wickedness, or whatever else is on offer that meets a need within the context of their own temperament and circumstances. Some kind of story and meaning is required to explain life's pleasures and, much more so, its suffering. Uncertainty and ignorance tend to be painful, even intolerable. Philosophy and theology can greatly tax the mind and heart. Thinking for oneself is very hard work. 'Finding oneself' is a popular contemporary slogan, but it is an exhausting struggle. It is generally much easier to seek out someone else who may be only too willing to tell us who we are.

We mostly prefer to have thinking about fundamentals done for us. We mostly adopt a system of meanings 'off the shelf' rather than go to all the trouble of making our own. Thus we sit with the warm reassurance of believing that our teacher/priest/therapist knows, better than we do, what life is all about. The democrats among us assume that our systems of checks, balances, mechanisms, meritocracies, qualifications, accreditation and external quality assurance systems will keep out the cold of corruption, ignorance and human folly. As it is in therapy now, so it has been in theology for millenia. The difference lies in the words, rather than the underlying reality. Therapy *is* our current theology.

Manoeuvring in the marketplace

Consumers do not always require research evidence before making their purchase. Even if there are strong indications that it is doing them harm, customers may still go on enjoying the product. As Freud so rightly argued, the rationality and rationale of our actions are not always strikingly evident.[16] Products, nonetheless, have to go on being sold if life as we know it is to continue, even if many are frivolous, trivial or downright useless. The marketplace is a shrine and worshippers believe that, with brisk competition, all is for the best in the best of all possible worlds. Supply, we hope, will match demand. How far either matches *need* is not on the agenda of economists, executives, accountants and other contemporary high priests.

Competition is most intense when no runner is conclusively ahead of the pack. If one brand of therapy really were far better than the others, it would by now have swept its rivals into extinction. Furthermore, if this favoured therapy ever became conclusively preferable to other ways of spending money, it would dominate cultures and liquidate many other goods and services. There would be tens of thousands, millions, of therapists, and the entire world would do therapy along with school. Instead of a parish church, there would be a local therapy centre.

If therapy were conclusively valuable, no person or institute could dominate it for long, and no research would be needed into its efficacy. Demand and supply would grow together, exponentially. Competition would centre around price and delivery. In this respect, as Gellner suggests, the Japanese might well become leaders in efficiency, training, marketing and value for money.

Advertising often works by insinuating that customers will finally come to terms with themselves, and receive public respect, when they buy the right car, house, coffee, holiday and leisure activity. None of these actually delivers as promised. So, the manic search for wholeness and peace continues, and new brands appear all the time. Ever hopeful, we reach out once more.

When the *real* goodness of a product is uncertain, it is all the more necessary that customers *feel* good about it. Perhaps they have no good reason to feel that way. Perhaps; but it is not a question that market researchers are in a hurry to explore. The customer must feel satisfied, with or without good reason. If the benefits decay as quickly as is decently possible, the supplier is on to a good business.

Advertisements are full of whole, 'self-actualized' people who appear to have sorted out their lives. If only I could find the product or person that would make me, too, feel complete, clean and clear. Yet one product is generally only slightly better than another, and therapists are, at best, only marginally superior to clients in sorting out their lives. We discover that we have a bar of chocolate, not a south-sea island dream. We end up with a fallible human being, not a superhuman therapist-wizard. This may be disappointing, but it does not have to be disastrous. The therapist, having no special vantage point, is down on the sod like the rest of us. The therapist may be able to help me. I may be able to help the therapist. No-one has any privileged access into the soul and circumstances of anyone else. Each of us, therefore, will need to think for ourselves. Regression to a child-like state, wherein we put ourselves blindly into the hands of others, will be a risk best avoided unless and until we really have failed to cope as independent adults.

'Brian', the reluctant guru in Monty Python's *Life of Brian*, (Methuen, 1979) tries to make this simple point to the eager crowd waiting for enlightenment:

BRIAN *Good morning.*

CROWD *A blessing! A blessing!*
(More pandemonium)

BRIAN *No, please. Please listen.*

(They quieten)
I've got one or two things to say.

CROWD *Tell us. Tell us both of them!!*

BRIAN *Look… you've got it all wrong. You don't need to follow me. You don't need to follow anybody. You've got to think for yourselves. You're all individuals.*

CROWD *Yes, we're all individuals.*

BRIAN	*You're all different.*
CROWD	*Yes, we are all different.*
DENNIS	*I'm not.*
CROWD	*Sssshhh!*
BRIAN	*Well, that's it. You've all got to work it out for yourselves.*
CROWD	*Yes, yes!! We've got to work it out for ourselves.*
BRIAN	*Exactly...*
CROWD	*Tell us more.*
BRIAN	*No, no, that's the point. Don't let anyone tell you what to do. Otherwise... Ow!*
MANDY	*That's enough.*

(She propels him out of sight)

The notion that Monty Python and other wise clowns may have as much or more to offer us than anyone else is a sobering reality that for many people is quite simply unacceptable. Acceptance of it is the major transition towards genuine adulthood. The analyst Wilhelm Reich made the point more systematically in *Listen, Little Man*[17] which warned against guruism and dictatorship. I fear, however, that most of us do not want to grow up and think for ourselves. Instead, we want to be released from doubt, ignorance and uncertainty, and we want someone else to do the job for us. With the right therapist, surely, we could finally see ourselves as we really are, shorn of all defences, rationalizations, games and manoeuvrings. With the right therapist, we could pass through a kind of psychic 'sheep dip', and be born again, renewed, reinvigorated and inspired.

This final graduation day tends to be postponed further and further into the future. Certainly, the trainee analyst must be immersed in this psychic cleaning, clipping and dipping process for years at a stretch. Few patients are wealthy or persistent enough to complete the whole course. Neither insurance companies nor the State could ever afford to fund such an unending inner quest. Only millionaires can sustain a complete 'Dyno-rod' style of cleansing process among the sewers of the psyche, and, even then, they do not necessarily look much improved.

Queues will form, even if only five minutes are available from a psychotherapist over the radio. David Viscott is one such guru in California. He described his approach to Jonathan Miller in BBC2 television's *The Talking Cure* (27 October 1991):

Everybody tells a lie.
I have a nose for when something is a lie.
I never attack the person, I always attack the lie…
…They all back off and they hear the truth underneath it.
That's what the therapeutic act must be… giving the opportunity for the person to be more honest.
I invade the lie when they're being phoney, that's fair game. Because that's what people recognise. People recognise the ability inside themselves to hear a greater truth.

If only it were true. The therapist sees the heart of our reality, attacks our lies, brings us to truth and sets us free. The listeners all applaud, and it's all done in five minutes!

Perhaps three minutes would be enough if the client were not so much burdened with problems. Analysts, certainly, believe that most progress is made by the 'YAVIS' patients: those who are young, attractive, verbal, intelligent and successful. These are the clients with the cash and ego strength to make full use of the therapist's skills. Perhaps they should be given a masters degree in self-awareness at the end of the treatment. Psychoanalysis, it seems, is just too difficult for most people. They do not have the brains and maturity to explore subtleties of psyche and circumstance. No wonder, then, that analysis tends to be a cultural marker worn by intellectual and artistic élites.

What's new? It was always the king, his courtiers, barons and assorted glitterati who monopolized the demand for astrologers, sages, philosophers, physicians, seers and saviours of one kind or another. The peasants, as ever, got on with planting and harvesting the potatoes, yams or rice. Their healing came from the rhythms of spring and autumn, sunrise and sunset, and from whatever love, care and support they found within their family, village or tribe. So it is today, for the vast majority. So it will be tomorrow. If they have enough to do and enough to eat, that will be therapy indeed. And if a parson, or other official care person, can bless and bury them in the appropriate seasons of existence, that will remain as much as most can ever realistically expect.

Notes

1 These days, psychology tries to show how advanced it is by modelling human beings on computers.

2 Presumably lower animals, like worms, are not conscious either, but this scarcely means that they have an 'unconscious'.

3 Gilbert Ryle, *Concept of Mind.* Hutchinson, 1949.

4 David Smail, *Taking Care: An Alternative to Therapy*. Dent, 1987.

5 Ernest Gellner, *The Psychoanalytic Movement*, p. 137. Paladin, 1985.

6 See, for example, Peter Rutter's *Sex in the Forbidden Zone*. Mandala, 1990.

7 In the early 1990s, this company was extremely skilled in constructing an aura of steamy youthful eroticism around their brands of cold product.

8 Freud initially thought that many of these claims were genuine, but he later changed his mind and described such confessions as female imagination. Jeffrey Masson argues, in *The Assault on Truth: Freud's Suppression of the Seduction Theory* (London: Faber & Faber, 1984), that Freud backed down not because he genuinely changed his mind, but through moral cowardice in the face of a society that did not want to hear about sexual abuse. In his most recent work, *Final Analysis* (Addison-Wesley, 1990), Masson shows how power and status are still given priority over truth. He was expelled from the psychoanalytic community for daring to produce evidence from the Freudian archive suggesting that Freud colluded in ignoring the widespread abuse he knew to be occurring.

9 Hence the sigh of relief when the 1994 Chicago study of sexual habits revealed that most of us lead humdrum, routine, monogamous sex lives far removed from torrid scenes in fiction and the media.

10 The media 'feeding frenzy' around Bhagwhan Shree Rajneesh during the 1980s is a recent example.

11 Oriental methods are having more success in the West than psychoanalysis has achieved in the Orient.

12 See, for example, the journey of Jesus into the Wilderness (Luke iv. 1–13).

13 I expect that the criticisms within this book will lead some therapists to search for signs of personal 'deficiency' in its writer rather than face the questions and arguments themselves. Self-evidently, a critic must be a neurotic. This is highly impertinent in human terms, and thoroughly dishonest intellectually.

14 Any ordinary mortal who makes a claim like this is liable to be diagnosed as psychotic, never mind arrogant.

15 Counsellor trainers are convinced that candidates need far more training than they themselves ever had or needed. This, of course, is in the interests of trainees and clients. The income and status it provides trainers is quite secondary and does not make them biased in any way.

16 To be fair, if we always waited for conclusive evidence, we might wait forever.

17 Wilhelm Reich, *Listen, Little Man*. Pelican, 1948, reprinted 1979.

Chapter 7

Transpersonal approaches

Religion, n.   A daughter of Hope and Fear, explaining to Ignorance the nature of the Unknowable.
(Bierce, 1881–1911)[1]

Transpersonal approaches within therapy have grown from a variety of roots and alliances. The green movement in politics joins loosely and intermittently with the human potential movement in psychotherapy, feminism and mystical traditions in religion. The result brings together arts, humanities and social sciences. Capra, Zukav and Bohm argue that this transpersonal vision is consistent with modern physics. It speaks of the 'quiet revolution', in values and actions, away from materialism, egocentricity and impersonal organizations, and towards spiritual regeneration and more humanized living. At one extreme, this 'new age' may hover among broken down caravans and bedraggled travellers. At another, it has been celebrated by smash-hit, million-seller writer–prophets on an international lecture circuit. It speaks of cooperation rather than confrontation, and the abandonment of attachment to conventional personal and social identity.

This is a deeper challenge than the traditional radicalism of Left and Right. The New Age prophet tells us that a phoenix needs to arise from the ashes within and around us so that the old ideals of peace, freedom, justice, community, love and truth can be restored and nurtured.

Popular paperbacks on this theme include Marilyn Ferguson's *The Aquarian Conspiracy* (1980), Fritjof Capra's *The Turning Point* (1982), and Ken Wilbur's *Up From Eden* (1981). There are many others. The New Age, new-dawn, 'the-Sun-is-coming-up-soon' message competes with the gloom, doom, 'survivalism-in-disaster' genre for top sales ratings. Charles Reich's *The Greening of America* (1970) provided what is now a vintage version of this declaration of a new beginning. He compared the rough frontier figure of nineteenth-century America with the mid-twentieth-century 'organization man' from executive suburbia. Both scored low compared with the 'love-is-all-you-need' youth celebrating outside his window on campus lawns during the humanistic festival of the late 1960s. This vision of Utopia, shared for a few months by an overly indulged and indulgent élite around 1968, passed quickly into myth and then became the subject of a great deal of understandable ridicule. The sixties may soon have their turn, however, as the next performer for the nostalgia industry.

The 1990s were labelled by journalists as the 'caring decade', when 1980s' promises and excesses turned sour and stale. So will we now search for values and spiritual direction? Or just another stylish façade? Do we want to live, breath and sweat in search of a new way? Or are we just looking for more fashion accessories, new designer components for the radical chic lifestyle?

Fritjof Capra's *Uncommon Wisdom*[2] is, unwittingly, an excellent warning of the dangers of 'designer spirituality' and hollowness within transpersonal psychotherapy. In sharp contrast to his previous efforts[3] it reads like a version of the magazine *Houses and Gardens*. The reader is regaled with reverential accounts of the tasteful, graceful guru homes he visits. We share his initiation as celebrity on the international lecture trail. The name-dropping is intense: Heisenberg, Krishnamurti, Chew, Bateson, Grof, Laing, Simonton, Lock, Schumacher, Henderson, Dimalanta, Schlain and, finally, Indira Gandhi herself. Capra's excitement about his own personal awakening, to royalties, sunshine and the jet-set, leads him to forget that this dazzling vision of opportunity is never going to be part of most people's agenda. Marilyn Ferguson, Jean Houston, Sir George Trevelyan, and too many other New Age celebrities, have, within their own lectures and writing, made the same mistake.

Capra's conversations and encounters with transpersonal psychotherapists are invariably conducted among stunningly beautiful settings, with select Californian or Mediterranean sea vistas, fine wines, charming décor and, unavoidably, an asset base, real estate value and travel budget that really would overwhelm planetary resources if too many others managed to join the party. Yet Capra and other green celebrities do not seem to see the irony. They fly in and out of Western campuses and conference centres, preaching the virtues of simplicity, cooperation and environmental friendliness. The audiences are impressed. We, too, want to sit by Pacific sunsets, with fashionable ethnic décor, if only we could afford it. We want to have exciting conversations, holistic visions of unity with the cosmos and meaningful encounters with beautiful people. We want to join Capra and company, look at the sunrise from 35 000 feet, make lots of money and sign autographs. We want, quite casually, to mention all the star names who know us and the lovely places we know. We want to be able to say… of the 'Big Sur' dialogues:

> I chose a beautiful secluded estate on the Big Sur coast near Esalen… a large enclosure designed in the typical Big Sur style with lots of redwood and an expansive glass front overlooking the ocean

of Stan Grof:

> I drove south along the sparkling Pacific coastline to visit Stan Grof at his home in Big Sur… as I caught glimpses of magnificent vistas of the ragged coast, fanning out before my eyes and disappearing into shades of grey at the horizon, my body relaxed and my mind expanded. I felt inspired and excited by my memories and even more excited by the expansion of consciousness which, I knew, was in store for me on this trip

and of Stan Grof's home:

> It is one of the most beautiful and inspiring places I have ever seen: a simple redwood frame with a spectacular view of the Pacific Ocean, perched on the edge of a cliff a couple of miles north of Esalen. The exterior walls of the living room are almost entirely of glass, with doors leading out to a wooden deck overhanging the breaking waves. One wall of the room is dominated by a huge Huichol yarn painting in brilliant colours, depicting people and animals on a sacred vision quest. There is a large fireplace, built of rough stones, in one corner; a comfortable couch surrounded by shelves of art books and encyclopaedias in the other; and throughout the room are objects of religious art, pipes, drums, and other implements of shamanistic rituals, which Grof collected on his journeys around the world …After showing me the house and telling me several anecdotes relating to his art collection, Stan offered me a glass of wine on the sundeck, and we sat down in this magnificent spot for our first long conversation.

It is a sparkling vision to upmarket Western consumers, envious of the celebrity lifestyle, and wanting more class than *Dallas, Eastenders* or an exclusive *TV Times* celebrity offer of collapsible TV-dinner tables 'in a choice of four veneers'. The real stars of Capra's *Uncommon Wisdom* are not the gurus and their psychology, but their beautiful homes and gardens, fine wines, tapestries and other paraphernalia. The natural redwood is particularly rich. Having been unnaturally logged out by greedy capitalists with no thought for Nature, it again becomes desirable once set in Stan Grof's home or the conference centre home of Capra's dialogues. Sophisticated consumers, with New Age and designer-living pretensions, may drool at this litany of names and places.

Of R. D. Laing:

> Jill Purce, who is a writer and editor with many connections in London's artistic, literary and spiritual circles, had met Laing through the anthropologist Francis Huxley, whom I also knew.

> Laing sent word that he could see me and that I should meet him on a certain day at 11.00 a.m. in his house in Hampstead, not far from where I had lived before leaving London ...He inquired whether I had had breakfast and when I told him I had, he asked me whether I would mind going to a nearby restaurant with a nice garden where he could have breakfast and I could join him for coffee or a glass of wine ...he ordered a bottle of red wine, which he recommended as the specialty of the house. Sitting in the lovely garden on that beautiful, sunny, late morning, we engaged in an animated conversation that would last for over two hours.

Breakfast wine and animated conversation about the New Jerusalem. I can see a big future in such stylish, consciousness-raising autobiography:

> The conference took place near Saragossa at the Monasterio de Piedra, a beautiful twelfth-century monastery which had been converted into a hotel. The array of participants was very impressive ...During that week I experienced a wonderful feeling of community and adventure generated by the extraordinary group of participants and the magnificent setting of the conference. Lectures were held in the old refectory of the monastery, often by candlelight; there were seminars in the cloister and in the garden, and informal discussions on a large balcony until late at night.

> [Laing] had come to the conference with a large entourage of family, friends, former patients and disciples, including even a small film crew ...He spent many evenings in intensive discussions with small groups of people, which usually ended in long monologues when everybody else had become too tired to continue the conversation...[! (*my* emphasis)]
> 'Any experience!' Laing shouted ...'Any experience of reality is indescribable! Just look around you and see, hear, smell, and feel where you are.'

What fun! ...To monopolise the conversation with extensive accounts of your own ideas and experiences, to have the entire event filmed, and then to declaim about the impossibility of describing reality! How unreal, for the rest of us at least, but how desirable. Who can avoid wishing they were important enough to be followed around by a film crew? Who can avoid the appeal of occupying the moral high ground while at the same time having exhilarating conversations about holistic consciousness in Pacific hot tubs or villas in Tuscany? Capra's eulogies of brilliant minds and beautiful homes and gardens go on and on:

> Schumacher's home was idyllic. The rambling Edwardian house... comfortable and open to the outdoors ...as we sat down to tea we were surrounded by an abundance of nature. The vast garden was luxuriant and overgrown. The flowering trees... warm spring sunshine ...peaceful oasis.

So much for homes and gardens. Yet there is a serious point to be made here. Capra's pageant of transpersonal psychotherapists and New Age philosophers all talk about sustainable lifestyles and ecological consciousness, but all are living a lifestyle that is quite beyond the reach of the vast majority, even of more wealthy Westerners. In other words, these teachers simply fail to practise what they preach. What would the world's peasantry think of this promise of a New Dawn? Capra, and too many others like him, remains charmingly, disarmingly, yet infuriatingly, naïve and ignorant about how his message comes over to more ordinary mortals stranded in less stimulating and aesthetic environments.

New Age conferences and gatherings of transpersonal therapists declaim about the need for a whole integrated vision of humanity, society and the environment, but the lifestyle to be observed does not conform to the ideal being preached. This Garden of Eden contains no inner cities, for example. What is to be done with these? Are they to be demolished? What is to become of their inhabitants? Will they ever find employment? Capra's work is full of sublime experience, to a ridiculous degree precisely in that it ignores the sordid, stupid, plain, poor, oppressed and criminal components of existence. Growth, apparently, is about peak experience. The sinister, silly and malevolent facets of all humanity are not built into the picture. So much for a whole/holistic vision.

To illustrate the point, I noticed, as a trainee in psychosynthesis years ago, that staff members were so busy envisioning humanity-and-the-planet that they gave insufficient attention to the humdrum ways in which they were getting on each others' nerves. Sure enough, a year later, they had mostly parted company, to develop a (re)vision of unity.

Genuine Fake[4], Monica Furlong's compassionate, yet searing, biography of the New Age megastar Alan Watts, similarly explores the painful ironies of guruism. Watts wrote with power, clarity and ease about the illusions of a separate self, universal love, celebration and compassion. Thousands came to sit at his feet, to hear him on the radio, to watch him on television or to read his many books. Yet what was the reality? Monica Furlong portrays a soul tortured by a deep sense of aloneness, weighed down by financial problems, unwilling to confront the hostility of his wives, or the neglect and abuse of his children, confiding in no-one, dishonest in his autobiography and addicted to vodka. He praised the ability to live in the 'here and now' but ignored his doctor's 'here, now' warning that his liver was swollen and overloaded with alcohol. He sang his message of liberation on a celebrity swirl of unending engagements. Yet Watts, a bright light of love, joy, union and communion, drank himself to death in 1973 aged fifty-eight.

In praise of simplicity?

Few progressive conferences meet in places like Gateshead, South Shields or Pittsburgh, and most growth aficionados like to progress their way out of such places. Who can blame them? I do sometimes think, though, that when I say something silly to a group in Gateshead they will pick it up and throw it back to me more quickly than will others in more exotic locations. I can explain why by refering to Hazel Henderson, another acclaimed New Age speaker, who entranced the 'Young Lochinvar', Fritjof Capra:

> As Hazel entertained me with lively stories about her experiences in Africa, Japan, and many other parts of the world I realised with amazement the truly global scale of her activism.

Henderson coined the concept of 'entropic work'. This, translated into common speech, is 'daily grind'. It is the labour that has to be done over and over again. It's never done, because as soon as it is done, it comes undone and has to be done again – cooking a meal that is immediately eaten, washing clothes, cleaning and clearing up after the children. Anyone short of servants will know what it is. These are generally low-status tasks, yet essential to basic well-being and survival. Henderson argues, rightly, that they are the bread and butter of existence, while the more sophisticated and high-status work provides the icing on the cake. In our hierarchy of needs, they are lower than, yet ahead of, more privileged or peak experiences.

Ordinary work has often been seen as the most reliable route to spiritual development. It connects us to the natural order of growth and decay, birth and death. In *Monty Python and the Holy Grail* (London: Methuen, 1977), kings are distinguished from the peasantry in that they are (I quote) 'not covered in shit'. Liberal kings and aristocrats, however, often seem to have envied the honest earthy connection of those closer to the sod. They have been seen as nearer to God and Nature than priests, kings and courtiers, and more resistant to verbal diarrhoea.

This vision of peasant wisdom can become overly romantic. Even if it exists, the privileged can never attain it while retaining their privileges. Why? Because being down is different from dressing down, daily experience of a slum differs from slumming for the experience, and growing potatoes because you have to is never the same as growing them during a break from your word processor.

Many of us can see that the simple life has its virtues and attractions. We love rural existence within small communities, especially if we can add a telecottage, two cars or visit at weekends from a gentrified quarter of the big city. I prefer to stay quiet about such ecofriendly idealism, since my lifestyle, like Hazel Henderson's, although with fewer air miles, so obviously does not live up to it.

Facile visions of Utopia in the village have appeared and reappeared within salon society as a cultural conversation piece ever since life, for some, became more comfortable. Rousseau, for example, (1712–78) addressed fellow sophisticates on the virtues of the 'Noble Savage'. Voltaire, a contemporary, got the measure of him with observations that still ring true today:

> I have read your new book against the human race, and thank you for it. Never was such cleverness used in the design to making us all stupid. One longs, in reading your book, to walk on all fours. But as I have lost that habit for more than sixty years, I feel unhappily the impossibility of resuming it. Nor can I embark in search of the savages of Canada, because the maladies to which I am condemned render a European surgeon necessary to me; because war is going on in these regions; and because the example of our actions has made the savages nearly as bad as ourselves. (quoted in Russell, 1946)[5]

The simple life is itself becoming a scarce and therefore expensive commodity. When population densities are low, even the poorest can enjoy fresh air, peace, quiet and an excellent view. Produce will be home-grown, and everyone will use stone, leather and wooden goods. All these are now moving upmarket because, as demand exceeds supply, costs rise. Hence the twentieth-century peasantry lives with concrete, plastic, noise, fumes and a view only of some other concrete apartment and the traffic below. The English countryside and village is ever more beyond the reach of the English yeoman. Mr and Mrs Everyman live neither in the castle nor at the rich man's gate, nor in Rose Cottage next door. They may well dream of the opportunity and read of the dream, but they will achieve, at best, a prime site in 'Tudor Grange', that high-density, executive heritage property looking in on itself and away from the nearby motorway. With their mortgage repayments, they may find that the dream holiday in a simple village community by the sea is more than they can afford. They may have to settle for concrete high-rise, a crowded beach or a leisure complex with wave machines. At times, we would all love to get back to Nature, but, in a crowded world, the privileged feel forced to fence off their own prime cuts from the rest of the proletariat.[6]

The New Age movement tends to ignore such dilemmas and difficulties, and becomes entrapped within a childish and impractical Utopianism. Some look back on the past with rosy spectacles and a soft focus. Others anticipate a future of fully realized beings whose highly developed consciousnesses interact in an ecotopian paradise of warmth, caring and sharing.

Even advertisers now acknowledge that paradise may never reach the people of Peckham; they will have to settle for *Bacardi* rum. The good life is certainly available, however, for those who can pay. For example, consumers can purchase caring therapy, group hugs, transpersonal meditation, loveable peasant settings and Mediterranean sunshine any time they want. Just provide your credit card number and, as soon as the computer has cleared your credit rating, you can fly away and experience 'all the care we have to offer you'![7] Given the fierce competition for a discriminating consumer market, the quality assured may very well be delivered. However, let's not pretend that any of this portends a new dawn of higher consciousness.

Christopher Lasch in *The Culture of Narcissism* and *The Minimal Self*[8] described the 'me' generation of the 1970s and 80s. Lasch saw it not as an advance into higher consciousness, but as a retreat into a private world of introspection, the result of decay in the family and society. He saw New Age joy and celebration as a thin veneer masking collective despair and emptiness. Lasch's analysis deserves attention, but it offers little in the way of hope.

Ken Wilbur, in *Up From Eden: A Transpersonal View of Human Evolution*[9] provides what for me is a more balanced analysis and assessment of the New Age movement. He argues that real changes are taking place, and proposes that the development of consciousness is an important stage in evolution that is by no means complete. Most human beings, he suggests, have reached the stage of being self-conscious, and pretty well all their actions are a means of extending and protecting their conception of who they are. This, however, is not the last word in consciousness and its evolution. The next step, he suggests, is for us actually to experience (rather than just think of) ourselves in a 'transpersonal', 'transegoic', way. With a transpersonal experience of self, whatever this may be, we would no longer see ourselves as separate from, and at odds with, the world as a whole, but as an inseparable part of one whole living process. 'Self' and 'other' would then be experienced as a seamless web, one whole interconnected unity, rather than as a heavily guarded boundary to be extended and defended as much as possible. This is all very well, but it is very difficult to describe what we, or others, have not experienced. Transpersonal experience is certainly a very long way from being a routine part of our daily lives!

Wilbur attempts to give a clear and explicit account of the ineffable, mystical apprehension of life known, most probably, to only a handful of people down the generations. He readily acknowledges his debt to nineteenth-century Hegelian philosophy, from which he draws heavily, but which, until recently, has been a most unfashionable voice in contemporary thinking. He is certainly not another Utopian promising some magical turn-around or breakthrough in personal and social life. On the contrary, his is an evolutionary perspective operating over a very long timescale, with no facile belief that progress is inevitable. He suggests that visionary thinking long predates, but is no substitute for, a general ability to put sublime ideas into everyday practice. Far from claiming that we are all about to become mystics, Wilbur considers that only a tiny fraction of one per cent of any population has the smallest apprehension of the 'transpersonal'. Intellectual debate about mysticism might precede, but cannot be a substitute for, felt experience and committed action.

Wilbur does not expect an outbreak of genuine joy and celebration, a beatific vision on every street corner and a felt sense that all of humanity is my brother and sister. On the contrary, he suggests that it would be a marvellous achievement if most people could at least manage an ordinary, common-or-garden sort of everyday rationality, coupled with a mild degree of empathy, and free of the more grotesque, but 'normal', extremes of paranoia, prejudice and projection. This, he argues, would be progress enough and would at least lessen the likelihood that we will eventually destroy ourselves.

Is a new age of caring, sharing humanity really dawning? There would appear to be no cause for immediate celebration. Never mind peak experiences; it looks as though a great deal of hard work will be needed just to ensure clean water, clean air and other basic necessities and freedoms. If the sunshine of the transpersonal is rising on our planet, its dawning is likely to be a very slow process. People have long hoped that the vision of the saints would permeate and express itself among us all. If this ever happens, it will do so no faster than the rise of a new chain of mountains. In a few thousand years, which is a mere twinkling of the eye in terms of species evolution, we may see definite signs of such profound change, but, in the meantime, our first priority is to ensure that the planet remains inhabitable. Mass celebrations concerning holistic visions will have to be postponed far into the future. There is a great deal of ordinary work to be done.

A small proportion of practitioners and theorists have long been interested in spiritual dimensions to healing. Jung is perhaps the best known, arguing that the bulk of his older patients were facing a spiritual crisis that needed to be identified as such. Roberto Assagioli, too, who was studying under Freud in 1910, considered that psychoanalysis was limited in its vision and coined his own term: psycho*synthesis*. For Assagioli, analysis was just a starting point. It could help us build, embrace and harmonize the various facets of our personality, but it was of no use when, having found ourselves, we wished to move beyond self-preoccupation. Similarly, Jung argued that, once we had constructed, asserted, accepted and adapted ourselves, we sought transcendence, some kind of union with nature, concord rather than conquest.

This view of therapy as harmony with the world has a long history. Traditional approaches to healing, particularly in the East, stress this spiritual dimension. Acupuncture, for example, seeks balance within ourselves and our wider surroundings. Likwise, aikido, tai chi, yoga, indeed all the oriental body therapies and martial arts, attempt to integrate our limited idea and sense of self with larger forces and circumstances of existence. Progress, within these traditions, comes through action and silence more than talk, during many years of practice. Martial artists learn to experience how real strength is received, rather than asserted. They become receptive and available to the forces and possibilities of nature. Self-centredness merely cuts them off from life's potential. They therefore stop forcing some idea of themselves onto others and (to cite Luke Skywalker from the box-office hit film *Starwars*) 'let the force be with them'.

Within these traditions, strength derives from knowing its true source beyond the defined self we think we are. It is similar to the Quaker tradition of alert receptivity and stillness, in which one waits for a felt sense of what is possible and appropriate, rather than indulging in a noisy, lunging, mind-centred, 'head-banging' aggression that seeks ascendancy over others.

Meditation, in its various forms, seeks to foster detachment from our imagined dreams, schemes, success, failure, comfort and discomfort. With such a perspective, we can experience the cacophony of personal experience arising and passing away, like sunrise and sunset, or leaves on the wind, or water in the river. Assagioli described such an outlook as 'dis-identification'. It lies at the heart of transpersonal therapy.

Self needs to be constructed, however, before it can be transcended. Small children and wise persons are much less self-preoccupied than are most adults. The cause in children is innocence and ignorance of the self. The reason among the wise is that the self is too narrow a stage on which to move. Baby and Buddha have a similar facial expression. One has not yet reached an idea of self, the other has gone past it, although without actually rejecting it. Only the latter has achieved transcendence.

This idea of 'me and mine' takes years to construct. In youth and early adulthood we 'get our act together', build an idea of who we are, what we want, where we want to go, what is ours and not ours. We make something of ourselves, develop our reputation and achievements, hope to build some weight and influence, and leave a mark behind us. We try to become successful, functioning, adults and may turn to a counsellor or therapist if we fail to make this normal adjustment.

Having built my castle of self, I seek to extend it or build an even bigger 'me and mine' on newer ground. Ultimately, however, we may tire of entrapment within our own self-preoccupation. Dreams, even realities, of super achievement begin to pall. We may feel gaoled in our castle of self, however large, comfortable and envied by others it is. If only we could get away from ourselves entirely, and escape into the open air. This wish to shake off some of the personal baggage of me-and-mine is quite understandable, because, if we stay too long with our self-conscious, self-centred and self-seeking activity, we become weighed down by our own weight, walled in by our own reputation and blinded by our own achievements. To put it most crudely, clients in a personal crisis are trying to get in touch with themselves, whereas clients in a spiritual crisis are trying to let go of themselves – counsellors need to recognize the difference.

Every child must form a conception of its own identity as it moves away, step by step, from its parents. We go forth, seeking trophies, achievements, status and a position in the world. We pursue what we hope can be ours, and, if successful, hang on to it as though it were a core of our identity. 'I have ...therefore I exist' lies at the heart of secular consciousness, each of us hoping that we can become market winners within whatever fields of competition we choose to perform.[10]

The tyranny of the marketplace

Every culture has its marketplace. Contrary to myth, this is not a gladiatorial arena within which anyone can do anything they like to defeat competitors, nor is it a product of nature and evolution that must be just left alone if it is to operate effectively. Markets are inherently human creations, a product of the society to which they belong. They can only function within a framework of (formal and informal) rules governing how stallholders must conduct themselves. The rules are consciously created in order to serve the interests of the whole community, or, more often, powerful élites within it. They can be changed if they do not achieve these purposes or if other interest groups wish to gain more benefit. Markets can be more or less humane according to the rules and underlying morals that govern them. These rules produce the market; they are not a product of it. They can be more or less just or exploitative, depending on the ethics from which they are derived.

Every culture also needs its sacred places and sacred moments. Are these commodities that can be bought and sold in the market? For how long can a civilization survive if it allows the sacred to fall into decay? What happens to civilizations that turn their sacred places into market-places or, worst of all, look upon the market itself as a holy shrine?

When markets rule the whole of life, who will rule the market? By what rules will it operate? Will it become amoral and anarchic? Will it become authoritarian, with rules fixed to suit the interests of the powerful? If everything and everyone is transformed into a saleable commodity, what happens to our sense of awe, wonder and reverence for life? Can life and its value be identified with its price? A few pounds for the chemicals? A few pounds an hour for unskilled labour? In this way, people are turned into things, objects of manipulation and self-promotion. Life loses its soul and meaning.

If the market is the whole of life, with no existence beyond it, how can people be any more than agents and objects hassling for an advantage? How can value be anything other than price? If this is true, an object or person that cannot be sold is worth nothing. This is what was meant by idolatory, the worship of idols. These do not have to be wooden poles; they can be credit ratings, or skills portfolios. The story of Mammon is of a false God who kills life and replaces it with gold. Is this a story or our present reality?

When the market becomes a shrine, how can human values survive? Are we valuable if we fetch, or command, a high price? Are we without value if we are a cheap or unwanted labour commodity? Are the old to be seen as a useless burden on the able? What if we have no cash? Does this mean that we have no needs?

According to the market, with its current rules, governors and beneficiaries, there is no 'effective demand' for food or clean water from millions of people who are dying from the lack of both. What does this mean? Are the people ineffective for not being able to signal an effective demand? Or is the market, with its current rules, ineffective for not being able to detect and respond to such obvious and gross needs?

When the market takes over the whole of life, needs, desires and values have no existence until they can be expressed through cash. This would not matter if power and cash were fairly evenly distributed and if people always knew what they needed. As it is, economies respond to frivolous demands from people who have more money than sense, while ignoring the real needs of those who have no credit.

The same process is observable in relation to care, which itself has become yet another commodity to be bought and sold. Nobody needs care, we are to believe, if they cannot pay for it. The wealthy need the lion's share of care and attention. Hence legions of counsellors, therapists and lifestyle consultants cluster around the more bloated corners of the West, while care for the poor becomes a low-status activity, uneconomical and unrewarding. The National Health Service will go the same way if it allows itself to respond to 'effective demand' (cash) instead of need. It will also stop being national, or a service or, for that matter, healthy. It will become a private sickness contract.

We are so imprisoned within the indecent values of our present marketplace that the resultant absurdity goes unnoticed. Apparently it is impossible to find work for tens of millions of unemployed people even though millions of others are seriously overworked. At the other extreme, I heard a 'countryside officer' on the radio saying that 'this moor has been very successful this year'. I had never previously heard of tracts of moorland succeeding or failing at anything. Did he mean that it was awe-inspiring, beautiful, healing? Of course not. He meant that it had attracted more than its planned quota of visitors and had thus helped to stimulate the local tourist economy. Therefore it did not need to be ploughed or built upon. Its role as a service commodity was established. A North of England moor was not something to wander in or wonder about. It was not a minor wonder of the world, since wondering and wandering are time-wasting irrelevancies in the marketplace, unless they can be transformed into saleable leisure projects. This is a world in which the best people to help you will be those with the largest accredited skills portfolio. Those who do not have a portfolio will not have a credit card or a job. According to this way of being, they will not exist at all.

To exist, it seems, is to be accountable to an internal and external validator and supervisor. Ultimate reality becomes the 'bottom line', the figures on accountancy spreadsheets. Flesh and blood, truth and lies, beauty and ugliness are pale fantasies compared to these. In the beginning was the Word, at the end was the Spreadsheet. Moorlands, counsellors, care programmes, everything and everyone, must be accounted for if it is to be of any account. Uncharted wondering and wandering count for nothing when chartered and certificated accounting reign supreme.

Of course, we cannot spend all our time in retreat within the quiet tranquillity of a temple, moor, mountain or lakeside. The market has its place, but it has to be kept in its place. It should be bound by rules. Currently the rule is that the poor are best served if the rich are allowed to look after themselves first. This, supposedly, will be in the interests of society, if society exists at all. Such madness is what happens when merchants and entrepreneurs become the arbiters, proprietors and privateers of ethics. They have become a kind of priesthood and philosophical school in their own right. The ancient Greeks, Romans, Chinese, Indians would instantly have regarded this as preposterous.

Counselling and prayer

What have people sought in faith and prayer? A supernatural parent figure? Shall we ask for Divine assistance when we cannot make it on our own? Do we want, and deserve, special favours and support? Is there a 'Father in Heaven', and are we like a large family of demanding children? Do we want special attention, special good fortune, and a special dispensation from pain and the consequences of our own folly? Do we want daddy to make the pain go away by magic and lift us out of whatever pit we fell in? Do we fear this divine daddy? Is he wild, inconsistent and unpredictable? Shall we placate him with a sacrifice? Will this minimize the punishments even if it brings no rewards?[11]

What about faith? Is this a reckless declaration of belief despite the overwhelming evidence of our ignorance? Will injustices be corrected, and life really begin, after we have died? Will there be pie in the sky when we die? What has any of this to do with harmony, awe, mystery and spirituality? Do we seek a prop in order to avoid standing on our own feet:

Our father, who art in heaven
Brush us down,
Give us a big kiss,
Mend all the broken toys,
And set us on our feet again
Thank you very much.

Do we want a god who can make us immune from the laws of Nature? Should he intervene on our side at the expense of others? Do we think he *is* on our side? Shall we now look for a counsellor instead of a priest? Whose side will he be on?

Intelligent opinion has, I hope, gone beyond medieval dogma and superstition about divine father figures. It may not yet have reached a transpersonal apprehension of humanity as belonging to, rather than battling against, the world. This 'vision statement' may become a necessity for our survival now that we really do have god-like abilities to remove mountains and change the entire world climate. It is difficult to know what proportion of religious teachers have sought to pass on this transpersonal apprehension of life. The message is there to find but has often been lost within the institutions, ritual and theology designed to preserve it. Will the great power provided by science and technology be matched by great wisdom provided by the Church or spiritual teaching? Do counselling and psychotherapy have a role to play?

In a world where everything and everyone has been turned into a commodity, transpersonal experience, too, has become marketable as a desirable item of sale: Whole Earth catalogues, One World collections, astral tapes, herbs, essences, crystals, simple homeware from worthy ethnic origins, designer sportswear for jogging, cycling or aerobics, a personal mantra tastefully displayed, a personal development programme for you on a two-year course in desirable surroundings, a holiday of a lifetime on a beautiful island centre for holistic studies with a charming local peasantry who will love to welcome you, a lifestyle consultant for busy executives who wish to take stock and reorient themselves on their lifepath. The list of desirable goods and services offered on holistic and transpersonal stalls in the marketplace grows longer and longer, always providing you can pay. You can even have white light and ecstasy, for an affordable £14.99:

Liquid Light: The High Consciousness Video ...Amazing liquid light video can make you happy! Life affirming subliminal messages! (from some of the greatest minds of all times). Your conscious mind is enchanted by a beautiful light show of shimmering shapes and colours, a kaleidoscope of ever changing 'liquid light', while your inner-conscious mind is gently showered with words of elegance, grace and delight. Enclosed are two pairs of special 'aura glasses' that refract the polarised light of the video itself causing it to expand and spread out from the television set in a most pleasing manner ...Share it with someone you love.

Warning: This mind altering video may raise your consciousness forever! (Presented by *Altered States* direct from America)

With virtual reality computer graphics, we will soon be able to wear rather than watch television. The television, in a helmet, will be placed over our eyes. Goodbye real world. Welcome to a three-dimensional electronic creation. The first marriage in cyberspace has already occurred with priest, bride and groom each donning helmets and sharing a computer-generated environment. Further possibilities can be left to your imagination.

Back in the real world, after hours in front of – or wearing – a screen, you may choose to take a bit of exercise, relax or embark on a little home study. You need a personal development plan. You can choose from a wide range of programmes, packages and modules. How are we best to actualize ourselves? A little psychosynthesis here? Calisthenics there? Aerobics, Jogging, Tai chi, Yoga? A consciousness-raising group? Some co-counselling? DIY acupuncture? Which would be the best institute, health, recreation or growth centre locally available? And what do I wear? Let's see, what hints can I get from the brochure.

Perhaps my problems are more serious. I feel I am cracking up. Is there anything available from my local community mental health centre? Yes, I am lucky. They are offering a variety of care *packages*. Like vegetables, the care programme is plastic wrapped, validated and quality assured by the 'personal services team (caring)'.

Everyone is now keen on personal development. The bigger corporations, indeed, want to develop, rather than exploit, the entire planet. Their services will make you a better person. Their products are kind to the environment and fair to Third-World producers. Companies are advised that it is quite outmoded to portray themselves as big, mean and ruthless. Senior executives are no longer warriors boldly going out to conquer and subdue. They are sages, elders, philosophers, weighed down by their awesome responsibility as stewards of the planet.

In the 1960s, it was fashionable to be pink or red and in the 80s to be radical blue and right; in the 90s, green has been the colour of choice. Colours change. Shall we be green within, or just wear the colour loosely as a surface emblem? Green has certainly been the premier marketing miracle in recent years. If it's green, it's good. If it's not green, it's bad. 'Modern' has become dated. No longer new and good, it now tends to sound old, ugly and exploitative.

Can green notions of a 'global village' be realized? Can I make a bond of shared humanity with every stranger? Can the world be brought together in love and a shared purpose, rather than through *Coca Cola*? Or is this green, as in naïve? In seeking a green and transpersonal experience, are we looking for a quiet life, a retreat from the pain and ugliness around and within us? Do we hope that, through spiritual development, our lives will be more pleasant and peaceful, or that, as decadent versions of Buddhism maintain, we can make suffering unreal?

With greater sensitivity, we may experience more pleasure, and more pain. With greater empathy, the suffering as well as the joy of another can feel like our own. Along with the peaks of existence, a whole vision must know and experience the troughs. Growing sensitivity enhances our ability to celebrate, *and* to grieve:

> When his mother Flo died, the young male chimpanzee Flint exhibited many of the behavioural patterns we associate with grief in humans. He avoided others, stopped eating and spent many hours a day sitting in a hunched posture, rocking back and forth. After some days, he died. (*New Scientist,* 4 February 1992)

We, like chimps, grieve when our mother dies. Our greater powers of imagination allow us to share sorrow on many other occasions, too:

> no chimpanzee has ever been reported to have consoled a grieving companion. Although chimpanzees have mental states and grieve at the loss of close friends, they do not seem to recognise the same mental states in others. As a result, they are unable to share another's sorrow or show empathy towards others. (ibid.)

When consciousness expands, it soaks up more joy and more pain. This ability has evolved and it serves a positive purpose. Pain is a lifesaver. Without it, we would not notice when we had wounded ourselves. At present, when the body politic becomes wounded, we seek to insulate ourselves from the painful consequences. Millions have no work and little opportunity. The environment faces serious damage.

We turn away. To face up to such problems is painful, it makes us feel bad. Well, perhaps we ought to feel bad sometimes. Perhaps we are going to have to feel planetry and collective pain if we are to avoid fatal injury to the human species as a whole.

Most of the counselling industry seeks to help clients to feel good. Politicians, too, want their constituents to feel good. Fire and brimstone preachers, on the other hand, tend to want parishioners to feel bad. Is there not a balance to be found here? Can we avoid Buddhist evasion, Christian masochism and humanistic hedonism? Pick up thy cross and walk, but do not play the martyr in the process: enjoy the sunshine and whatever other pleasures are available and appropriate.

Perhaps the art of effective living is to establish an appropriate balance of feeling good and feeling bad. People become demoralized and ineffectual when they feel too bad about themselves, yet we become shallow and ineffective if we feel inappropriately good about ourselves. High self-esteem, by degrees, transforms into smugness, selfishness and complacency. Counsellors, a product of our contemporary feel-good obsession, just do not seem to have grasped this at all. Repentance and the role of suffering are rarely part of the agenda within counselling theory. Mystics imaginatively connect to the joys of collective humanity. They also hear the cries of collective suffering. What kind of faith is it that only seeks to hear of good news?

Whole industries are now available to help consumers escape from, rather than engage with, the real world. Soon, we may spend more of our waking lives relating to electronic images than to flesh and blood individuals. More energy, attention and raw cash seems to be given over to the pursuit of plausibility rather than truth:

> Even when we meet in the flesh, that flesh itself might no longer be as natural and unadorned as it may seem. For example, the average American cosmetic surgeon at the end of the nineteen eighties was making a million dollars a year. More than two million Americans (mainly women) underwent cosmetic surgery in 1988, a figure which had tripled in two years. Americans were undergoing 160,000 breast operations a year and 67,000 face lifts, and, in 1989, five contestants for Miss America e.g. Miss Oregon, Alaska and Florida were surgically reconstructed by a single Arkansas plastic surgeon! (Wolf, 1990)[12]

In a crowded and noisy world, peace and quiet are becoming saleable, scarce, and therefore increasingly expensive, commodities. If you are very rich, you will be able to buy them through your exclusive use of the best seacoast, moorland, mountain or select residential neighbourhood. But if there is not enough empty space available near where you are, you can try a mask and ear plugs, or watch a video of quiet countryside and a tinkling stream. This may sound unglamorous and a poor substitute for the real thing: it will have to be made more alluring with suitable marketing skill. Thus, peace and quiet may have to be replaced by 'restricted environmental stimulation therapy', (REST© ?); designer masks and earplugs will be made available with suitable logos, packaging, add-on accessories, cans of fresh air, sunbeds and an illustrated explanatory booklet introduced by a New Age celebrity. For those who want even more, withdrawal tanks will be made available at appropriate therapy centres, where, under supervision, people will be able to float in warm water and seek nirvana, either in total blackness and silence, or, for the less hardy, with suitably restful or inspiring video accompaniments.

There has never been a necessary connection between stewardship and equality of opportunity or basic humanity. The élites of many civilizations (the British aristocracy, for example) have quite often had a sincere understanding of the need for stewardship of Mother Earth. Yet this has not necessarily made them very liberal or benevolent to their own tenants. The nobility in Eastern and Western empires have often lavished far more care on their land and animals than on the peasantry, and it may happen again. Thus forests might be carefully tended, but children left to starve (they add to carbon dioxide emissions, do nothing to control sea levels and consume scarce resources). In South America, there is already evidence in some big cities that the police have been shooting young beggars to clear the streets of such polluting influences.

Actions will count for more than words. In this respect perhaps, the following computer program has something to teach us:

> Eurisko was so clever that the first golden rule it generated was that all machine-generated instructions were rubbish, and with this flash of inspiration, it dutifully shut itself down. (Edwin Galea, *New Scientist*, 8 September 1990)

Notes

1 Ambrose Bierce, *The Devil's Dictionary*. Castle Books, 1881–1911.

2 Fritjof Capra, *Uncommon Wisdom*. Flamingo, 1989.

3 See, for example, Fritjof Capra, *The Turning Point: Science, Society and the Rising Culture*. Flamingo, 1984.

4 Monica Furlong, *Genuine Fake*. Unwin, 1986.

5 Bertrand Russell, *History of Western Philosophy*. Allen & Unwin, 1946.

6 On a recent US holiday, I noticed that at every desirable beach resort, with its natural setting, low-rise skyline and tasteful décor, there was a police patrol in tactful, and regular, attendance. These 'unspoilt' environments were crafted and guarded like medieval castles.

7 On Earth, if not in Heaven, the gateway to consumer paradise is found in cyberspace, within the global banking system that instantly checks every purchase against your credit limit, from any part of the world. Hell in the twenty-first century will be electronic expulsion from Gold Card spending, care and opportunity.

8 Christopher Lasch, *The Culture of Narcissism*. Abacus, 1989; *The Minimal Self: Psychic Survival in Troubled Times*. Picador, 1984.

9 Ken Wilbur, *Up from Eden: A Transpersonal View of Human Evolution*. Shambhala, 1981.

10 Sussex psychologist Helga Ditmar, author of *The Social Psychology of Material Possessions: To Have is to Be*, found that teenagers' impressions of other people were more strongly influenced by their possessions than their behaviour. She filmed a young man and woman in two situations. The wealthy setting included a carved pine kitchen with high-tech appliances, a well-decorated living room with television, video, hi-fi stack and CD, an expensive squash set and a Ford Granada. The poor setting included a narrow galley kitchen with basic appliances, a lounge with small television and record player, a swimming outfit and a small Volkswagen. The actors were filmed after work, making tea, checking television channels, listening to music, packing sports equipment and carrying it to their car. More than one hundred 16- to 18-year-olds, half from East Sussex public schools, half from a working class comprehensive, were shown the videos. All assumed that the people in the wealthy settings were more intelligent, successful and educated, as well as more in control of their life and environment. The people in the poorer setting were described as 'warmer, friendly and more self-expressive'. (*Times Higher Education Supplement*, 4 December 1992)

11 Peter Cooke and Dudley Moore got the measure of this kind of belief in their television sketch on religion. Asked by Dud if he believed in God, Pete replied: 'Well, Dud, when I'm in a tight spot, I say a little prayer. I say, "Please God help me out …if you're there. If you're not, then don't bother. But if you are there, please make me better by next Tuesday, and I'll know it was You, and I'll promise to believe in You, and thank You very much, and I'll know you're there for future reference".'

12 Naomi Wolf, *The Beauty Myth*. Chatto and Windus, 1990.

Chapter 8

Conclusion

It would be better, and more honest, to say to the patient: 'I have so many personal difficulties of my own that it is only with great difficulty that I can hear about yours'.

(Ferenczi, letter to Freud, 1989)[1]

Conference for Carers (1988)

The Carnival is over
New Age Aquarians
Wild Affairs, Affrays, Excitements
Gone

To a staid sensibility.
Ageing, anxiety-managed,
And managing children, chores, departments, teams
Committed and rooted, or gently rotting?
On from Right On to Right thinking, Right wing?
Well wrought or, if over-wrought
It's decorously hidden.

We've become decent, established, stable
Able enough, our path defined and finite
Well within the Pale
We no longer rail against humdrum limitation
Except quietly, in committee and a memo.
Held firm in our tracks
Do not de-rail us.

We moved from Flower-Power to Power Ploys
From Joy to Jargon
From doing it in the road
To keeping a Neighbourhood Watch.
We gave Peace a chance
Now little's left to chance.

The New Age
is another age.
We moved from innocence
to common-sense
From Be-ins to
Has-beens with accreditation.

Of course, I'm being unreasonable;
We grew up, that's all
Or so we've said.

Perhaps it's just me
Do you understand? Do you hear?
Of course you do.
Your listening skills
And powers of non-directive empathy
Are soberly supervised
Every two weeks.

So will you help me?
What do you propose?
Shall I pull myself together

Give up this childish blether?
Find life beyond my tether?
Indulge and sulk forever?

(Inspired by the annual gathering of the BAC)

Fashions come and go, but certain basic human needs remain immovable and unchanging. Human warmth is one; did humanity really need a Carl Rogers to remind us? Security in childhood is another. Do we require a Rank, Klein, or Bowlby to tell us that our parents are important?

Compassion and consolation have always been in heavy demand, especially when times get tough, and, if we are to survive at all, somebody or something always has to be found to provide. When a culture is besieged by fear and insecurity, people go on hoping that they can at least stave off the worst of their catastrophes, hence the

sacrifices and ceremonials designed to placate vicious and unpredictable gods in the belief that, even if the harvest is still going to be bad,
it may not be as bad as it would otherwise have been. With this kind of
reasoning, any theology remains impregnable.

The need to feel consoled about the past, reassured about the present
and hopeful about the future is almost irresistible. Without these props,
it is difficult to carry on. On sunny days and with a fair wind behind us,
the evidence of our own senses provides grounds for optimism. But
when life gets tougher, when we notice our decay, decline, loss, illness or
impending death, some kind of theology is generally invoked to fill
what can otherwise appear to be a gaping void of meaninglessness and
hopelessness.

In an age steeped in state welfarism and the secular professions, it is
easy to forget the role of the clergy, which has, down the centuries and
before all others, provided sanctuary, forgiveness, pastoral counselling
and consolation to its battered flock. How could psychoanalysis have
had any success if not for the decline of the Church? In another century,
Freud would have been a priest who would have developed his own ideas
by offering innovative interpretations of the sacred texts and attractive
variations on public ritual and private confessional. Behaviourism, too,
surely owes much of its success to the failure of the competition,
appealing to those impatient with the indulgent speculation of Freud.
Finally, the client-centred school has thrived by presenting itself as warm
and human, for those frustrated by cold scientism.

Different personalities have always wanted, and needed, divergent
styles of caring. Some want, and will always want, a warm, passionate
and intimate ally; others prefer to be supported by a cool, dispassionate, detached authority who can be admired and trusted. Some
need to express their emotions; others require a disciplined perspective
on their feelings or need to take urgent action. Some want a parental
figure they can actively lean on; others prefer a seasoned guide to climb
with them or provide no more than a map. Less genuine seekers after
truth may opt for a magical mystery adventure to take them as far away
as possible from painful or routine reality. Similar variations can be
found, historically, within the different styles of care offered by, for
example, low and high Churches.

Regardless of our needs, we are unlikely to find that they can all be
met by just one person, since different facets of our personality are
drawn out, or inhibited, in the unique personal chemistry that develops
between individuals. There is not even a neat dividing line between

helper and helped, since all are supported in a constructive relationship and no-one can be sure what will result from our encounter if we are really open to each other.

Even when we can identify the help we need, it is difficult to know where we can best find it. Friends and family cannot live up to perfectionistic ideals and, at worst, may be more of a problem than a consolation. They are still, nonetheless, the most important source of material and emotional support when functioning 'well enough'. The list of potentially healing, therapeutic influences is, however, almost endless.

Professional discussion of the nature of healing tends to focus on particular specialist approaches to psychotherapy or medicine, yet when lay people consider what keeps them sane, they generally think of less technical, more ordinary, strategies: they have danced, sung, swum, made love, loosened their inhibitions with drink (then, too often, lost control through drunkenness). They have made music, made some kind of constructive contribution to their community, and felt a sense of achievement and due consolation. They have found a place and a role in their daily routine, village and wider society. If they ever had time, they developed recreational interests that recreate themselves, take them out of their day-to-day cares and give them perspective and/or the company of others.

People stay sane and find motivation and inspiration by laughing and crying, working and playing together. They have been healed by contemplating the world around them in quiet reverence. They have been healed by participating in committed, positive activity. Alternatively, they have been consoled by thinking of others worse off than themselves. Schadenfreudean therapy.

Most forms of healing, then, do not belong to professional specialists at all. They arise from living our lives with courage, commitment, compassion, integrity, good humour and a due sense of proportion. Virtually anything can be healing when now is the right time and place to be doing it. And anything can be harmful when the time and place is wrong.

To repeat, the whole of life is psychotherapeutic when we are living with commitment, compassion, courage and a sense of place and timing. It is not so much what we do, but the attitude, or spirit with which we do it. We can be healed when we can recognize a time to work, a time to play, a time to laugh, a time to cry, a time to withdraw from others, a time, even, to die. There may, however, be severe limits on our ability to save our souls when we are trapped in a soul-destroying environment that is poisoning our bodies, minds and spirits.

Perhaps I might move nearer to insight and enlightenment if I shared with, and belonged to, a wider community abundant in its love, care, compassion and honesty. But in the real world, such abundance might not be found, and so I must accept my tendency to behave destructively and foolishly, and talk nonsense, either because I have cut myself off from others or because you, being no nearer to the truth than I, are actively colluding in our collective folly.

Hence the shared delusions of, for example, the Rogerians who, anaesthetizing themselves from awareness of the society around them with all its evil, suffering, power ploys and games, imagined that they could become clean, caring and nondirective just by talking about it. Authenticity includes sordid as well as sublime aspects of existence. Growing up incorporates decay, decline and destruction, as well as growth and creation. Therefore, we need to guard against anyone who too confidently assumes that they are empathic, real, warm, caring and trustworthy. Any special claim to virtue deserves a sceptical response. Integrity and insight can never be guaranteed in a world that, although bright, wholesome and honest, is also full of fractures, darkness and deceit.

Let us be wary of any group that accredits itself as able to provide love, or a substitute, and which siphons off ordinary humanity and sells it back for a fee. Human compassion is not a commodity to be bought and sold at all, even though many of its imitations fetch a high price in the marketplace. In an imperfect world, there is no caring 'microclimate' or oasis immune from pernicious influence. We can, and do, damage each other as well as heal. We can suffer exploitation and remorse about our own wrongdoings. Sicknesses in society can be like air we have to breathe. No-one, including counsellors, can free themselves from this pollution and its consequences. Perhaps they will provide a cleansing perspective on a mad and muddy world. Or just raise more mud.

Our *dis*-ease lies in our own blood and in the air we breathe. We are victims of soul-destroying circumstances, and also of the wholesale 'soul sale', by ourselves, of ourselves, to the highest bidder. We need, therefore to look both within and beyond ouselves. Psychotherapy and introspection have their place. So, too, do political, social, legal and moral remedies.

Nothing and no-one is intrinsically therapeutic, but almost anything and anyone can be, when the time, place and chemistry are right.

Therapy may need to focus on bodies, feelings, minds, rights, obligations or some combination of these, which are each cause and effect of the others. Sometimes, paradoxically, our own healing will not take place until we forget our individual preoccupations for a while and pay more attention to the needs of others. Talking can be therapeutic, but so can walking, running, climbing, fishing, dancing, playing or working. Being cradled safe and warm can be therapeutic, but so can braving a storm on a mountainside, or looking out onto a peaceful country scene. A bath can be therapeutic, but so can working in muck if the work seems worthwhile. A good cry can be therapeutic, but so can a decision to avoid letting tears and fear get on top of us when the time requires that we take courage and determination in our hands. A break from all responsibilities can be therapeutic, but so can a quiet recognition of the need to shoulder our burdens and responsibilities, to avoid shirking our duties and to live with honour and dignity. By recognizing my own duties to others, I will be healing myself in the very process of helping you. Every client, then, is a therapist for every therapist. We all have powers to heal and harm.

Can any society produce enough paid counsellors and therapists to meet the demand? Should it try? Who will pay? Most people cannot afford personal help, however low the wages, say, for a cleaner. Yet counsellors are generally middle class. Their fees are not affordable by clerical, blue-collar and no-collar classes.[2] The problem is shifted, but not solved, via taxation. Could the public pay? Will the rich pay taxes to support counselling of the poor? Tax-paid counselling, like tax-paid education, would be more likely to involve a net subsidy to the middle class. White-collar clients are heavily overrepresented as users of counselling.[3] Therefore public provision makes a net transfer of resources from the average taxpayer to relatively wealthy and assertive clients who expect, and receive, more personal attention and who will not accept just medication. Could private insurance cover everybody? Only if the wealthy pay premiums that subsidize the poor. Will they do this? I rather doubt it. Even schemes for the privileged are tottering before ever-spiralling health costs. Poor people, almost by definition, cannot afford professionals unless richer people pick up the bill. Whatever counselling they get will most probably, as ever, be within self-help groups. Hence, the higher the status of the counsellors, the more they tend to be monopolized by clients who, from a global perspective, fret that their spoonful of circumstance is only silver, and that the golden opportunities of their dreams elude them. Those who could, for a while, be at peace with their 'wooden spoon' consolation prize, if only it had food on it, somehow, once again, get left behind.

Therapy is a contemporary form of the perennial effort to find a 'Kingdom of Heaven' within each of us[4], but, with its focus on the individual 'I' and its disregard for the social, it is a journey of the camel through the eye of a needle. Too many within the counselling and human potential movement have tended to imagine that, to express myself, all I have to do is to let go, let rip, let it all hang out and just 'be'. Through my spontaneity, it is argued, I will automatically discover my creativity and my authentic self. This, unfortunately, leaves out self-discipline altogether.

I may wish I could release the child in me, and that, certainly, needs its time and place, but society and democracy already have more than enough childish behaviour to cope with. Adult healing and social progress require adult behaviour, not child-like naïveté. The adult self is not something that can simply be unleashed. It has to be cultivated; it has to learn, revise, reflect and develop poise, grace and dignity. Otherwise what do we find? Self-expression becomes a juvenile confessional devoid of perspective, wit or wisdom. A sweaty armpit is offered to the world as 'my authentic self'. Without self-discipline, authenticity becomes melodramatic and attention-seeking, and is unworthy of our real potential and integrity. So what is to be done with the client who goes on behaving like an indulgent child? Unless such behaviour is challenged, it may continue indefinitely, and the counsellor will then be colluding with the client.

Clients may want easy answers. Will the counsellor oblige? Is there a reliable, real, intuitive, 'organismic' self within each of us? Or is Rogerian belief in such a self just another easy response? How, for example, do we distinguish between authentic intuition and real prejudice except by hindsight? And there is always more hindsight lying in wait for us in the future; it may yet cause us to alter our views.

In our indulgent consumer culture, with its thirty-second attention span, we may need to get a grip on ourselves instead of trying so much to 'let go'. Pulling ourselves together, although vague, old-fashioned and inadequate, may be nearer to what is needed than letting go. Letting it all hang out does not help slovenly individuals in real danger of making an indulgent mess of themselves and their disintegrating life.

Christianity promised an afterlife of Heaven or Hell, according to your present behaviour. I am more impressed by the hell on Earth consequent on our foolish, indulgent or wicked decisions and actions – bad karma, as the Buddhists call it. Counsellors, if they are to be of any use to clients, must surely assist them in exploring consequences of their decisions. How is this to be done? Can, and should, counsellors avoid imposing their own values on the client? Can, and should, counsellors keep their own values to themselves or take a 'value-free' approach? A value-free counsellor, I suggest, is either amoral, a coward or a fool. Judgements, implicit or otherwise, run like a spine through all our perceptions, choices, acts and words. We are judging all the time. Our presence, our values, influence clients, whatever we think or do. We are often most influential precisely when we avoid pushing ourselves on to others.

In search of a formula

Can a 'good enough' service be secured within counselling and psychotherapy? The success of these professions seems to be fatally dependent on their being executed in the right spirit, and with the right human qualities. Are they professional service commodities at all?

> One central conclusion which seems to me inescapable is that fundamen-tally psychotherapy cannot satisfactorily be cast in terms of anything other than a personal relationship, so that any attempt to standardise or techni-cize therapy is certain to detract from its proper understanding. (David Smail, in Pilgrim, 1983)[5]

> The assumption that human life could be generalised, and that therapists possessed its secrets, has been widely abandoned ...In psychotherapy it is now widely assumed that deep meaningful learning can occur only in the context of a genuinely personal relationship. [This requires] the genuine presence of the therapist as a particular human being. (Phillida Salmon, in Pilgrim, 1983)[5]

Many clients speak sincerely, and with feeling, about the help given by their therapist. Others say the same about friends and family. Sometimes, however, our own networks do not exist or do not function. They may not be appropriate. On such occasions, we may well need to turn to a helpful third party. Every culture provides such roles. The case for them is unassailable, but how far can, or should, they be professionalized, organized and purchased? Do professional therapists do the job better than lay people or other professionals? The evidence in their favour is uncertain. The mediocre theory underlying their work and their frequent inability to describe what they are trying to do ought, often, to be a cause for great concern.

I do recommend particular professional counsellors, and I have made good use of some myself, but I have come to realize that I am not thereby endorsing counselling. I am recommending *particular individ-*

uals whose wisdom and compassion I respect. These people constitute a minority of names on a large database. I have found no relationship between the qualifications of a counsellor and the quality of his or her work. Consequently, I find it impossible to either recommend or warn against counsellors I do not know personally.[6]

Luck, mainly, will determine whether or not you can find a genuinely personal relationship with a counsellor or anyone else. This ought not to come as a surprise. How can we possibly produce a technique that, once learned, will reliably turn people into more genuine, warm, personal, helpful human beings? If anything, the acquisition of new techniques, skills and status will tend to accentuate narcissistic pride and arrogance. What could be more phoney, and absurd, than the claim that 'I am a certified genuine person'? In our current obsession with mechanisms, we have succumbed to the grotesque illusion that basic human qualities can be instilled into people on a production line of counsellor training. Priests and philosophers have struggled for centuries to persuade citizens to be good. The effort is always worthwhile, but we are mad if we imagine we have found a successful formula.

If we cannot reliably *produce* the right kind of counsellor, can we at least *discover* them among candidates? How many saints are we likely to find? And how do we find them? Moreover, how do we decide whether the clients are good enough for the service being provided? How many clients can, or wish, to help themselves, face their own shadows, dilemmas, fears, fantasies, defences and delusions? It is not a task for weaklings. Freud, T. S. Eliot and many others suggest that only a small proportion of humanity is willing to face the realities of existence. Freud thought that most people were not good enough for psychoanalysis; they simply did not have what it takes. If so, psychoanalysis cannot be of much use to most people. Freud dwelt less on that side of the equation.

Paul Halmos focused on counsellor qualities back in 1965 in *The Faith of the Counsellors*[7]. He observed that counsellors, by general consent, need a rounded-out personality, enabling them to combine knowledge with creative intuition; they have to be capable of empathy, to identify easily with their clients, to be kindly without expecting anything in return and to avoid taking remarks personally. More recently, Gerard Egan, in *The Skilled Helper*[8], made similar observations. The list of desirable human qualities goes on and on. Counsellors and psychotherapists need to be creative, to transcend the narrow self with its defences and narcissistic concerns; they need to see the loveable soul that lies at the centre of some otherwise less-than-loveable personalities; they must endure all kinds of attack and resistance on the part of the client; they must separate their own needs and responses from the needs of the client; they must be intelligent without making a show of their intelligence; they must be loving without getting enmeshed in their own, or the client's, emotions and needs; they must be close and intimate, but not too close and intimate; they must be able to set up suitable boundaries between themselves and the client, and know that flexibility and sensitivity is needed in setting such boundaries. Finally (except that the list can be extended on and on), they must have real humility (in the face of a truly awesome list of personal qualities!). To repeat, it is best if counsellors are saints.

A little more saintliness would be desirable in all of us, but in practice, of course, saints are in short supply. Generally, however, the world of work requires skills that can be learned and practised independently of our desirable and ugly personalities. You can be a tinker, tailor, soldier, sailor, butcher, baker or candlestick-maker without having to be a pleasant person. Everyone would prefer it if you were warm and genuine as well as proficient in baking, but, either way, we'll get bread.

Yet if the right personal qualities are absent in a counsellor, we will not get bread, beef or anything of value. This is because, at the root of all care, is care that, in a world obsessed with the buying and selling of commodities, is not actually a commodity at all. Consequently, it cannot be turned on and off like a tap, or trained or accredited into existence. At a price, though, we can all go through the motions of caring and, in the absence of anything better, this may provide consolation of a sort. If no-one really cares for us, we might pay someone to pretend, and at least then we will not have to pretend to care for them. If we have busy lives, we might actually prefer to pay for a friend, since then we retain full control and can pay off the counsellor at any time without any sense of obligation. Pay me £20 or £50 an hour, and it's the least I can do to give you time and attention. I'll even try to care about you because, if I could manage it, the next hour would be easier for me as well as more beneficial to you.

In fact, we cannot make ourselves care. Either we care a lot, a little or not at all, and that's the bottom line; that's the hard reality. We can try to delude ourselves about it (and much of the counselling industry is engaged in a mammoth exercise of collective self-deception), but we cannot change the bottom line. If we don't care, we don't care, and if we are to be human we are going to have to face this hard reality. It's a

problem when you're employed by Megacare plc and you've got certifi-
cates on the wall that tell customers you're a caring person.

The future of counselling and therapy as marketable professions,
therefore, is very questionable unless they confine themselves to clear,
limited, practical tasks. There is no evidence to suggest that you would
be better, or worse off, if you went for a walk, took a holiday, had a bath,
saw some friends, got a job or got active in politics. For the unemployed
or homeless, psychotherapy is no substitute for job therapy or housing
therapy. We cannot simply talk our way out of trouble and overcome
real adversity just by changing our attitudes.

I doubt that these observations will deter people from counselling.
If they can find no-one else to turn to, who can blame them? We will
actively choose placebo and phoney personal contact if this is the only
way of maintaining hope, meaning and human contact. Yet the growth
of counselling seems more a symptom of, than a remedy for, a sick and
unhappy society. Surely we should pay more attention to the sickness
itself? The problem is a collective one; how are we to humanize our
relationships generally and ensure that our society is a humane place to
live and work? These questions are not addressed, and the problems are
not solved merely by purchasing individual attention for ourselves.

In a mechanical world, the search continues for some kind of skills-
based mechanotherapy, with reliably measurable outcomes and tick-
boxes of achievement. Institutions offer portfolios of care programmes
and action plans to their staff and clientèle. Tenderness, it is hoped, will
be resolvable into its mechanical parts and then reassembled into an act
of tenderness. Or will it? Halmos thinks not and quotes Sidney Jourard
who observed that:

> The 'technical' therapist is striving to manipulate himself and his patient
> rather than respond to him... I have come to recognise that those who
> habitually strive to manipulate others in one way or another, do violence
> to their own integrity as well as to that of their victims. (I–Thou relation-
> ship versus manipulation in counselling and psychotherapy, *Journal of
> Individual Psychology*, 1959, vol. XV, pp. 174–179)

In any case, therapists do not necessarily do what they say they are
doing:

1 Practitioners using the same theory may not do the same thing in
   practice. Their work may be very similar to a rival who, in theory,
   is supposed to be working differently.
2 Experienced therapists tend to be more flexible.
3 Personal qualities count for more than technical skills.

4   Experience helps, except when it breeds arrogance.
5   Therapists are not necessarily more skilful with, or understanding of, clients than are other professionals.[9]

There are huge concentrations of therapists in big cities such as London, New York, Los Angeles and San Francisco. California and Connecticut, too, are well supplied. What has been the result of all this labour? These intensively therapized societies are suffering accelerating social decay. Their inhabitants experience ennui, loss of purpose, perspective and collective responsibility. They retreat into their own private worlds. The therapy is a symptom of this decay; a sign that a broader social and spiritual vision has been lost. Instead of seeking organismic warmth and other individualistic paraphernalia, we need to see that Cities and Societies are themselves cell-like organisms that, without due care and attention, can wither, decay or disintegrate.

In our disintegrating society, social responsibility has given way to career mobility. As a result we have lost public space, political commitment, families and friends. Instead we have 'networks', manipulated by single players to suit themselves. Each manoeuvres within a nexus of atomized individual contracts, connections and deals, rather than any organic sense of 'us'. The mobile phone has replaced the public meeting.

Sometimes, it seems, we have even forgotten what friendship actually means. Love is difficult to express, even to understand, when we do not know how to give or receive. Because so much of life has been commercialized, we think that giving puts us in credit, and receiving leads to debt. We thus confuse generosity and gratitude with the investing and borrowing, buying and selling of commercial existence. So we try to buy a friend or sell ourselves as the friend of someone else. This leads to illusions of intimacy and commitment when really there is nothing, over and above the commercial contract:

> In an increasingly wide range of settings – from evening classes to church congregations – lonely people are propelled into a mutually self-deceiving 'togetherness' by means of superficial 'techniques' and games (eg. 'ice-breakers'). Instant intimacy becomes something you can buy from your local encounter group centre. (Smail, 1987)[10]

It is hard to give up a lucrative enough career after years of training. To begin at all, we have to believe in ourselves and our skills, and to question such belief can be very demoralizing. What is it to be helpful and human? What is it that can heal or harm us as individuals? How can other individuals help? These questions are always worth asking, but artists have generally been wise enough to know that categorical answers to such imponderables of existence cannot be given. Psychotherapy, like literature, provides a choice of stories, or myths, within which a person's life can be told and made meaningful. Artists know that, although powerful and practical, their story is 'just' a story. Therapists, too often, fall into the trap of believing that their story is true.

Counselling and crises of faith

Hope springs eternal, within counselling as elsewhere. It has to, if life is to continue at all. If we lose heart, the light drains from our eyes and our whole body tells the tale. Loss of hope is like a hole in the fabric of our identity through which our life bleeds away. We may become manic, we may distract ourselves, we may be openly despairing, but whatever we do, there will be no healing until we can rekindle our spirit of hope.

Major journeys, and crises of faith, are not easily negotiated. They are not resolved by thin platitudes, cosy nostrums or tidy accreditation programmes. If we are to deal with crises that challenge our very identity and sense of meaning and purpose, we will need a philosophy of life that really is life-sustaining, and which can provide faith and support self-esteem when circumstances are tough. Are we, currently, living in a culture whose philosophy can help us through such tough times? I think not. With our obsession with celebrity, youth, beauty, wealth, power and success, we seem to be fixated on warm and shallow waters, sunny days, big dinners and comfort generally. Life is good, we are to believe, providing life goes on being kind to us, and we feel a fair wind of fortune behind us. Then we can feel good about ourselves and really live – as seen on television.

But what do we do when we face decline, defeat, disaster and death? What about problems that have no solutions? How do we cope with failure, doubt, despair and depression? What about the times when our self-esteem is profoundly battered? How do we sustain life, faith and hope when we are caught in a severe storm? Our shallow secular consumerism is then about as adequate as a Mississippi paddle steamer trying to negotiate Cape Horn in a force twelve hurricane. It is no longer life-sustaining since it is not sea-worthy as a philosophy of life. It is a philosophy that worships good fortune and all the good things that come with it. It is of no use to people caught in rough waters or to those who, jaded by too many easy days, are searching for a deeper sense of significance in their lives.

Those whose vision of themselves and their lives is neither deep nor robust are likely to be overwhelmed when circumstances become tough for them. Sympathy from others may help, and the trained ear of a counsellor might provide a limited amount of support, but counsellors cannot very easily help people to help themselves if neither counsellor nor client has a vision that can sustain them through tough times. It is relatively easy to keep morale and self-esteem high when all is going well for us. What, however, are we to do when faced with more radical challenges and pressures?

In a major crisis it may not just be that my circumstances seem to fall apart. Worse than that, my notion of myself may disintegrate. For example, what if I lose (too many of?) the following: my spouse, my job, my hope, my home, my picture of the past, present and future? Who am I then in all of this? What happens to me as subject when the key objects of my existence unravel? The philosopher Descartes told us that 'I think, therefore I exist'. But perhaps he should have said 'I exist because the little bit of world of concern to me, that fills my thoughts and actions, seems fairly stable'.

Our language is constructed by 'subjects', 'verbs' and 'objects'. Is this the way the world is or just the way we talk and think of it? Philosophers may propose a world of verbs and events. Maybe changes and events are fundamental, and stability and objects just an illusion? If this is reality, can we take it? Philosophers ponder the question. People in crisis suffer the experience. Are we in the world or of it?

Our ancestors believed that, when the 'self-I-thought-I-knew' starts to disintegrate, we need to turn to the larger mysterious forces of the life within and around us if we are to survive. Every religious tradition will advise of the need to understand the power of prayer for support, guidance and inspiration. No mere human will be sufficient, be he an accredited counsellor, priest or ordinary lay person. The notion of prayer, however, generally has no place among what is a mainly secular counselling community. Yet what are we to make of prayer? What, if anything, do we understand it to mean? Shall we dismiss it altogether, on the grounds that counselling is an entirely secular matter designed for postmodern, postreligious people? Some will certainly see it that way, although many counsellors are in fact practising Christians who therefore, presumably, look upon counselling as a much weaker intervention than Divine support. If we are confident in the power of prayer, why turn to counselling at all?

Of course, it all depends on what is meant by prayer. Too often it has been of the petitionary variety where one shuffles deferentially in search of this, that or another special favour, bowing, scraping, apologizing, hoping not to offend, and trying to show how duly grateful we would be if we could just ask...

Yet there are more significant ways of understanding prayer. Perhaps it is what(ever) we do that connects us to power, insight, courage, compassion and wisdom beyond the self-I-think-I-know? People have spoken of pregnant powerful silences, inspiring scenery or works of art. Some have referred to the expression of all humanity on a single face, or 'the face of Christ' on every human being. For others, inspiration is a well from which they can draw. Martial artists feel strength, not from themselves and their own conscious efforts, but from forces welling up from the ground, or from a stream of energy rushing through their arms. Are these just daydreams? Or is self within a larger flow of existence more real than what Einstein called the optical illusion of a self apart?[11]

What is most real? Do we move through life (the secular view), or does life flow through us? Should we try to be a star performer or are we the stage on which life is performed? To change tone for a moment, shall we sing 'Oh, I do like to be beside the seaside' or, 'Oh, I know that I am being-with-the-seaside.'? Maybe where, what and who we are is more interconnected than we thought? Could we become a window through which power, light and life can move? Writing, running, walking, talking; everything can be experienced in this way. The egocentric experience is of a self struggling and battling, forcing a way through a resistant medium. The self-transcendent experience is of a flow of words, ideas and actions coming from who knows where?

How do such speculations relate to the routine of day-to-day counselling? Not very much if counselling is a primarily secular activity confined to utilitarian tasks and targeting. Yet the secular vision of human beings as consumers and commodities to be bought and sold is inherently constricting. If you are not aware of this, you will almost certainly have been bought by it, and you will unwittingly sell the same lack of vision to others.

Capitalist consumerism reigns supreme at present. It is part of the air we breathe, so its smell and pressure is difficult to detect. It permeates everything we do, think, feel, believe and hope for. It constructs and constrains almost every version of counselling and psychotherapy. It has changed counsellors and therapists far more than they realize and far more than counselling has managed to change consumerism. It is widely believed that there is no alternative. Indeed, many do not even *ask* whether there is an alternative, since the very possibility is not part of their thinking. With the overshadowing or collapse of radical alternatives, it is extremely difficult to take any kind of perspective on our all-pervading status quo. Yet current levels of consumption, materialism and secular preoccupation are unsustainable.

Mystical, spiritual dimensions of human encounter are not very compatible with the routinizing, professionalizing and bureaucratizing of counselling. They may not interest those who just want to make a living, or who have become attached to a shallow agenda of care and a facile vision of themselves as caring persons. Nor does the transcendental belong to any narrow vision of what is normal, sensible and proper. It challenges those who wish to counsel others to conform to a plastic, tawdry status quo.

Radical, spiritual, challenges are not new. In the nineteenth century, Nietzsche castigated the conformist, supine, manipulative mediocrity and hypocrisy he saw in Christianity. He felt loathing and contempt for the super-ego of Victorian Christianity, which, he thought, debased humanity rather than inspiring it. Nietzsche, I am quite certain, would have felt a similar disgust for the underlying ethic of so much of our contemporary humanistic counselling. He would have poured scorn on those bland therapists who tried to defend themselves by saying that they are innocent because they are nondirective. He would have demolished that feeble plea of the mediocre: that their own vision, or the lack of it, was of no consequence in their contact with others; that they didn't mean any harm; that they were only trying to help and that they didn't want to get in anyone's way.

The questions raised in these pages make life more difficult for counsellors and clients. Many have no easy answers or no answers at all. One professional reader of the manuscript warned that the book could be a devastating experience for people in distress. How much reality, individually and collectively, can we take?[12] Perhaps, as a potential client, you would have preferred to be soothed with reassurances that new professional carers have arrived on the scene and that, once you have checked their credentials, you can sit back and trust that a quality consumer service will reliably be delivered.

I have argued that there is nothing final, neat and tidy about the mystery of being helpful, loving and caring, and that such services can never be straightforwardly sold or purchased in the marketplace or provided free by a caring State. I have thereby placed what I hope is a hefty spanner in the works of those agencies who would like to set up a smooth scheme that will manufacture and sell caring people, mechanotherapists or tutors in tenderness to those millions who would undoubtedly appreciate such a service were its delivery ever possible. Instead, I have argued that we cannot, and should not, be freed from the untidy and inherently chaotic responsibility of caring for each other. I hope I have laid to rest the idea that people skills can be neatly arranged and delivered by appropriately trained service professionals.

Some readers may find these observations gloomy and depressing, but I think they are cause for optimism and reassurance. The good news is that the whole mysterious business of living, loving and learning from each other will never be boiled down into a formula, however complex. If it could, we would eventually be able to programme machines to tell us how to live our lives, and the new Church of Life would no doubt be containable, and contained, within a consortia of corporations.

Salvation, mechanized or otherwise, is not around the corner. Why feel dismay? It is a source of great relief. Of course, counselling may well succeed as a profession despite its failure to deliver as promised. Desperate customers have nowhere else to turn. Counselling, like medicine, may build its status even though 'most of the common and incurable diseases remain common and incurable'.[13]

The consolations of counselling

The very fact that others are trying to be helpful is comforting to us, even if they are unskilled and unsuccessful. If they add a little flattery, and carry some authority, they may win us over completely. We are easily swayed by authority. Stanley Milgram, in a classic series of experiments[14], explored our tendency to defer to people in white coats, even when their instructions were outrageous. 'Technicians' urged participants to give electric shocks to 'subjects' who incorrectly answered questions. Sixty per cent complied. The actors feigned agony. Only those inflicting what they thought were high voltages suffered, yet they obeyed. They assumed, of course, that those in authority knew what they were doing.

How much more compliant will we be if the authority is an ally, is warm and pleasant and makes positive remarks about us? How many of us can resist a charm offensive from an authority figure? Ross Stagner explored this question. Would we accept inaccurate but favourable impressions of ourselves from experts? He gave sixty-eight personnel managers a 'personality test'. The 'results' were identical, faked, flattering and woolly. Stagner asked them to assess each statement according to whether it was: (5) amazingly accurate, (4) rather good, (3) about half and half, (2) more wrong than right or (1) almost entirely wrong. The table opposite (*Personnel Psychology*, 1958) shows (in percentages) how these managers assessed the accuracy of these statements.

Hypnotists make bland statements, knowing that subjects will unwittingly fill in the details themselves. Counsellors can impress clients with the same strategy. Two general rules provide a powerful means of manipulation: the bland is experienced as specific; the positive is perceived as accurate.

Clients want to believe in the counsellor and, of course, counsellors want to believe in themselves. People just do not know how easily they can deceive themselves and be deceived by others. This knowledge is best understood by professionals in advertising and public relations. We easily forget what we have been told. We prefer to believe that the counsellor is discovering rather than reflecting the client's meaning, but even plain reflection is pleasurable. At least it proves that we have been heard, which itself provides relief and reassurance.[15] The result, in these circumstances, is mutual self-deception. It is all the more effective because the counsellor is as deceived as the client.

Counsellors are rarely aware of their own flattery, and its effects on clients. They will say, 'I don't flatter clients; I respect them enough to know that they would not appreciate it'. This, of course, is itself highly flattering to any client. Who wants to admit, even to ourselves, our vulnerability to undue compliments? Hence adulation is unwelcome, but only if it is observable.

Clients want to be challenged, but not demolished. Counsellors do not want to lose too many clients. Within all these principles is a formula for a successful career, a good feeling for the patient, but not a physical cure or social remedy if these are needed. Every client is prized by every counsellor, if only for having the courage to come for counselling in the first place. Immediately, therefore, the relationship is established on a positive rather than an impartial footing. Remember, all you have to say to clients, following Stagner's survey, is that 'You prefer a certain amount of change and variety and become dissatisfied when hemmed in by restrictions and limitations'. With this and similar observations, you will impress over 90 per cent of your clients.

Clients want to feel they are receiving close, individual attention. This can be achieved without really knowing anything important about the client.[16] How? It's not too difficult. Just watch and listen to the client to see how they respond to your general (Stagner-style) observations. Some will strike a chord with them. Play the chord again.

	% Response				
	5	**4**	**3**	**2**	**1**
You have a great need for other people to admire you	39	46	13	1	1
You have a tendency to be critical of yourself	46	36	15	3	0
You have a great deal of unused capacity which you have not turned to your advantage	37	36	18	4	1
While you have some personality weaknesses, you are generally able to compensate for them	34	55	9	0	0
Your sexual adjustment has presented problems for you	15	16	16	33	19
Disciplined and self-controlled outside, you tend to be worrisome and insecure inside	40	21	22	10	4
At times you have serious doubts as to whether you have made the right decision or done the right thing	27	31	19	18	4
You prefer a certain amount of change and variety and become dissatisfied when hemmed in by restrictions and limitations	63	28	7	1	1
You pride yourself as an independent thinker and do not accept others' statements without satisfactory proof	49	31	12	4	4
You have found it unwise to be too frank in revealing yourself to others	31	37	22	6	4
At times you are extroverted, affable, sociable, while at other times you are introverted, wary, reserved	43	25	18	9	5
Some of your aspirations tend to be pretty unrealistic	12	16	22	43	7
Security is one of your major goals in life	40	31	15	9	5

Source: Stagner, 1958: *Personnel Psychology: A Journal of Applied Research*

They will be struck again. Soon you will be in tune with them and will learn what tunes they prefer to hear. They will be impressed by your ability to see into them.

Too much flattery, however, can become visible and therefore offensive and unbelievable. Clients do not want a diet of pure sugar. Explore their dietary preferences and give them what they want. Their responses will show what they do and do not like. They will remember what they liked and forget what they disliked, especially when you repeat one and avoid the other. Give them enough raw truth to stimulate and challenge them, but not so much as to overwhelm them. Avoid the following; they are almost never welcome:

- You have little capacity for independent thought and accept other's statements without satisfactory proof.
- You are rather a superficial and unimaginative individual, lacking capacity for insight into yourself and others.
- Your achievements are somewhat mediocre, yet you appear to have exhausted most of your potential.
- You have few means of overcoming your inherent weaknesses.
- You show little talent for, or interest in, self-discipline.
- You seem unwilling or unable to take responsibility for yourself, your life and the tragic mistakes you have made.
- Your life seems very dull, but perhaps you would not welcome much of a jolt to your routine.
- Deep down, you seem to be rather shallow and superficial. You copy others rather than have any original thoughts of your own.
- Your aspirations are limited but realistic.

Genius and saintliness are rare. The painful corollary, perhaps, is that mediocrity, timidity and lack of vision are common and 'normal'. Yet clients tend to be described as extrovert, intelligent, sensitive, appreciative, cultured, decisive, quick and impatient with trivia and superficialities. Their weaknesses and blind spots are mentioned too, but the criticisms, however superficially dramatic they may appear, are usually presented so that the overall feedback is highly complementary. Clients like to see themselves in a 'heroic' mode when they tackle their weaknesses. Counsellors are usually happy to support them within this metaphor.

We commonly believe the medicine must taste sour if it is to do us any good, but a coating of sugar is welcome too, along with a heavy dose of warmth and optimism. Thus scientology assaults its initiates with searing accounts of their weaknesses and failings. It is a big stick. It needs to be balanced with a large carrot. This is the promise that, once trained, initiates will become clean, clear, fully realized beings. Graduation day needs to be postponed more or less indefinitely since the vision, the hope and the promise always greatly exceed any achieved reality. Also, it makes for better business to keep your clients in training more or less forever. The techniques listed here have been familiar to gurus for generations. Every entertainer has heard the old adage, 'Make them laugh, make them cry, make them wait', and these principles may be equally important in maintaining client attendance during counselling.

At its worst, counselling is just another way of distracting ourselves, playing games and avoiding important truths. Since we are all, necessarily, accomplished in the arts of self-deception, it is very difficult to know, and rather unsafe just to assume, that we will be any the more real with ourselves in the role of client than we are in other contexts. We may simply invent new ways of being phoney. Counsellors, too, cannot escape being human any more than their clients can, so no-one can ever be sure whether their claims to authenticity, warmth, wisdom and sincerity are one iota more sincere, accurate and authentic than anyone else's. There simply is no way of training people to be more honest, either with themselves or with anyone else.

Consequently, counselling is, at root, just another arena within which the perennial human dramas of good and evil, truth and lies, warmth and hostility, love and indifference are played out. It is not a vehicle for resolving such issues, since they are by their nature irresolvable. If our counselling goes well, it will be because we and our counsellor, as people, are being real, open, honest and supportive of each other. If it goes badly, it will not be because the counselling is not working. It will be because we are not working well together. There is no intrinsically good or bad mechanism of counselling; there are merely people willing, or unwilling, to be open with each other for whatever reasons.

Inevitably, then, the overall verdict has to be a mixed one. Counselling can help us face ourselves, or fill in time. On its own, counselling is a hopelessly vague word denoting a huge variety of methods, activities and contexts within which human beings can tell the truth or lie to each other. When defined in broad terms, it excludes nothing, and becomes merely a vague restatement of virtue. Counselling on its own is rather like a one-legged stool: it does not stand up very well. Adverbs and adjectives provide a few more legs, and the future may require them – for example, *debt* counselling, *careers* counselling, *genetic* counselling. If the defined task is reasonably clear, utilitarian and dependent on factual information possessed by the counsellor, we get a clearer picture of what counselling as a professional activity may be. However, psychotherapeutic counselling, involving healing rather than advice and guidance, is concerned with a deeper exploration and negotiation of meanings within our lives. We are light years away from making this a tidy professional activity, and I, for one, very much doubt that the task can, or should, be achieved, even in principle. This book, I hope, has managed to show why.

Counsellors are neither better nor worse than the rest of humanity. What else could we possibly expect? They are no less and no more caring than anyone else, and no more immune from 'compassion fatigue' than the rest of us. This will be an insuperable problem if they expect to deliver compassion day after day, year after year, at regular fifty-minute intervals. Counsellors have a future if they can deliver effective skills and insights even when feeling less than compassionate, but counselling has bolted like a beanstalk in a hothouse of expectation and lacks adequate roots.

Notes

1 Jeffrey Masson, *Against Therapy*. Collins, 1989.

2 Even though its counsellors are unpaid, *Relate* marriage guidance in 1992 needed donations of £10–20 per hour to cover its overheads.

3 See Albee in D. Cohen (ed.), *Challenging the Therapeutic State: Critical Perspectives on Psychiatry and the Mental Health System*. Special issue of the *Journal of Mind and Behaviour*, 1990.

4 See Luke xvii, 20–37.

5 David Pilgrim (ed.), *Psychology and Psychotherapy*. RKP, 1983.

6 Neither can I be certain even of my own personal recommendations. I withdrew one name from my list when I heard a spate of stories that this counsellor was sexually abusing clients. He subsequently resigned from the BAC just before being disbarred from membership.

7 Paul Halmos, *The Faith of Counsellors*. Constable, 1965.

8 Gerard Egan, *The Skilled Helper*. Brooks/Cole, 1985.

9 For summaries of research results, see D. Pilgrim and A. Treacher, *Clinical Psychology Observed*. Routledge, 1992; and S. Bloch, *What is Psychotherapy?* OPUS, 1982.

10 David Smail, *Taking Care: An Alternative to Therapy*. Dent, 1987.

11 The most recent examination of this notion of 'flow' is to be found in Mihaly Csikzentmihalyi, *Flow: The Psychology of Happiness*. Harper & Row, 1992.

12 For example, what about the 'here–now' reality of our most intimate encounters? '*Psychological Bulletin* journal reports that 95% of men and women have sex fantasies throughout the day, and that 85% have fantasies

while having sex. The most common fantasies involve having sex with a past, present or imaginary lover.' ('Gut Reaction', *Guardian*, 30 May 1995). How far is it wise to discuss the reality, and meaning, of fantasy? With whom? When? With what result?

13 See Rose, 1990, in Scambler (ed.) *Sociology as Applied to Medicine*. (Baillière Tindall, 1991). Richard Peto, an Oxford statistician and pioneer researcher on medical effectiveness, has confessed to what he claims to be the 'completely trivial' insight that most treatments do not work very well: 'If they did have a huge effect, then doctors aren't stupid, and they would probably know about them anyway. They wouldn't be doing trials.' Peto has discovered that the effects of treatment programmes can be so small that very large samples (up to 20 000 patients) may be needed to detect them. Not surprisingly, even doctors have been disappointed to hear this. Peto quotes one as saying, 'Look, if a treatment's effects aren't obvious on 100 patients, then it may be of statistical interest but it's not of any medical interest'. Peto considers this to be 'statistical unwisdom', but it certainly seems like human wisdom (Peto interview, *Times Higher Education Supplement*, 27 November 1992).

14 Stanley Milgram, *Obedience to Authority*. Harper & Row, 1974.

15 The construction of plausibility within hypnosis is brilliantly explored in John Grinder and Richard Bandler, *Trance-Formations*. Real People's Press, 1981.

16 This explains why the most superficial astrologer can be avidly read by millions. Even computer programmes designed to ape counsellor behaviour can be of interest to people only too willing to suspend disbelief.

Summary questions

Introduction

1 Why do you think the word 'counselling' is used so often and so broadly?

2 Do you think the scope of the word should (and could?) be made more narrow?

3 Would a 'moratorium' on the word be useful? Should we insist that anyone found using the word be required to explain themselves in some other (clearer) way?

4 How far do you think it is reasonable, or appropriate, for counsellors to become friends with, or substitute friends for, clients?

5 Is there a 'real self', to be found like a gem amidst the mud of delusion? Is there a kaleidoscope of 'selves'? Does 'self' exist in, or emerge from, its environment? Do you prefer one or none of these metaphors?

Chapter 1

1 How great, do you think, is the danger that counselling may oversell itself and create unrealistic expectations?

2 How reassured do you feel by all the promises of corporate care now put out by advertisers?

3 Does counselling face a backlash? Does it deserve it? Is there a middle way?

4 Can counselling and psychotherapy be expected to provide love on demand?

Chapter 2

1 What happened to modesty and understatement?

2 Are counselling and psychotherapy too dependent on the virtue, as opposed to the virtuosity, of the counsellor?

3 Is it sufficient just to accumulate a minimum number of hours of theory and practice in order to qualify as a counsellor? Will any theory suffice? Any practice?

4 If some theories and practices are to be disallowed, who will decide, and on what grounds? According to what assessment of what outcomes?

5 Is there a problem in drawing a boundary between counselling and other activity? Does it matter?

6 Do we have any reason to believe that a trained counsellor is less likely to be an abusing counsellor?

7 Is virtue managing to keep pace with (psycho)technology within counselling?

Chapter 3

1 To whom should the counsellor be answerable, and in what circumstances?

2 Where in the status hierarchy should counsellors be placed?

3 What do you think of the idea that people should be 'counselled in and out' of various options?

4 Is there an adequate way of categorizing all the various schools of counselling?

Chapter 4

1 'The Rogerian vision of humanity does seem to be a vision of the innocents, and therein lies their guilt.' Do you agree?

2 Does anyone actually achieve the ideal of 'unconditional positive regard'? Should they even try?

3 Is the counsellor a sort of friend?

4 Is counselling changing society, or is society changing counselling?

5 Should the counsellor prize and nurture every whim, fantasy, emotion and opinion?

6   Do you think that counsellors can, or should, take a 'value-free' approach to their clients?

Chapter 5

1   Do cognitive behaviourists take a 'purely objective' approach to human beings?

2   Are they better judges and observers than others?

3   Are they more self-aware than others?

4   Is psychology more like a science or an art? How far does it depend on the personal creative genius of exceptional individuals?

5   How far is it possible and desirable to judge and observe impersonally and dispassionately?

Chapter 6

1   How much will remain of Freud's reputation in the twenty-first century?

2   Does the training of psychodynamic therapists give them exceptional powers of observation, introspection and understanding?

3   Does *anybody* have any special and reliable ability to see into others?

4   Does it make sense even to try to imagine a 'final' and objective understanding of human beings?

5   Can anyone reliably rise above the fog of human interaction?

6   Isn't 'awareness of my blindspots' a logical contradiction?

7   Do you have to be a psychoanalyst in order to understand and criticize psychoanalysis?

8   Who will decide whether the analyst has got it right or wrong?

Chapter 7

1   Do we seek the transpersonal or the comfortable?

2   Is a 'New Age' dawning in psychotherapy?

3   Is 'being normal' all there is to life? Is 'normality' enough?

4   'Self-actualisation' …is this a useful goal to aspire to?

5   Does *repentance* have a role within counselling?

6   Can we find a useful, practical, way of talking about, and demonstrating, the spiritual context of existence?

Chapter 8

1 How far has the rise of psychotherapy been dependent on the decline of the Church?

2 'We prefer warm and shallow waters, sunny days, big dinners and comfort generally.' Do you agree?

3 'Our shallow secular consumerism is sometimes about as adequate as a Mississippi paddle steamer trying to negotiate Cape Horn in a force twelve hurricane.' Is it?

4 Could tenderness be resolved into its mechanical parts and then reassembled into an act of tenderness?

5 'The good news is that the whole mysterious business of living, loving and learning from each other will never be boiled down into a formula, however complex.' Will it not? Is this good news?

6 'Counselling has bolted like a beanstalk in a hothouse of expectation and lacks adequate roots.' Does it?

7 Where does counselling go from here?

Suggested reading

Argyle, M. *Social Skills and Health*. Methuen, 1981.

Audit Commission *Finding a Place: A Review of Mental Health Services for Adults*. HMSO, 1994.

Balint, M. *The Doctor, his Patient and the Illness*. Pitman, 1957.

Barker, I. *Power Games: A Workshop on User Empowerment*. Pavilion, 1991.

Beck, A. *Cognitive Therapy and Emotional Disorders*. New American Library, 1976.

Becker, E. *The Birth and Death of Meaning*. Pelican, 1980.

Belfrage, S. *Flowers of Emptiness*. Women's Press, 1981.

Berne, E. *Games People Play*. Grove, 1964.

Berne, E. *What Do You Say After You Say Hello?* Corgi, 1975.

Berrios, G. E. and Freeman, H. (eds) *150 Years of British Psychiatry, 1941–1991*. Royal College of Psychiatrists, 1991.

Berryman, J., Hargreaves, D., Howells, K. and Hollin, C. *Psychology and You*. BPS & Methuen, 1987.

Black, D. *Inequalities in Health: Report of a Research Working Group*. DHSS, 1980.

Bleakley, A. *Earth's Embrace: Facing the Shadow of the New Age*. Gateway, 1989.

Bloch, S. *What is Psychotherapy?* OPUS, 1982.

Bohm, D. *Wholeness and the Implicate Order*. Routledge, 1980.

Bowlby, J. *A Secure Base*. Routledge, 1988.

Brown, D. and Pedder, J. *Introduction to Psychotherapy*. Tavistock, 1979.

Brown, J. A. C. *Freud and the Post Freudians*. Pelican, 1961, 1983.

Brandon, D. *Zen in the Art of Helping*. RKP, 1976.

Capra, F. *The Tao of Physics*. Fontana, 1976.

Capra, F. *The Turning Point: Science, Society and the Rising Culture*. Flamingo, 1984.

Capra, F. *Uncommon Wisdom*. Flamingo, 1989.

Clare, A. *Psychiatry in Dissent.* Tavistock, 1976.

Clare, A. and Thompson, S. *Let's Talk about Me.* BBC Books, 1981.

Clark, A. *The Want Makers.* Hodder & Stoughton, 1988.

Cohen, D. *Psychologists on Psychology.* Ark, 1985.

Cohen, D. (ed.) *Challenging the Therapeutic State: Critical Perspectives on Psychiatry and the Mental Health System.* Special Issue of the *Journal of Mind and Behaviour,* 1990.

Cohen, J. M. and Phipps, J. F. *The Common Experience.* Rider, 1979.

Corey, G. *Manual for Theory and Practice of Group Counselling.* Brooks/Cole, 1985.

Csikzentmihalyi, M. *Flow: The Psychology of Happiness.* Harper & Row, 1992.

Dass, R. *Be Here Now.* Crown Publishing, 1971.

Dass, R. and Bush, M. *Compassion in Action.* Rider, 1992.

Dass, R. and Gorman, P. *How Can I Help?* Rider, 1985.

Davis, H. and Fallowfield, L. (eds) *Counselling and Communication in Health Care.* Wiley, 1991.

Doerner, K. *Madmen and the Bourgeoisie: A Social History of Insanity and Psychiatry.* Basil Blackwell, 1981.

Dryden, W. (ed.) *Individual Therapy in Britain.* Harper & Row, 1984.

Dryden, W. (ed.) *Marital Therapy in Britain.* Harper & Row, 1985.

Dryden, W. *Therapists' Dilemmas.* Harper & Row, 1985.

Dryden, W., Charles-Edwards, D. and Woolfe, R. (eds) *Handbook of Counselling in Britain.* Tavistock/Routledge, 1989.

Dryden, W. and Feltham, C. (eds) *Psychotherapy and its Discontents.* Open University Press, 1992.

Duck, S. *Relating to Others.* Open University Press, 1988.

Easwaran, E. *Meditation: Commonsense Directions for an Uncommon Life.* Routledge, 1979.

Elder, A. and Samuel, O. *While I'm here, doctor.* Tavistock, 1987.

Ellis, A. and Harper, R. *A New Guide to Rational Living.* Institute for Rational Living, 1975.

Ernst, S. and Goodison, L. *In Our Own Hands: A Book of Self-Help Therapy.* Women's Press, 1981.

Ewles, L. and Simnett, I. *Promoting Health: A Practical Guide to Health Education,* 3rd edn. Scutari Press, 1991.

Eysenck, H. The effects of psychotherapy: an evaluation. *Journal of Consulting Psychology,* **16**: 319–24, 1952.

Eysenck, H. The Effects of Psychotherapy. *International Journal of Psychiatry,* **1**: 99–142, 1964.

Eysenck, H. *Decline and Fall of the Freudian Empire.* Pelican, 1986.

Farrell, B. A. *The Standing of Psychoanalysis.* Oxford University Press, 1981.

Featherstone, M. *Consumer Culture and Postmodernism.* Sage, 1991.

Ferguson, M. *The Aquarian Conspiracy: Personal and Social Transformation in the 1980s.* Paladin, 1983.

Ferrucci, P. *What We May Be.* Thorsens, 1982.

Ferucci, P. *Inevitable Grace.* Crucible, 1990.

Frankl, V. *Man's Search for Meaning.* Hodder & Stoughton, 1987.

Fransella, F. *Need to Change?* Methuen, 1975.

Freire, P. *Pedagogy of the Oppressed.* Penguin, 1975.

Freud, S. *Totem and Taboo.* Routledge, 1919.

Freud, S. *Introductory Lectures on Psycho-analysis.* Allen & Unwin, 1922.

Freud, S. *Two Short Accounts of Psycho-analysis.* Pelican, 1962.

Freud, S. *Civilisation, Society and Religion, Civilisation and its Discontents et al.,* vol. 12. Freud Library, Pelican, 1985.

Fromm, E. *Psychoanalysis and Religion.* Yale, 1977.

Fromm, E. *The Crisis of Psychoanalysis.* Pelican, 1978.

Fromm, E. *To Have or To Be?* Abacus, 1978.

Fromm, E., Suzuki, D. T. and Martino, R. *Zen Buddhism and Psychoanalysis.* Condor, 1977.

Fulder, S. *How To Survive Medical Treatment.* Century, 1987.

Furlong, M. *Genuine Fake: A Biography of Alan Watts.* Unwin, 1986.

Gellner, E. *The Psychoanalytic Movement.* Paladin, 1985.

Gordon, T. *Parent Effectiveness Training: The Tested New Way To Raise Responsible Children.* Plume, 1975.

Greening, T. (ed.) *American Politics and Humanistic Psychology.* Saybrook, 1984.

Grinder, J. and Bandler, R. *Trance-Formations.* Real People's Press, 1981.

Halmos, P. *The Faith of the Counsellors.* Constable, 1981.

Hampton, C. *Socialism in a Crippled World.* Pelican, 1981.

Hay, D. *Exploring Inner Space.* Pelican, 1982.

Health Education Authority *Report on National Mental Health Promotion Conference.* University of Salford, HEA, 1989.

Heather, N. *Radical Perspectives in Psychology.* Methuen, 1976.

Herink, R. (ed.) *The Psychotherapy Handbook: The A–Z Guide to More than 250 Different Therapies in Use Today.* New American Library, 1980.

Hesse, H. *Siddhartha.* Picador, 1979.

Hewitt, J. *The Complete Yoga Book.* Rider, 1983.

Hillman, J. and Ventura, M. *We've Had a Hundred Years of Psychotherapy, and the World's Getting Worse.* HarperCollins, 1993.

Hind, D. *Transferable Personal Skills: A Tutor's Guide.* Business Education Publishers, 1989.

Hopson, B. and Scally, M. *Lifeskills Teaching.* McGraw Hill, 1981.

Hopson, B. and Scally, M. *Build Your Own Rainbow: A Workbook for Career and Life Management.* Lifeskills Associates/Open University, 1984.

Howard, A. *Finding a Way: A Realist's Introduction to Self-Help Therapy.* Gateway, 1985.

Howard, A. Psychotherapy: status symbol or cure? *Openmind,* **28**: 9, 1987.

Howard, A. The necessities and absurdities of accredited helping. *Counselling,* **64**: 19–22, 1988.

Howard, A. *Anatomy of Errors.* Gateway, 1989.

Howard, A. Counselling p.l.c. *Counselling,* **1**: 15–16, 1990.

Howard, A. *Getting Through to You.* Gateway, 1991.

Howard, A. What, and why, are we a©©rediting? *Counselling,* **3** (2): 171–3, 1992.

Howard, A. A Fairy Story. *The Psychologist,* **6**: 268–70, 1993.

Humphrey, N. *Consciousness Regained: Chapters in the Development of Mind.* Oxford University Press, 1984.

Hunter, R. and MacAlpine, I. (eds) *Three Hundred Years of Psychiatry.* Oxford University Press, 1963.

Illich, I. *Deschooling Society.* Pelican, 1971, 1978.

Ingleby, D. (ed.) *Critical Psychiatry: The Politics of Mental Health.* Penguin, 1981.

Inglis, B. *The Diseases of Civilization.* Paladin, 1983.

Jackins, H. *Fundamentals of Co-Counselling Manual.* Rational Island Publishers, 1970.

James, W. *The Varieties of Religious Experience.* Longman, 1902.

Jenkins, D. *The Contradiction of Christianity.* SCM Press, 1976.

Johnston, W. *Silent Music.* Fontana, 1976.

Jordon, N. *Themes in Speculative Psychology.* Tavistock, 1968.

Jung, C. G. *Memories, Dreams, Reflections.* Random House, 1961.

Jung, C. G. *Man and His Symbols.* Aldus, 1964.

Jung, C. G. *Answer to Job.* Ark, 1984.

Kaptchuk, E. *Chinese Medicine.* Rider, 1989.

Kennedy, I. *The Unmasking of Medicine.* Paladin, 1983.

Khan, H. I. *Spiritual Dimensions of Psychology.* Sufi Order Publications, 1981.

Khan, P. V. *The Call of the Dervish.* Sufi Order Publications, 1981.

Kirby, R. and Radford, J. *Individual Differences.* Metheun, 1976.

Kopp, S. *If You Meet the Buddha on the Road, Kill Him!* Sheldon Press, 1974.

Kovel, J. *A Complete Guide to Therapy.* Pelican, 1978.

Krishnamurti, J. *Commentaries on Living.* Quest, 1981.

Krishnamurti, J. *Last Talks at Saanen.* Gollancz, 1986.

Lasch, C. *The Culture of Narcissism.* Abacus, 1980.

Lasch, C. *The Minimal Self: Psychic Survival in Troubled Times.* Picador, 1984.

Le Shan, L. *How to Meditate.* Sphere, 1978.

Levine, S. *A Gradual Awakening.* Rider, 1980.

Levine, S. *Meetings at the Edge.* Anchor, 1984.

Levine, S. *Who Dies?* Gateway, 1988.

Mackay, D. *Clinical Psychology: Theory and Therapy.* Methuen, 1975.

McFadden, C. *The Serial.* Pan, 1978.

Malcom, J. *Psychoanalysis: The Impossible Profession.* Picador, 1981.

Margolis, J., Manicas, P. T., Harre, R. and Secord, P. F. *Psychology: Designing the Discipline.* Basil Blackwell, 1986.

Masson, J. *The Assault on Truth: Freud's Suppression of the Seduction Theory.* Penguin, 1985.

Masson, J. *Against Therapy.* Collins, 1989.

Masson, J. *Final Analysis.* HarperCollins, 1991.

May, R. *Power and Innocence: The Search for the Sources of Violence.* Fontana, 1976.

Meehl, P. E. Discussions of Eysenck's *The Effects of Psychotherapy. International Journal of Psychiatry,* **1**, 156–7, 1965.

MIND and WEA Yorkshire North District *Experiences of a Changing Kind: Adult Education in Psychiatric Hospitals and Day Centres.* MIND/WEA, 1985.

Monty Python *Life of Brian.* Methuen, 1979.

Munro, E.A., Manthei, R. J. and Small, J. J. *Counselling: A Skills Approach.* Metheun, 1979.

Murgatroyd, S. *Counselling and Helping.* BPS & Routledge, 1985.

Murray Parkes, C. *Bereavement: Studies of Grief in Adult Life.* Penguin, 1987.

Needleman, J. *The New Religions.* Dutton, 1977.

Nelson-Jones, R. *The Theory and Practice of Counselling Psychology.* Holt, Rinehart & Winston, 1982.

Nelson-Jones, R. *Human Relationship Skills.* Cassell, 1986.

Newton, J. *Preventing Mental Illness.* Routledge, 1989.

Passons, W. *Gestalt Approaches to Counselling.* Holt, Rinehart & Winston, 1975.

Peck, M. Scott *The Road Less Travelled.* Hutchinson, 1978.

Peck, M. Scott *People of the Lie.* Rider, 1983.

Perls, F. *Gestalt Therapy Verbatim.* Bantam, 1976.

Perls, F. *The Gestalt Approach & Eye Witness to Therapy.* Bantam, 1976.

Perls, F., Hefferline, R. F. and Goodman, P. *Gestalt Therapy.* Pelican, 1979.

Pilgrim, D. (ed.) *Psychology and Psychotherapy.* RKP, 1983.

Pilgrim, D. and Treacher, A. *Clinical Psychology Observed.* Routledge, 1992.

Porket, M. *The Theoretical Foundations of Chinese Medicine.* MIT Press, 1978.

Priest, R. G. (ed.) *Psychiatry in Medical Practice.* Macdonald & Evans, 1982.

Quilliam, S. and Grove-Stephenson, I. *The Counselling Handbook.* Thorsons, 1990.

Radford, J. and Kirby, R. *The Person in Psychology.* Methuen, 1975.

Rainwater, J. *You're in Charge.* Thorsens, 1981.

Reich, C. A. *The Greening of America.* Penguin, 1972.

Reich, W. *Listen, Little Man.* Pelican, 1948, 1979.

Rhinehart, L. *The Book of est.* Abacus, 1977.

Ries, A. and Trout, J. *Positioning: The Battle for Your Mind.* McGraw Hill, 1981.

Rieker, H. U. *The Secret of Meditation.* Rider, 1978.

Rogers, C. *On Becoming a Person.* Constable, 1967.

Rogers, C. *Encounter Groups.* Pelican, 1973.

Rogers, C. *A Way of Being.* Houghton Mifflin, 1980.

Rosen, R. D. *Psychobabble.* Avon, 1979.

Rowan, J. *Ordinary Ecstasy: Humanistic Psychology in Action.* Routledge, 1976.

Rowan, J. *The Reality Game: A Guide to Humanistic Counselling and Therapy.* RKP 1983.

Rowan, J. *The Transpersonal: Psychotherapy and Counselling.* Routledge, 1993.

Rusk, T. *Instead of Therapy.* Hay House, 1991.

Russell, J. *Out of Bounds: Sexual Exploitation in Counselling and Therapy.* Sage, 1993.

Rutter, P. *Sex in the Forbidden Zone.* Mandala, 1990.

Ryle, G. *The Concept of Mind.* Hutchinson, 1949.

Salmon, P. *Living in Time: A New Look at Personal Development.* Dent, 1985.

Sarason, S. *Psychology Misdirected.* Macmillan, 1981.

Saxe, L. *The Efficacy and Cost-effectiveness of Psychotherapy.* Office of Technology Assessment, Congress of the United States, Washington DC, US Government Printing Office, 1980.

Scambler, G. (ed.) *Sociology as Applied to Medicine.* Baillière Tindall, 1991.

Schaef, A. W. *Beyond Therapy, Beyond Science.* HarperSanFrancisco, 1992.

Schutz, W. *Joy: Expanding Human Awareness.* Pelican, 1973.

Schutz, W. *Profound Simplicity.* Turnstone, 1979.

Sedgwick, P. *PsychoPolitics.* Pluto, 1982.

Sennett, R. *The Fall of Public Man.* Knopf, 1977.

Sharma, S. L. *The Therapeutic Dialogue.* University of New Mexico Press, 1986.

Shepard, M. *Do-it-Yourself Psychotherapy.* Optima, 1988.

Shepherd, M., Wilkinson, G. and Williams, P. *Mental Illness in Primary Care Settings.* Tavistock, 1986.

Sherrard, C. The Rise in Demand for Counselling. Unpublished paper, Leeds University, presented to British Psychological Society, Lincoln, 1991.

Shotter, J. *Images of Man in Psychological Research.* Methuen, 1975.

Siegel, B. *Love, Medicine and Miracles.* Arrow, 1988.

Siegel, B. *Living, Loving and Healing.* Aquarian, 1993.

Skinner, B. F. *Beyond Freedom and Dignity.* Pelican, 1979.

Sloan, T. D. *Deciding: Self-Deception in Life Choices.* Methuen, 1987.

Smail, D. *Illusion and Reality: The Meaning of Anxiety.* Dent, 1984.

Smail, D. *Taking Care: An Alternative to Therapy.* Dent, 1987.

Stafford-Clark, D. and Smith, A. *Psychiatry for Students.* Allen & Unwin, 1964, 1983.

Stalker, D. and Glymour, C. (eds) *Examining Holistic Medicine.* Prometheus, 1989.

Storr, A. *Human Aggression.* Pelican, 1979.

Storr, A. *The Art of Psychotherapy.* Secker & Warburg, 1983.

Storr, A. *Solitude.* Fontana, 1989.

Storr, A. *Churchill's Black Dog, and other essays.* Fontana, 1990.

Sutherland, I. *Health Education.* Allen & Unwin, 1979.

Sutton, C. *Handbook of Research for the Helping Professions.* Routledge, 1987.

Szasz, T. *Ideology and Insanity.* Pelican, 1973.

Thera, N. *The Vision of Dhamma.* Rider, 1986.

Thorne, B. *Person-Centred Counselling: Therapeutic and Spiritual Dimensions.* Whurr, 1991.

Thornton, E. M. *The Freudian Fallacy, Freud & Cocaine.* Paladin, 1983.

Townsend, P. and Davidson, N. *The Black Report.* Pelican, 1982.

Trungpa, C. *Cutting Through Spiritual Materialism.* Shambhala, 1973.

Tulku, T. *Skillful Means.* Dharma Publishing, 1978.

VandenBos, G. R. (ed.) Special Issue: Psychotherapy Research. *American Psychologist,* **41**: 111–214, 1983.

Van Der Post, L. *Jung and The Story of Our Time.* Penguin, 1978.

van Deurzen-Smith, E. *Existential Counselling in Practice.* Sage, 1988.

Veith, I. (trans) *The Yellow Emperor's Classic of Internal Medicine.* University of California Press, 1972.

Vivekananda, S. *What Religion Is.* Advaita Ashrama, 1972.

Viorst, J. *Necessary Losses.* Simon & Schuster, 1988.

Watts, A. *The Wisdom of Insecurity.* Rider, 1954.

Watts, A. *The Way of Zen.* Pelican, 1976.

Watts, A. *Tao: The Watercourse Way.* Cape, 1976.

Watts, A. *The Meaning of Happiness.* Pelican, 1987.

WEA North Western District *Health Education for Women: A Report and Evaluation of Work in the WEA North Western District.* WEA, 1988.

WEA North Western District & Health Education Authority *Women and Health: Activities & Materials for Use in Women's Health Courses and Discussion Groups.* WEA, 1986.

Whitehead, M. *The Health Divide.* Penguin, 1992.

Wilbur, K. *Up From Eden: A Transpersonal View of Human Evolution.* Shambhala, 1981.

Wilbur, K. *Eye to Eye: The Quest for the New Paradigm.* Anchor, 1983.

Wilbur, K., Engler, J. and Brown, D. *Transformations of Consciousness.* Shambhala, 1986.

Wood, G. *The Myth of Neurosis.* Macmillan, 1983.

Woolfe, R., Murgatroyd, S. and Rhys, S. *Guidance and Counselling in Adult and Continuing Education.* Open University Press, 1987.

Yalom, I. *Love's Executioner and Other Tales of Psychotherapy.* Penguin, 1989.

Index